Social Agency Policy

Consulting Editor: *Beulah R. Compton,* University of Alabama

The Nelson-Hall Series in Social Welfare

John P. Flynn

Social Agency Policy
Analysis and Presentation
for Community Practice

Nelson-Hall Publishers ⬛ Chicago

Library of Congress Cataloging in Publication Data

Flynn, John P.
  Social agency policy.

  (The Nelson-Hall series in social welfare)
  Bibliography: p.
  Includes index.
  1. Public welfare—United States. 2. United
States—Social policy. I. Title. II. Series.
HV95.F53 1985   361.6'1'0973   84-25561
ISBN 0-8304-1088-0

Manufactured in the United States of America

10 9 8 7 6 5 4 3 2

™ The paper used in this book meets the
minimum requirements of American
National Standard for Information
Sciences—Permanence of Paper for
Printed Library Materials, ANSI
Z39.48-1984.

Contents

List of Outlines
and Checklists

Preface

Social Agency Policy: Analysis and Presentation for Community Practice provides theoretically based, practical models for the analysis and presentation of social policy in legislative, administrative, and interagency areas at the small-scale or local (including state or regional) levels. The book focuses on both the content and process aspects of social welfare policy analysis and provides outlines that will serve as models for analysis and presentation of policy at the small- as opposed to the grand-scale (national) level.

This book is intended as a text for undergraduate and graduate courses in social welfare policy and for those courses in public administration, counseling and personnel, or other human services areas concerned with social policy practice at the local level. It is also intended as a helpful tool for those social agency professionals who are called upon to provide policy analyses in their work but who have had no preparation in its practice. The lack of such preparation affects virtually all social welfare practitioners, given the relatively recent emphasis on social welfare policy analysis in general, and the absence of tools for small-scale policy analysis in particular.

We see an immense need in the area of social welfare policy analysis. Traditionally, social welfare or human service policy has been taught from a descriptive or historical perspective; that is, various important events or structural features of legislative and service agencies have been chronicled. This approach, while important in identifying the social, political, economic, or philosophical foundations of policy, generally lacks an emphasis on critical analysis as it pertains to policy work at the local level. Consequently, professionals who find themselves with the responsibility for social welfare policy analysis do not have the guides or tools to meet their responsibilities and ethical mandates. The models for analysis that have emerged in recent years have been geared to national or grand-scale content and processes; they have limited value to the local level practitioner. Very few of us, for example, have the opportunity to go to Washington to rewrite the Social Security Act or to design a jobs and employment policy and program for the nation. The vast number of social and other human services workers must meet their policy responsibilities at the local level—in cities, counties, states, or regions of states.

This book, then, attempts to provide human services professionals with the ability to analyze and present both the content and process of social policy—in their own organizations and interagency activities and in the legislative arenas (e.g., city ordinances, county resolutions, state legislative proposals) that are meaningful to their professional lives. Local or small-scale issues, such as personnel policy matters, interagency social action positions, information security and client confidentiality, regulatory legislation, and accountability policies are some of the policy analysis issues that we will address.

Every author of a professional book or article owes acknowledgments to more people than can be recalled and to more experiences than can be described. This book is no different; it represents the accumulated contributions of many friends, colleagues, and former students. Thanks are due to the anonymous readers whose critical review and comments gave helpful direction to this work, as did the careful reading given by two of my colleagues, Doris Greene and Edward Pawlak. Thanks also go to the people at Nelson-Hall, particularly Ron Warncke for his thoughtful encouragement throughout this effort, to Dorothy Anderson and Elizabeth Rubenstein for their editorial help, and to Tamra Campbell for the book's design. It is my special pleasure to acknowledge two groups, in particular, however. The first is my family—Fran, Paul, and Bridget—whose patience and good humor contributed in many ways to this project, though their efforts may not be evident in the final product. The second is the students who have provided many applications of various drafts of my models and outlines to their agency placements in the field and have taught me the reality of these policy analyses and presentations. Many of the case illustrations that follow have been drawn in varying degrees from the work of Ed Bottum, Mary Brandt, Irma DeYoung, Marge Dokter, Louise Dunbar, Terry Kuczeruk, Peter Matchinsky, Regina McClurg, Paul Miller, Jamie Muller, Michele Rutherford, and Cathy Ur. To all the rest who may recognize themselves in me or in my work, I say "thank you for your help."

1

Introduction

This book is written for social workers and other human service practitioners who wish to influence, or are influenced by, the analysis of social welfare policies. We envision the reader as *anyone* in the field of social welfare, since every person and every program is affected by social policy. Many practitioners are also in a position to effect changes in social programs and social policies, either by themselves, in coalitions, or in other cooperative efforts. While the book is especially written for those who engage in policy-as-practice at the local—interagency and intra-agency—level, it is also intended for practitioners at the regional or state levels of policy analysis.

Social workers and other human or social service personnel have come to recognize that social welfare policy directly affects their day-to-day practice; and—that as individuals or members of groups or organizations, they have the opportunity to actively participate in policy analysis and change. A problem, however, is that many practitioners are not accustomed to viewing social policy as a close-to-home phenomenon that can be developed, altered, or shaped (as well as tolerated!) in and through their day-to-day routines.

Social welfare policy has traditionally been perceived as something "up there" or "out there,"—a mandate or constraint from on high or from some external system. While this perception is sometimes accurate, policy frequently comes from the environment immediately around us—decisions made by city councils and county commissions, mandates of central administration, decisions of a local or regional policymaking board, rulings of an administrative law judge or agreements made by local, regional, or state agencies acting together. The impact of such policy is felt largely in the environments of "small-scale systems." At times, the social worker may attempt to influence these policy processes by analyzing their impact for his or her employer.

Many practitioners, however, fail to recognize the impact of their participation on small-scale policy systems, probably because policy work has not been viewed as one of their interventive methods, as has management, administration, or the provision of direct services. This alienation or perceived distance from the policy aspects of living systems belies the fact that practitioners are actually very close to social policies at the agency level. For example, many psychiatric inpatient facilities or residential care programs for children have (or should have) formal policies on the use of seclusion and restraints. These policies intimately affect social practice and can be effected by human service practitioners. Many have had to develop and/or operationalize policies in their own areas of practice that pertain to the policy principle of "the least restrictive environment," whether in an elementary school setting providing special education services, a juvenile detention facility, a partial day care program for developmentally disabled adults, or an activity program for senior citizens. Or, we find policies requiring team assessments and case planning by a number of disciplines, as in an acute care medical facility. The detail of agency-based policies and the concommitant procedures generated are very much a part of the "policy life" of social agency practice.

Lack of awareness of the role practitioners play in policy may also be due to the manner in which many have been socialized regarding the content and process of social welfare policy. That is, the practitioner is more likely to view social welfare policy content and process as that huge mass of information that constitutes the backdrop for learning about social welfare services. Policy might be seen as synonymous with information about the various social services fields, the structure of national service programs, or principles involved in various social issues such as poverty, racism, or sexism. Certainly, this is important information; it helps to give us a full policy perspective. But social agency policy is more than the substantive content handed down by generations of accumulated programs, or the principles articulated in social legislation. There are specific opportunities for policy analysis and policy change in the day-to-day provision of human services. The direct service practitioner has a concrete opportunity to "occupy the policy space" when, for example, an agency establishes policy for psychotherapy services in which fee negotiation with the client is required as part of the therapeutic process; or to determine agency policy regarding visitation in an inpatient substance abuse treatment center.

Other examples may be found where both agency administrators and direct services staff participate in shaping agency policy concerning negotiations with outside funding sources, such as developing contracts for such policy issues as obtaining global assessment scores on agency clientele and providing the results to a funding source, or drafting interagency agreements about case management responsibilities or case conferencing. These opportunities for policy analysis present themselves through both existing policies and new developments in policymaking.

From another perspective social welfare policy *process* (as opposed to *content*) is often seen as "politics." The tendency here is to characterize policy process as something that only happens in and around the nation's capitol and about national issues such as social security, national health insurance, and public assistance. Little wonder that we tend to look beyond our immediate environments in search of what is happening in social welfare policy.

Yet the processes of policy development are often very close to home. For example, social agency coalitions sometimes unite to persuade a city commission to budget a fixed percentage of general revenue sharing funds to local human services programs. Both the content and the process of that policy principle and goal require analysis and action at the small-scale level. For example, policy processes are undertaken by local child care agencies when assisting a state social welfare department to alter its policies and to allow for *purchase* of services, as opposed to only *direct provision* of services by state agencies.

Historical-Descriptive Approaches to Policy

Our understanding of social welfare policy relies, in large part, upon recognition of significant social policy actors who appeared in social welfare history, or upon an accumulation of policy events occurring over time. It is a fitting and at times exciting experience to recall the contributions of people who have shaped social policy over the years: Jane Addams, Florence Kelley, Frances Perkins, Bertha Reynolds, Eugene Debs, Clarence Darrow, Edwin Witte, and others come to mind. Remembering these people and their impact on American social welfare policy not only gives recognition to their contributions but also provides a vehicle for identifying the policy issues and programs that have emerged over time. This approach to learning social policy is valuable; it enables us to maintain our rich policy heritage.

A similar approach is that of viewing social policy as the accumulation of a series of particularly important events — the chronological view of social welfare. One example is found in reviewing the establishment of the state chargeback system in developing mental health policy. This came about when states levied charges upon localities for the care of indigents and the mentally ill. This fostered the dual roles of states and localities. Another example is the fundamental policy principle established by the Social Security Act of 1935 of building in mandatory conditions for grants-in-aid to the states or the concept of categorical approaches to assistance. Grants to states for assisting special groups were made contingent upon accepting other policy, such as requiring state program administration by civil servants. Much of our policy process understanding is based upon major and visible events and their associated activities, such as the activities of Dorothea Dix and the Pierce Veto, for example, or the intriguing interplay of the Ford Foundation's Grey Areas Project, the President's Commission on Juvenile Delinquency and Youth Crime, and the development of the Economic Opportunity Act. Certainly all of these approaches, taken singly or in combination, provide frameworks for either descriptive or critical analyses of social welfare policies.

Living Policy

Past policy processes are not the only factors that affect the present. As human services practitioners, we are active participants in our current policy environments. In our day-to-day work we have the opportunity to support existing policies and generate change for new ones. We do not suggest that earlier or external policy events are not important in our lives. Rather, we see the significance of another aspect of policy that is potentially within our understanding and, at times, even within our control.

A common and useful conceptualization is that social welfare policy is made in three arenas: **(1)** legislative, **(2)** judicial, and **(3)** administrative. Policy analysis must take both the opportunities and constraints of these arenas into consideration. Legislated policy not only means state or federal laws but also local ordinances or resolutions — and the rules and regulations that derive from these laws. In fact, the regulatory area, often overlooked, is perhaps far greater in size and scope for the social welfare analyst than the body of legislated policy taken by itself, since laws or statutes often demand and generate a vast body of regulatory policy. Furthermore, the policy set forth by legally constituted boards of directors and/or commissions may be seen as legislated policy in the sense that board policy governs all other agency policy and either delineates or makes new opportunities for social action in policy processes, as for example, when coalitions interact. As is well known, legislation provides the right and responsibility for action and, at times, **(1)** gives credibility to policy analysis, and **(2)** even mandates that the analyst review and evaluate policy.

Judicial policy is set both by courts and court agencies: judges decree social-welfare policy in contests over statutes and regulations; court agencies, such as juvenile or domestic relations courts, set forth policy which approximates the force of law (at least until it is contested). In the local policy arena this could, for example, entail the clash between individuals who seek a new home as a result of deinstitutionalization and neighbors who contest zoning ordinances in court. Another is edicts by juvenile courts which variously limit either the rights of children or their parents. Rules or procedures concerning commitment or guardianship that differ from court to court provide other examples for judicial policy analysis and policy action at the local level.

Administrative policy, whether set by the administrative branch of governments or the executive or program levels within agencies, constitutes perhaps the largest body of policy providing grist for the analysis mill. Administrative policymaking takes the form of policy manuals for an organized set of interrelated organizational policies, or ad hoc and ephemeral policies sent by memo as administrative directives. Administrative policy is generally the level of policy closest to the direct practitioner since it is only one notch above the "front line" of practice.

Most of us fulfill our professional responsibilities to social-welfare policy with other people like ourselves in small-scale legislative, judicial, or administrative policy systems. By this we mean that much of what we do occurs with individuals, groups, social agencies, and other organizations and is part of our routine professional responsibilities. While these elements, appearing with some regularity within identifiable boundaries (i.e., within these "systems"), are influenced by broad and large-scale social policies, these small-scale policy systems also generate and respond to their own realities at the local, small-scale policy level: we generate our own policy environments and constraints at the local or small-scale level. In fact, opportunities for the analysis, development, and articulation or presentation of policy are present virtually all the time in our local-level practice. We cannot only participate in and influence the play of policy at this level, but policy participation is often either part of our job expectations or at the least a part of our responsibility as active participants in our agencies and our professions. A major part of human services work is participation in social agency policy, ranging from analysis of that policy for the mere sake of understanding to the analysis of policy for purposeful change.

Working at the Policy Level or Policy Space

What is meant by the "policy level?" *Policy* refers to *those principles which give expression to valued ends and provide direction to social welfare action.* "Policy level" on the small scale is comprised of all those resolutions, orders, rules, guidelines, or other statements of principle that derive from councils and commissions, courts, boards, executives, or interagency compacts that guide and direct our professional activities in community social welfare. For purposes of this book, the small-scale policy system that comprises the social welfare community refers to the local, regional, or state levels of activity. Our focus is on those policy actions that center around intraagency, interagency, and group policy action. "Policy space" refers to situations in which we have the opportunity to effect the nature or shape of policies affecting us or those for whom we act as advocates by altering the interrelationships of the elements in interaction, such as people, programs, or resources.

Our attention is given to policy practice at the local level, because that is where the vast majority of human services practitioners devote their professional lives and the vast majority of social services clientele interact with human services systems. It is also the place where most practitioners meet their ethical and professional commitments. The Code of Ethics of the National Association of Social Workers, for example, provides a number of mandates for its members to take on responsibilities for initiating and shaping social welfare policy. Another, and perhaps more practical reason is that many practitioners are called upon to analyze the content and/or the process of those policies arising out of local activities; they are sometimes asked to provide reports or presentations on those analyses. For example, they are often asked to analyze potential policies being considered by our own governing boards; or to respond to a formal request on a proposed policy published by a state agency by review and comment within a sixty-day period; or to give an expert opinion on the potential impact of proposed legislation upon client services that our interagency task force wishes to address.

In the area of social policy process, we might be asked to analyze the role or influence of key actors or events in a community issue, such as the merging of a number of human services agencies, or the application by a new agency for membership in the local United Way or community welfare council. Practitioners may be required to provide leadership in a social action process aimed at purposively affecting community welfare policy; their ability to analyze the policy process might be crucial to goal achievement.

Clearly, if social and other human services workers are to influence policy decision making, they must possess or develop skills in the analysis of policy content and process. Mayer and Greenwood (1980) contend that policy research is goal-oriented, requires the analyst to be familiar with a systems perspective, demands the ability to manipulate a large number of variables, is focused on both content and action, and must be conducted in multidisciplinary situations. But do practitioners have the skills to meet those obligations? As Ziter (1983) notes, social workers have developed policy skills to only a limited extent, despite considerable attention to policy content in social work curricula. It would seem, then, that concerted efforts must be made to develop skills in the area that Ziter refers to as "policy analysis and synthesis."

The Need for Small-Scale Policy Models

Many social workers have the ability needed for such analyses. They have the broad system knowledge, the accumulated experiences necessary for understanding, and probably the analytical skills to do the job. However, it is likely that many do not have the policy analysis models needed at the small-scale level for precisely the reasons stated above: practitioners have perhaps been socialized to believe that social policy only happens somewhere beyond or outside of their immediate environment. And, if they have been inclined to take an analytical approach to social welfare policy, the literature has been helpful only to the extent that it has provided large-scale or national system models for analysis. In all likelihood, many (if not all) of those models have been pitched at large-scale, national-in-scope social welfare issues and systems; such models are limited as tools for small-scale policy analysis.

This book will provide direction for the analysis of policy content and process—both the substance and the activity of social welfare in small systems. We will review what the literature has to offer us and, at some points, extract what is relevant to our own needs for small-scale policy analysis, but we will essentially be forging our own tools. And that is exciting. We will not only develop that set of tools but also share in the development of that area of social intervention that might be called social policy practice or social welfare policy practice.

Policy Work

Heretofore, social policy has been seen by and large as an area of substantive information in support of the various methods of social work practice, such as social treatment, planning, community organization, or administration. One could argue that the analysis of social welfare policy has really existed in other forms or in other methodological orientations, such as social welfare administration or social welfare research and evaluation. Or it might be said that the analysis of the process aspects of such policy has really been the business all these years of the community organization method of practice. In fact, Ziter has said that, within what is called "policywork," are the three practice areas of community organization, administration, and "a technical component, policy analysis and synthesis" (Ziter, 1983, p. 39). Nevertheless, it does appear that the essentials of analysis (analysis and synthesis for our purposes here) have received the least attention in terms of skill development.

Our intent here is not to stake out any territory or domain. The essential point is that we are in need of models for analysis of small-scale social policy and we will have to develop these models ourselves if we are to be policy practitioners. To see policy, to know policy, to feel policy, is not enough: we find ourselves doing policy and we need the tools, including models for small-scale policy analysis and the presentation of those analyses, to do our job. We need to know how to conduct those analyses and how to convey them to others. As we recognize more and more that there are identifiable and essential sets of knowledge, skills and abilities associated with the "doing" of policy, we come to realize that, indeed, social policy work is social policy-as-practice. This book is written from that perspective, i.e., that social policy is a part of social work practice and an essential element in all human services practice. The business of small-scale policy analysis — of policy content and policy processes — is central to the work of policy practice.

This book also takes a general or human systems perspective throughout, at some points explicitly and at other points only implicitly. The systems approach here is not the common or typical linear approach of stating goals or objectives, identifying alternatives, developing feedback mechanisms, and so forth. Rather, we will summarize the underlying principles of systems thinking and weave those principles into the outlines for analysis provided in later chapters. These human system principles will be made explicit in chapter 5 when we identify value elements for policy analysis.

Chapters 2 and 3 contain a review and summary of approaches to policy analysis in social welfare and an inventory of models for analysis currently available. Chapter 4 sets forth the essential elements of a model for the analysis of policy content and integrates case illustrations, along with the application of an outline for the analysis of content. Chapter 5 deals specifically with the value elements of policy analysis and is followed by expanded discussion of case illustrations, with an emphasis upon value considerations. Chapter 6 develops the model for the analysis of policy process at the local level and is followed, in turn, by process-oriented applications of case material. The rest of the book deals with situations frequently requiring the presentation of policy analyses: legislative analysis, giving testimony, and position statements. Again, the substantive chapters are each followed by case illustrations.

Each chapter that generates an outline for analysis also includes case illustrations. These case examples are either woven into the narrative or appear at the end of the chapter. Some cases illustrate both *content* and *value* analysis or *process* and *value* analysis. Cases 3, 6, and 8 all focus on the issue of an integrated policy for the downtown mall.

2

Approaches to Policy Analysis

In chapter 1, we discussed a number of approaches to the analysis of social welfare policy; we also briefly considered some of the contexts within which policy analysis in the social welfare area might occur. Now we will explore what social welfare policy is.

What Is Social Welfare Policy?

A conventional way of going about the study of social policy is to begin with a definition of basic terms. However, David Gil has shown us the tremendous range and number of options available to us if we wish to give definition to the term "social policy." In fact, in addition to citing numerous authors' definitions, Gil notes Freeman and Sherwood's observation that at least four "layers" of an understanding or definition of social policy exist, depending upon whether one emphasizes social policy as a philosophical concept, a product, a process, or a framework for action (Gil, 1976, pp. 3-10). Thus, one's understanding of what constitutes social policy greatly depends upon a person's perspective, which could be significantly determined by a task at hand, the job, or one's world view. It could also depend on whether one's focus is the substantive aspects of a policy or policies or the process aspects of policymaking.

Nevertheless, the policy definitions found in social welfare literature emphasize the broadest or highest level of human interaction, particularly national policies such as income maintenance, massive provision of social services, and various other questions about distribution of national resources. Very little is available to guide us in policy analysis at the local levels, due in part perhaps to a presumption that local policy analysis phenomena are too idiosyncratic or unique, or perhaps due to the presumed primacy of national policy. However, since our intent is to be of immediate and practical help

to practitioners at the local or community level, small-scale definitions are in order.

One-Liner Definitions of Policy

It is perhaps practical to think of social welfare policy in simple terms.
Generally speaking, the common ingredients in most definitions of
social welfare policy are that policies (1) set forth principles, and (2)
deal with human health, safety, or well being. More comprehensive
definitions would, of course, include some notions of social interaction, legitimacy, sanctions, availability of resources, and so forth.
However, the central concepts have to do with the fact that policies
set forth the values that give shape to ends or means; and that social
welfare policies relate to the health, safety, and well-being of human
beings in social systems.

One uncluttered approach to obtaining a definition of policy is
to establish a number of reasonable one-liners. For example, social
welfare policy (hereafter occasionally referred to as social policy) is
a set of goal statements about desired human conditions. Or, social
policy is a set of principles to guide social action. One definition is
goal oriented, the other means oriented. Looking at a combined
ends/means definition, we could say that policy is a statement of
desired ends, with selected alternative means. Another approach to
definition is to look at policy from a strictly empirical perspective
(i.e., what one can see or feel) and simply view it as a position taken
by an individual or an organization, either implicitly or explicitly.
Put another way, a policy is a decision made or not made, as Harvey
Cox (1966) would perhaps state it. Another approach is to look at
social policy from a technical, administrative, or planning perspective and refer to it as a standing plan (Kahn, 1969) or an organizing
principle to shape, for example, a service system, or for program design
purposes.

Since social welfare services tend to be inspired by socially sanc-
tioned goals often debated at the community or agency board level,
it could be said that policy is the ordering of priorities. The latter
would be a simple one-liner, process-oriented definition of social welfare policy. MacRae and Haskins have argued that these economic-
decisional orientations to policy analysis currently dominate the field.

Models based upon this approach emphasize criteria of maximization of social welfare as measured either by the value of outcomes or the satisfaction of preferences (MacRae and Haskins, 1981, p. 8).

In contrast to these more rationalist orientations to policy, DiNitto and Dye emphasize the political aspects of social welfare policy. They say that public policy is the "outcome of conflicts...over who gets what, and when and how they get it" (DiNitto and Nye, 1983, p. 9). For them, social welfare policy is "anything government chooses to do, or not to do, that affects the quality of life of its people" (DiNitto and Dye, 1983, p. 2). This is the conflict approach to social process.

Finally, policy has a special property in virtually any system: the ability to give order and predictability to a social system. In fact, it can be said that the purpose and desired function of all policy, whether legislation, judicial decrees or mandates, or administrative directives, is to give order and predictability to a system. The latter properties lead to the reduction of disorder. Consequently, a policy provides information to those who are likely to be subject to or influenced by it. Hence, a very practical one-line definition is that policy is (merely!) systematically ordered information. Policy, then, provides a signal, a direction, of what is expected of people—individuals, groups, or organizations.

The following list summarizes these definitions of policy:

1. A formal or informal expression of goals or valued ends.
2. A statement of desired ends with an indication of selected alternative means.
3. The ordering of priorities.
4. An organizing principle.
5. A standing plan.
6. A decision made (or not made).
7. A position—taken implicitly or explicitly.
8. The outcomes of social choice about who gets what, when and how.
9. Information ordered in a system.

The reader can no doubt develop a number of other one-liner policy definitions, perhaps more relevant to the context or responsibilities of his or her practice. For a definition to be useful, it must articulate the fundamental principles or values at stake and must relate to human health, safety, or well-being.

Power and Policy

Since social welfare policy can either move people to action or delimit their range of potential outcomes, a close relationship exists between policy and power. A definition of power that is particularly relevant to this discussion is provided by Polsby. Simply put, power is the "capacity of one actor to do something affecting another actor, which changes the probable pattern of specified future events" (Polsby, 1963, p. 5). As noted above, policy, by its nature, also introduces a stochastic process in human interaction. That is, policy provides for a certain lawfulness with respect to how people will behave, whether they are entitled to a particular service, whether staff can exercise a certain prerogative, and whether a particular agency is free to make a given decision within the promulgated rule or regulation. At times, policy allocates power to individuals or organizations; at other times, power legitimates the ability to make or enforce policy. When power legitimates in this way, individuals or organizations are given authority. Thus, power and policy are inextricably interwoven.

It may also be said that policy is information; it transforms data into information, disorder into order. Policy shapes information in such a way that people can communicate priorities and expectations. When policy is clearly stated and consistently administered, people know what is expected of them or their agencies.

Policy, Power, and Information

The power of policy lies in its ability to give order to and manipulate a system by providing information. This is possible due to the close relationship between policy, power and information. When a social welfare policy has clarity, consistency, legitimacy, and sanction, that policy may be said to be powerful. The test of a policy's power is found in the degree of salience it has for a large number of people or for a sustained period of time. Furthermore, the power of such a policy is evidenced by the degree to which people normatively behave according to the policy's mandates, which explains why policy is so vitally important to social practice professionals pursuing social goals.

The allocation of resources in our society is highly dependent upon the distribution and exercise of power by various interest groups. Policy gives shape, direction, and limits to that exercise of power: the actualities of the policy process frequently determine how or whether those in need will share in our society's resources. Consequently, in the context of power relationships, policy is a key vehicle for achieving social ends. This characterization of the role and function of policy is no less true in small-scale systems than in large-scale or national systems.

It may be said that policymaking is the processing of information wherein the communication obtained and promoted gives order (organization) to the system. Thus, social policy, when processed (as with information), becomes communication and gives order and predictability to a system or its members. It may also be said that the making of social policy is the management of social power, and the power of social policy lies in its ability to order or manipulate a social system: policymaking is the making of decisions and the making of policy decisions is the playing out of *influence*. As McGill and Clark (1975) have indicated, power is the *potential* for having or using resources, while influence is the actual exercising of power through the decision-making process. Therefore, while social policy actually constitutes the substance or content of a particular issue, it also constitutes the processing aspects of power and influence and the ordering of information in a system.

What Does Policy Do for Us?

As Alfred Kahn has indicated, policy enacts practice (Kahn, 1973). Policy shapes and delineates what the practitioner does, how he or she relates to the client group, and the manner in which discretion is allowed or exercised. Policy also provides the priorities within which the practitioner can allocate time and other resources and, consequently, provides a structure for how one's professional role is to be carried out. As policy shapes individual or group functioning, it also shapes the nature of things at the *program* level, setting the agency's direction, the content of services, and the tone and quality of the milieu within which work is accomplished and services provided. The workers influenced by policy reciprocate and have many opportunities to set, modify, and even negate social policy in both formal and informal ways. Thus, we may infer that social practitioners undertake policy analysis at all times, at least at some level of consciousness, as evidenced by their dutifully or creatively carrying out policy mandates or by their purposefully engaging in social action at various system levels to modify or even resist those mandates.

Dolgoff and Gordon (1976) have suggested that there is actually a continuum of reciprocity between the practitioner and the larger systems from which policy emanates. At one end of the continuum there are only client- and worker-specific policies, such as a mutual decision to depart from an agreed upon treatment-policy principle like the location or frequency of interviews. At the other end of the continuum, there are situations in which an entire service system is altered, as in redefining the authority and responsibility of state and local levels of government with respect to provision of a social service. At all levels the direct practitioner is actively involved in the making and ultimate success of policy decisions. For example, the worker and/or agency makes a policy choice by selecting a particular treatment modality, e.g., deciding to provide only behaviorally based treatment, or taking on clients only when the entire family consents to treatment. In such situations the worker or agency acts within the context of having performed a small-scale policy analysis (presuming that decisions are made with responsible forethought).

Along that continuum, workers may also make policy decisions that shape and define their own strategic roles, such as becoming advocates, brokers, mediators, therapists, facilitators, or change agents. The individual or the group makes choices regarding who or what the interventive target might appropriately be. The practitioner's choice of strategic role is itself evidence of the agency's and/or the practitioner's own policy position toward the appropriateness or preference of a particular intervention modality. For example, a school system's social work unit might arbitrarily or consciously select a child, the parents, a teacher, the school principal, or even the administrative structure as the target for intervention. Some practitioners routinely take on one or a selected number of these targets — as a matter of policy.

Finally, Dolgoff and Gordon suggest that what often really occurs is a blend of the three policy decisions, i.e., choice of treatment modality, worker role, and intervention target. Clearly, however, these three areas of policy decision occur at the smallest scale — that of interpersonal practice. For example, the worker makes a choice (hopefully after thoughtful analysis), about the appropriateness of assuming a broker, mediator, or therapist role. These role choices are partly determined by agency policy, e.g., what services are fundable or otherwise allowable. Treatment methodology is also limited or enhanced by agency policy and/or facilities as is the choice of clients and/or targets.

Perhaps an analysis of social policy at the program or agency level makes the policy analysis process clearer. Here, program coordinators are called upon to provide the agency director or task force, for example, with a detailed statement of the potential impact of a piece of pending state legislation upon the agency's mission or client population. Or an agency staff member is asked to provide an analysis of the ramifications of taking on a new service or establishing a new outpost at a branch location. In the context of policy process, an agency administrator may have to assess the possible social costs and outcomes of entering into a proposed or emerging coalition that results from current social action surrounding a policy issue. These situations clearly suggest that practitioners take implicit or explicit approaches to their analyses of policy.

Policy analysis has a range of functional utilities. Gilbert and Specht have pointed out that frameworks for policy analysis provide a meaningful set of concepts applicable to a wide range of situations, help to simplify a complex reality, and direct attention to certain elements while filtering out others (Gilbert and Specht, 1974). An explication of the elements for analysis also helps us to make our own assumptions known and to open our philosophical points of view to examination. Cates and Lohman (1980) have suggested that such analyses can serve to educate personnel to policy changes or consequences, provide a way to determine the local discretion available in new rules or regulations, allow clear position statements to be developed, and help client groups become more informed in order to enhance their ability to lobby more effectively. These are all rather practical utilities of policy analysis, which provide justification for efforts to build models or frameworks for the analysis of social welfare policy.

Approaches to Social Welfare Policy Analysis

As the reader is probably aware, there are many approaches, models, or frameworks for the analysis of social policy. In the discipline of political science, Thomas Dye (1981, pp. 19-45) has identified eight analytic models that are applicable here. These may be described as follows:

1. *Institutional model.* Policy is seen as the outputs of institutional events and processes.

2. *Rational model.* Policy is seen as the effects of efficient goal achievement.

3. *Process model.* Policy is seen strictly as political activity.

4. *Incremental model.* Policy is viewed merely as variations and modifications of past positions. *adding to program*

5. *Group model.* Policy is seen as the maintenance or outcomes of group equilibrium.

6. *Elite model.* Policy is seen as the preferences set and/or taken by elite community actors. *Powerful policy makers*

7. *Game theory models.* Policy is seen as rational choice-taking in competitive situations.

8. *Systems model.* Policy is seen as system inputs, throughputs, and outputs. *Popular*

The foregoing list makes it clear that there is no universal model for policy analysis. Which approach to take will depend upon an individual's situation—one's job responsibilities, level of functioning, philosophical orientation, and so forth. In this regard, Moroney cites Rein's observation that no single academic or professional discipline can adequately develop a universal appropriate tool. Rather, the analyst must select and apply the approaches used in the different disciplines and synthesize the analysis into a meaningful whole (Moroney, 1981, p. 78).

At the large-scale level of social systems, a number of successful approaches to the understanding of social welfare policy has developed, some of which are found in classic texts, such as Romanyshyn (1971), Dolgoff and Feldstein (1980), Kammerman and Kahn (1976), or Frederico (1980). These approaches to policy range from the historical/descriptive to the critical/analytical. Generally speaking, the approach to analysis has been to explore the various fields of service (e.g., child welfare, corrections, mental health, income maintenance, etc.), or to identify policy milestones in the chronology of American welfare history. Some approaches offer practical, descriptive information, such as details regarding the benefits or eligibility requirements of particular programs, while others provide critical analyses of the choices taken or the opportunities foregone in past policy and program development. It appears that most of the literature has focused on the content, as opposed to the process aspects of social welfare policy, though this is an impressionistic observation.

The shift has been away from an emphasis upon historical and descriptive approaches to social welfare policy and towards analysis of current policy impact or future policy choices. This newer theme is particularly evident in the emergence of model building in social welfare policy analysis. These efforts are of great value to us in developing our own models for small-scale policy analysis.

Models for Analysis

As noted above, a number of models are used in policy analysis. Models, of course, are merely temporary constructs developed to help us solve problems. Frequently we use models to aid us in our day-to-day problem solving. For example, if we find our housing inadequate, we might drive around on a Sunday afternoon and look for signs saying "Model Open." We can literally walk through and touch that temporary construction of reality; in so doing we gather data that narrows or expands our range of choices, and find further direction in our decision making. The model house suggests an awareness of a set of values that identifies a house as a dwelling for human satisfaction and includes some theoretical evidence about the utility, as well as the beauty, of a cantilevered roof. Perhaps the location of the lot is based upon empirical evidence of where and how the sun situates itself upon the house's windows, thereby suggesting that the architect (i.e., analyst) utilized data collection and analysis in development of the model.

A model for social welfare analysis is essentially the same. It is based upon certain values, certain theories about how things ought to work or go together, as well as upon some empirical reality. Basically, there is no difference between problem solving in technical and interactional areas.

> An explicit model, scientific or otherwise, however, introduces structure and terminology to a problem and provides a means for breaking a complicated decision into smaller tasks than can be handled one at a time. (Quade, 1975, p. 48)

This fundamental view of models is true whether our models are flowcharts, decision trees, or elaborate theoretical constructions without graphics.

In this book we will develop and use outlines as expressions of our models. However, whatever the approach, the process and the product still require the explication of what we value, what our hunches, hypotheses, or theories of cause and effect are, and rely upon the collection of empirical data. The models of social welfare policy analysis emerging in the current literature are all based upon these notions. And, while they differ significantly in their complexity, jargon, and emphasis, all make a contribution and each responds to the expanding recognition of our need for analytic tools and structure in presenting our policy analyses. While we will go into some detail in each of the models to which we refer in chapter 3, a limited number will be noted here for purposes of introduction. A more extensive list (and discussion) of authors and models is provided by Lyon (1983) in his report on a survey of required readings in social welfare policy courses in undergraduate and graduate social work programs.

The first model, selected for discussion here mainly because of its frequent appearance in the literature, was presented early on by David Gil (1976). Gil provides a highly elaborate and detailed framework for policy analysis, based on a perspective that certain social requirements are presumed to be universal. Gil stresses the repeated analysis and comparison of alternative policies in his problem-solving approach. Joseph Heffernan (1979) provides somewhat of an interactionist perspective; his focus is the analysis of the interplay of economic and political choice taking. Gilbert and Specht (1974) emphasize the inputs, processes, and outcomes (though not in those terms) of social welfare policy choices. Prigmore and Atherton (1979) provide an inventory of questions that are essentially basic value choices and practical political and financial parameters in a policy environment. Meenaghan and Washington (1980) provide a framework that derives from a set of basic and universal questions and a set of optional questions or concerns. While these models (as well as those presented in Chapter 3) are necessary to understand social welfare policy analysis, they all speak to and are designed for analysis at the grand- or large-scale policy levels. On the other hand, they provide us with direction in constructing another needed tool, a model for social welfare policy analysis at the small-scale level.

Dilemmas in Understanding

The reader should be forewarned that he or she will be faced by the same problems with which the aforementioned authors have struggled. As people, limited by thought and language, but needing to know and understand, we must make many choices as we proceed with our construction of a model for analysis. While these choices include many esoteric labels and tend to be seen as "intellectual concerns," if we look beyond the jargon and focus on the concepts, we can perhaps take more conscious responsibility for what we will set out to do. The latter refers to the range of choices all people make in their everyday lives, and to which they give little notice as they attempt to "make meaning."

We can create our understanding (i.e., our models) based upon the notion that there are certain objective facts and most of what we need to do is merely identify those facts. At the risk of over-simplifying, this is sometimes called positivism. An alternative, called a phenomenological approach, is to hold that objective understanding is found in the process of events, not the a priori conditions. This is one duality we face; we should be cautioned that we do not need to make any forced choices in this regard as our model will need to be eclectic.

Another classical duality is that of inductive versus deductive reasoning. Some models might emphasize beginning with a theoretical point of view and then proceeding to collect the facts appropriate to the theory. This deductive approach gives a good deal of direction to the practitioner and has led to many outstanding discoveries and analyses. The alternative approach, inductive reasoning, begins with the collection of a large amount of empirical data and then sets out to provide some shape and context to that data via movement towards theoretical explanation.

Yet another duality is the classical contest between a task and a process orientation so clearly treated by Roland Warren, for example (1972). The first tends to emphasize the goal, the second, the means of goal achievement. This duality seems to be clearly personified in social work practitioners. Some staff might be particularly task oriented, as opposed to others who might be particularly process oriented regarding what they emphasize, how they perceive their environments, and the importance of things and events in those environments. An excellent discussion of the conceptual and philosophical problems and pitfalls in explaining social policy phenomena is provided by Carrier and Kendall (1973), with particular emphasis on the contest between positivism and phenomenology.

We cannot totally avoid the pitfalls offered by these dualities. If we are honest, we will simply have to accept the limitations of our conceptual abilities and, as best we can, take what seems appropriate from the existing models in the field. The models that we choose must have their own integrity and logic. In chapter 3, a survey of the content and approach of what exists will hopefully assist us in making these selections.

Sources of Information

Where shall we get our information? In speaking of policy research, Tripodi, Fellin and Meyer suggest that three sets of information are available: "data on the target population, findings from studies of the use of intervention strategies, and information on costs, staff needs, and other organizational and administrative factors related to program delivery" (1983, p. 163). To this we would add the access to and knowledge of prior history, individual and collective biases in the organizational group(s) under analysis, and current political and economic pressures bearing on the issue for which the analysis is undertaken. In short, the policy analyst needs to have access to and a facility for the use of a range and variety of information resources in order to conduct an adequate analysis—or, more realistically, to at least be aware of the informational deficiencies that exist in the analysis when it is conducted. A big order—but let's begin!

Summary

In this chapter we considered a definition of social welfare policy and have provided a number of one liners. We also identified some interdependencies between policy, power, and information as an introduction to seeing what policy actually does for us as social practitioners. We looked at a few approaches to model building in social policy analysis and considered the conceptual and philosophical dilemmas posed for us in the dualities of positivism and phenomenology, inductive and deductive reasoning, and in the classical contest between task and process orientations to reality. From here we will take a more detailed look at some current large-scale models for analyzing policy content and process.

3

Current Models
for Policy Analysis

This chapter will provide a review of selected models for policy analysis in social welfare that are presently available to us. First we will review models that emphasize the analysis of policy content, then those that emphasize policy process. The chapter will help to identify the state of the art and will be helpful in mining the essential features or characteristics of various currently available models. Consequently, this chapter will provide a base for enumeration of elements thought by others to be essential, as well as what we might offer ourselves, and will provide a starting point for the models for small-scale policy analysis and presentation from which we will construct our own outlines.

While we must develop and construct our own models for small-scale policy analysis, there is a great deal of value in the social welfare literature to give us direction. The fact that much of this literature has been made available in recent years attests to the fact that the focus on policy analysis models in social welfare is a relatively recent development. However, although many of these models have much to offer, we still find it necessary to extrapolate from them to the small-scale situation if they are to be of any practical use for policy analysis at that level. Both the terminology used and its applications are large-scale, national, or even global in nature. These models often have limited direct relevance to the kinds of policy problems endemic to local agencies or statewide policy issues/action systems.

Before proceeding, however, we must make one note regarding the use of the term "models" as opposed to the choice of an alternative term, "frameworks." As noted in the previous chapter, models are taken to mean temporary constructions developed to solve a particular problem. Presumably, models are based upon one or more theories or set of propositions that make everything a coherent whole for problem-solving purposes. The term "frameworks" tends to have a similar meaning but is used in the literature to give recognition

and/or conscious visibility to the philosophical or world view as well
as the technical and theoretical features embodied in the model.
Perhaps we should more appropriately refer to our pursuit here as
the development of frameworks, rather than models, but the latter
term appears to have wider use in the field. For our purposes here,
when we refer to models we are also referring to those conceptual,
problem-solving devices that embody the values aspect suggested
by a philosophical or a world view. Additionally, we are taking our
task one step beyond conceptual model construction as we will
develop outlines for use in conducting analyses and presenting those
analyses.

Selected Models

In this chapter we will summarize and review both content and
process models for policy analysis. That is, we will look at models
that emphasize either substantive analytic content or the process or
activity aspects of policymaking. The tasks of policy analysis tend to
be either content- or process-specific; consequently, our task here is
to generate both types of models and outlines in order to help the
policy practitioner. We do not imply or suggest that content and
process are not interactive or interdependent. Indeed, one cannot
realistically focus on one to the total exclusion of the other. Content
and process are separated as a matter of emphasis for the purpose
of exploration and focus.

Cates and Lohman (1980) reviewed a number of frameworks and
found four different types of analytic categories emphasized by different schemes. There tends to be a focus upon (1) the policy values
or objectives, (2) the policy target groups, (3) the methods of
implementation of policy, and/or (4) the environmental impact of
a particular policy or policies. Any model or application of a model
can obviously emphasize one or any combination of these four
categories.

Haskins contends that whatever approach is taken to policy
analysis all analysts will agree that five basic activities of analysis
would include: (1) describing the problem situation; (2) specifying
criteria; (3) generating alternative strategies; (4) selecting a "best"
policy; and (5) assessing feasibility (Haskins, 1981, p. 203).

The simplest model would include the fewest number of elements or variables. That is, while some models have an elaborate number and variety of interconnected elements that facilitate a comprehensive and detailed analysis, some models provide a limited number of essentials. This is not to imply, of course, that a simple model is simplistic; it only indicates that some analysts tend to limit their number of tools in order to eliminate their workbench clutter. Put another way, some models are more or less inclusive, depending upon the number and variety of criteria employed for analysis. This does not suggest that anyone assumes that the job is any less complicated or complex.

Models Emphasizing the Content of Policy

Robert Moroney's approach to analysis provides a useful beginning in that, rather than setting forth outcome criteria or feasibility considerations at the outset, he bases his entire analysis on the premise that all "policy formulation is fundamentally concerned with making choices, and those choices are shaped by values" (Moroney, 1981, p. 99). In fact, Moroney emphasizes three basic values as being fundamental to social welfare policy analysis:

> Following this line of reasoning, I suggested that not only do values generate the criteria an analyst might use to evaluate existing policies or develop new policies, but also that three general values—liberty, equality, and fraternity—are the driving forces behind all policies, and that these three values cannot be maximized simultaneously. Whichever one is given primacy will result in limitations on the other two. (1981, p. 99)

While Moroney does offer some suggested criteria beyond the values preferences, his position is fundamentally to keep visible throughout analysis the primacy of values in choice taking and preference selection. This position is especially appropriate for a practice-oriented profession bound by its code of ethics to deal openly and aggressively with values. In fact, Levy (1979b) contends that values and ethics for professionals tend to converge in that the pursuit of valued ends becomes an ethical mandate for professional practice. That is, what we want (values) and what we must do about it (ethics) converge in professional practice, whereas values and ethics may be quite separate when dealing with these terms in a general sense.

An approach that utilizes a limited number of criteria is the model provided by Joseph Kelley (1975). Kelley, who offers what is called a change-related (as opposed to a past-oriented) approach, provides a limited number of criteria, each of which is undoubtedly familiar to all of us. His three essential criteria are adequacy, effectiveness, and efficiency. That is, any proposed or actual policy subjected to analysis must be assessed in terms of (1) the extent to which a specified need or goal is met if program objectives are carried out (adequacy); (2) the extent to which the outcomes obtained are a result of policy intent and program activity (effectiveness); and (3) the measure of goal attainment in terms of the expenditure of the least amount of resources (efficiency). One can hardly develop social policy of any kind without considering these basic criteria. Consequently, the three criteria might serve as a foundation for any model for social welfare policy analysis.

However, Kelley adds what he calls two key "subcriteria" called "identity" and "self-determination." That is, if the substance of the matter is of a social welfare nature, one must also consider the impact of the policy or consequent program upon the self-image of the beneficiary or target (the identity), and the right of consumers to a voice in the determination of those policies that might affect them (self-determination).

Given the nature of the code of ethics of such organizations as the National Association of Social Workers and other human services associations, it is little wonder that adequacy, effectiveness and efficiency are not sufficient criteria. The impact upon client identity and client self-determination are criteria that *must* be included in any model for social welfare policy analysis.

This particular model would, on the face of it, appear easy to apply to small-scale policy contexts. Surely an agency policy may be considered in terms of the current or potential adequacy of its benefits. Effectiveness might be determined by quantitative or soft measures within the local action system; and local measures that determine what constitutes desirable levels of efficiency could perhaps be agreed upon. At small-scale levels, the questions of impact on client or target identity and self-determination are perhaps more realistically pursued. The problem with the model, however, is that it posits only a limited number of criteria and is not in itself an adequate representation of reality for an inclusive or a comprehensive analysis.

A much more elaborate model is presented by Gilbert and Specht (1974) in which they suggest two levels for content analysis. The first is referred to as the foundations or major parameters of choice. It includes the identification of the major values at odds in the policy, the explicit or implicit theories giving rise to the policy issues, and the overarching alternatives that are possible. The second is what are called the "dimensions of choice." Those elements, labeled by Gilbert and Specht as bases of social allocations, types of social provisions, strategies for delivery, and modes of finance, essentially analyze the questions of who gets what, through what delivery mechanism, and how the program will be financed. These issues, for example, could be translated into questions of eligibility criteria, forms that benefits might take (e.g., social insurance or public assistance), questions of service system design (e.g., preventative, habilitative, or rehabilitative), and concerns about mode and manner of finance.

Gilbert and Specht suggest that their model embodies the social, political, and technical process aspects of policy as well as the performance outcomes of actual policies and programs. However, their emphasis seems to center around the substantive content aspects of policy rather than the process of policy development or change. Perhaps the greatest strength of their model is its emphasis upon the products of any given set of policy choices; however, that feature should be a strength of any model for analysis.

Meenaghan and Washington (1980) provide a framework that includes a mixture of generally applicable principles (e.g., concerns for ethics regarding work or individualism), basic criteria (e.g., fairness, adequacy, and equality), and generalizable design criteria (e.g., funding and allocation characteristics, types of benefits, or delivery mechanisms). This framework, while perhaps no more comprehensive than some others, does tend to be quite explicit and enumerates a range and variety of considerations in social policy analysis. In their basic framework, which they refer to as "lower levels of choice," they search for the fairness, adequacy, and equality in the basic thrust of any policy. They then examine the level of prevention desired, the goal mix, types of benefits (e.g., cash versus in-kind benefits or the redistribution of power), the delivery system design, financing considerations, and the like. Their "higher level" analysis suggests more detailed examination of these elements and examines both the historical and contemporary ramifications of various choices based upon the model's criteria. Their approach appears to be an attempt to strike a balance between content and process orientations to analysis.

Joseph Heffernan (1979), while giving extensive attention to the political-economic substance of social welfare policy, nevertheless tends to emphasize its process aspects. Heffernan suggests that the main issue in social policy is to link personal problems to public concerns and that this task and process evolve around two central concepts: political power and economic scarcity. He sees policy as the accommodation of competing and sometimes contradictory demands upon scarce resources, and policy analysis as the articulation of preferences among alternative values and options wherein policy goals, procedures, and consequences are constantly evaluated in terms of what is desirable and what is possible. The primary strength of Heffernan's model lies in the visibility given to choices among preferences, though relatively little (compared to other analytic models) is offered in terms of substantive criteria for analysis.

Another model is that of Prigmore and Atherton (1979). Their approach is unique in that they pose a set of questions that serve as an inventory or laundry list. Their model is comprised of approximately a dozen questions in four major areas: (1) considerations related to cultural values; (2) dimensions of influence and decision making (political acceptability and legality); (3) knowledge considerations (whether the policy is scientifically sound or rational); and (4) elements related to costs and/or benefits. Prigmore and Atherton's approach provides a range of criteria, which includes a questioning of basic values and premises as well as of those items frequently associated with the rational aspects of policy analysis, such as design principles, financing considerations, and delivery mechanisms.

A review of models for policy analysis would not be complete without acknowledging the model provided by David Gil (1970; 1976). Gil, taking a mixture of the classical structural-functionalist approach from the field of sociology and a mechanical view of systems analysis, emphasizes certain basic societal requisites such as resource allocation, rights distribution, status allocations, and the linkage between rights and statuses. Gil's outline for analysis essentially employs a rational and interactive problem-solving approach in which a variety of problem definitions and alternative choices are played out. Gil's model tends to be the one most frequently cited in the literature, perhaps because of its clarity and comprehensiveness. Yet its detail can be intimidating, if not somewhat impractical in terms of manageability.

There is one particular aspect of the Gil model, however, which is unique and receives little mention in the frequent references in the literature. We refer to Gil's contention that the fundamental purpose of policy analysis is to enable the analyst to become part of a counterculture through which those interested in maintaining the status quo might be educated to newly found self-interests. In other words, the policy analyst is seen as having a mission—to alter the system's organization of power and influence. Though Gil's approach to policy analysis is fundamentally rationalist in nature, his goals are value based and pursued in a phenomenological context—a rare mix.

As noted earlier, each of these models (and others in the literature not mentioned here) appears to have been created and developed with broad, large-scale, primarily national policy analysis tasks in mind. While most of the models are inclusive and comprehensive, their languaging and examples tend to relate to levels well beyond and outside the needs of the policy practitioner at the local or small-scale level. Nevertheless, each offers much to the development of policy analysis tools and we will rely heavily on these works as we develop our own model in later chapters.

Models Emphasizing the Process of Policy

Identifying a body of policy literature as policy *process* literature in social welfare is a difficult task. While many books and journal articles related to models and frameworks for the analysis of *policy content* are available, interest in policy process tends to be scattered among a number of fields, including the social problems area within sociology, the political economics area of economics and political science, and the decision-making and communication areas of management, planning, and administration. This may be due to the fact that certain substantive or content concerns of social welfare "belong" to that field while the process aspects of social interaction are endemic to virtually all behavioral fields. Nevertheless, our task here is to identify a range of process-oriented models that might serve us in model building for policy process analysis.

We have selected four process explanations to policy change that offer some promise as models for policy process analysis. These may be identified as (1) the action system model, (2) the competing problems definition model, (3) the sequential/incremental model, and (4) the leverage model. While we could have looked to the literature on power or community organization, for example, to find our material, we chose instead four disparate explanations of process in the policy context, since this variety promises a range of elements for our own model construction.

The *action system model,* originally developed by Sower and his colleagues (1957) and further refined by Warren (1963; 1977), is based upon the presumption that social policy action occurs in phase- or stage-like fashion over time. Certain tasks are performed over the life of the action system in order to accomplish the desired social change. An initiation set of actors is established, out of which a "charter" (i.e., a specific or general agreement upon a goal for action) is formed. Then sponsorship and legitimation are obtained, the action set is expanded, and the substantive matters are pursued by an "execution set." And, in a feature added by Warren, it is presumed that the action set is transformed into a new group within which new goals and charters are pursued. The essential elements to be gleaned here for a model of policy process are initiation, support, sponsorship, legitimation, and implementation of group decisions. The model has some utility and has provided the theoretical foundation for studies by Flynn (1973) and Whitaker and Flory-Baker (1982).

The *competing problems definition model* derives from the social problems literature. An excellent example is provided by Ross and Staines (1972): the central theme is that private (individual or group) concerns have a predictable life as they undergo the process of conversion from private to public issues worthy of consideration for public policy discussion. For Ross and Staines, key elements are the change agents' ability to enlist the awareness and support of key partisans, media, officialdom, and related interest groups for the purpose of placing the concern on the public agenda. This "agenda-setting" is prerequisite to formal and legitimate public consideration of policy goals and options. However, while Ross and Staines provide insights into what might be called a policy "preprocess," they do not concern themselves with the throughput processes of policy action; rather, they see only summary outcomes, such as negotiations obtained, legislation passed, and the like. Tierney (1982) used this model effectively in documenting the preprocess of establishing spouse abuse shelters in the United States. York (1982) used this model to analyze the politics of defining social problems.

A very elaborate and perhaps the most familiar model is the *sequential/incremental model* offered by Charles Lindblom (1967; 1975). In summary, Lindblom holds that the policy process is played out according to an established (albeit sometimes informal and implicit) set of rules in which the play of power is managed primarily by partisan analysts and proximate policymakers (e.g., executive staff members, legislative staff, or respected analysts). That is, partisan analysts become "the knowledgeables" around given issues wherein knowledge becomes power when exercised by those in positions immediately subordinate to policy decision makers. Hence, proximate policymakers sometimes play a greater role in the play of power and the policy process than do persons in nominal positions of decision-making authority. In his conceptualization, Lindblom includes a variety of strategies or "dodges" employed by policy actors. For our model-building purposes, however, the key elements are the role of partisan analysts, proximate policymakers, and the notion of rule-like behavior. We regard this conceptualization as inherently conservatizing, given that any policy change is seen only as an incremental change from previous states and/or conditions and because the process fundamentally evolves around compromise.

The *leverage model* offered by Kenneth Gergen (1968) is an elaborate one that seems to rely on an unusual language of its own. However, the concepts offered are highly generalizable. Gergen places primary emphasis for the explanation of policy upon (1) the personal efficacy of the individual actors, (2) the salience of the policy issue throughout the relevant social systems, and (3) the various resources available to the action system, such as time, people power, communication facilities and avenues, finances, technical capacity, and so forth. A distinguishing element in this broad and comprehensive model is the role of the individual, group, or organization vis à vis the personal efficacy (either charisma or credibility) of the key actors involved: the partisan analyst is seen as a resource in the policy process.

The Marxist or Socialist Perspectives

The reader may wonder why no attention has been given to Marxist or socialist models of policy analysis. After all, much in the literature expresses a Marxist or socialist perspective on the content and processes of social welfare. Notable examples can be found in the writings of Galper (1975; 1980) and Cloward and Piven (1971). However, the Marxist or socialist oriented literature belongs more in the realm of a *perspective*, a world view, or an overall framework for looking at reality rather than a *model*. While the socialist perspectives found in the literature provide an excellent overall context for *analysis*, or offer the basis for selection of criteria that we value or find compatible with our codes of ethics, as yet no Marxist or socialist *models* have been advanced. That is, the Marxist or socialist perspectives have not developed to the point of providing us with *models* that suggest specific decision-making variables that can be broken down for purposes of problem solving.

The socialist literature does, however, offer significant content. Galper speaks to the value of client self-determination and appropriately emphasizes the social control or regulatory functions of welfare systems and the external environment affecting clients and social service workers. He emphasizes the presence of class antagonisms among and between the sponsors, providers, and receivers of social services and the various degrees of competition and opportunity surrounding control of and access to resources. Of particular note is Galper's critique of the limits of reformism. However, Lyon refers to Galper as providing "the only openly socialist policy monograph" (1983, p. 388). If this is the case, Galper voices many sound criticisms of the bases and priorities of social welfare systems, but does not offer a *model* that provides direction at the practice level. Nevertheless, the socialist critique should be kept in mind; it does, in fact, provide us with a useful context for our own pursuit of model building.

Models Emphasizing Quantitative Approaches

A number of models are available that primarily take a quantitative approach to analysis. They tend to be used in large-scale policy analysis and, while we will not attempt to incorporate them here, some of these quantitative approaches will be summarized. For those who wish to pursue these models further and who might benefit from illustrations, an excellent primer is available, written by Stokey and

Zeckhauser (1978). The quantitative models may be characterized as both deterministic (wherein the outcomes are certain) and probabilistic (wherein the variables, as well as variable values, are unknown). They are often referred to as preference models since their analysis strategy consists of determining the available decision alternatives, followed by selecting a preference from those alternatives. We will summarize a few of these, below, in particular input/output models, the difference equation, queuing models, computer simulations, Markov chains and processes, benefit/cost analysis, linear programming, and decision analysis.

The model that appears to be the least quantitative is the ***input-throughput-output*** approach found in the literature. In fact, these input/output models are often mistaken for "system approaches." In social services, the input might be clients or funding sources, the throughputs the social treatment processes or techniques, and the outputs the solved problems, the satisfaction obtained from service, or other quantifiable measures of the results of the service process. Use of these models requires knowledge of the whole range and dimensions of the various inputs, throughput procedures and, of course, also demands creativity in making outcomes and outputs operational.

Difference equations are used to explore the changes in variables over discrete periods of time. This approach could be applied, for example, to the number of discharges from a hospital on a daily basis or at annual intervals. These equations are generally used only by mathematicians, perhaps due to the reliance upon the use of mathematical notation in the equations and a general lack of comfort with that approach by most policy analysts in the human services.

Queuing models are used to study situations in which the provider of a commodity or a service is faced with a demand that exceeds the supply or availability of what is provided. Key elements in using queuing models in human services, for example, might be the demands or applications (called "arrivals"), the time necessary to provide services (called "service time"), and the "queue discipline" or "queue characteristics," such as special treatment that needs to be made available for crises or emergencies, or priority problem conditions. Queuing models have been used to simulate decisions about the judicious location of satellite offices by a human service agency (Luse, 1982).

Computer simulations tend to be used when a large number of complex and interdependent variables are involved. Simulations are laboratory models in which the analyst attempts to reproduce real-life conditions as represented by an algorithm in the simulation. (An algorithm is a mathematical expression that presumably includes significant variables, with their proper weight and relationship assigned according to some theoretical understanding of the problem.) Simulations and algorithms have been used in decision support systems in making child placement decisions (Jaffee, 1979), in determining service awards for in-home relief (Boyd et al., 1981), and in modeling policy processes (Flynn, 1985). A summary review of a few applications to health and welfare problems has been provided by Luse (1980). As with queuing applications, computer simulations allow for an unlimited number of theoretical experiments under virtually an unlimited number of conditions. Their limitations come in not having relevant data in hand so as to construct useful algorithms applied to meaningful situations.

Markov models provide yet another approach. Markov chains are based on probabilities and are used to follow the flow of people or events through a system. For example, a Markov chain might be used to follow the transition of developmentally disabled adults through a residential training program that provides a continuum of care. While the Markov chain deals with the probabilistic movement of individuals through a system of events, Markov processes allow the analyst to study entire populations. Both approaches require knowledge of the properties of mutually exclusive states or events, the presence of uniform and fixed time intervals, and populations that are constant in size. Therefore, there are limited opportunities for application of these models in social welfare, though they are appropriate and useful in certain circumstances.

Benefit/cost models essentially determine the ratio of benefits to cost, with the favorable outcome being sufficiently higher benefits, presuming a system giving high priority to an economic efficiency principle. Benefit/cost models are perhaps the most frequently used mathematical approach to evaluating expenditures for public services. The difficult tasks in benefit/cost approaches involve specifying all the tangible, intangible, quantifiable, and nonquantifiable variables involved in achieving a net cost. Benefit/cost models have been applied to work training and other direct rehabilitation programs, perhaps because those programs tend to be better defined in terms of inputs and outcomes and, as noted, they are rooted in economic efficiency.

Linear programming is used by policy analysts to distribute a limited amount of resources (e.g., money, time, or staff) to a program or a problem resolution project. It is used to determine the optimum or minimum allowable resource or cost required to complete the range and sequence of tasks necessary for goal achievement. In human services, linear programming (as with PERT, flow charting or other work plan techniques) can be useful in project planning and demonstration efforts. Another application might involve planning for the carefully scheduled use of facilities by more than one group or agency program. A limitation, of course, is that not all social welfare problems, nor all variables associated with a particular problem, are linear. Some variables are nonlinear or the values associated with some alternatives are not acceptable to the program sponsor or the analyst in the context of a given situation.

A final model to be mentioned here is decision analysis. *Decision analysis models* help the analyst sort out the complexity of decisions that are contingent upon one another. Decision analysis is especially useful where decisions must be made sequentially, which is why these models are characterized by decision nodes and decision trees, all of which are contingent upon probabilities and potential payoffs. These models are appropriate in human services when working with individuals or programs wherein milestones are achieved and subsequent strategic decisions are made along the way.

Stokey and Zeckhauser (1978) quite properly acknowledge that no magic is involved in the use of quantitatively oriented models for policy analysis. In fact, as with all models for policy analysis, there is no substitute for having the necessary and sufficient information demanded by a thorough or knowledgeable analysis. And perhaps most worthy of all is the fact that all models require a conscious valuing ✓ of the ends that are sought and the means that are employed.

Summary

In this chapter we have discussed a number of models, some emphasizing the content aspects of policy analysis and others the process aspects. Each model gives evidence of having its own philosophical perspective and each is committed to a set of fundamental principles as well as its own concepts and jargon. We then discussed the Marxist or socialist perspective in policy analysis. We also summarized a number of quantitatively oriented models, though we will not draw on these in constructing our own outlines. In chapters 4 and 5 we will extract these principles, concepts and criteria, and add our own, in our efforts to build a model for small-scale analysis of policy content and process.

4

Content Elements
for Small-Scale Policy Analysis

Our next task is to combine a number of the content elements for small-scale policy analysis, borrowing here and there from what we have already seen or reviewed, and developing our own tools. To this end, we must first identify the basic core of content elements that constitute the essentials for a model for analysis.

Essential Activities in Analysis

Looking back on what others have already constructed in grand-scale models currently in use, we can see that content or process models require that the analyst give consideration to six areas or engage in six essential activities. These are:

1. Identifying the policy problem and/or the policy goals
2. Setting the criteria for review or choice
3. Assessing system functioning
4. Determining major strategies
5. Determining feasibility
6. Assessing congruence with desired values

Obviously, none of these six essential activities can be seen as discrete events experienced in a totally linear fashion; they are interrelated and occur in an interactive or circular fashion. For example, policy goals are intertwined, with values and strategies often dependent upon feasibility factors. What we will now need to do is identify the particular analytic tasks or substantive areas that are associated with each of the six major activities of small-scale policy analysis. In the discussion that follows, we will draw on the summaries of grand-scale models surveyed in earlier chapters as well as the brief guide for small-scale policy analysis provided by Flynn (1976). Since the topic of congruence with desired values demands special attention, we will treat it separately in chapter 5. In this chapter we will deal with the first five essential activities.

For illustrative purposes, we will also introduce a detailed case example in this chapter. As we move through the discussion and explanation of the elements of the outline for analysis of policy content, we will provide applications involving a policy situation.

Before introducing the case illustration material, one additional comment should be made regarding the application of each element of the outline for analysis. The reader should be cautioned that not every policy analysis needs to laboriously go through and apply each and every criterion that follows in this application. Rather, the outline serves as a problem-solving tool that should be applied as it appears appropriate to a given situation. For purposes of illustration, we have attempted to provide applications for each criterion for our hypothetical situation. No compulsive meta-message is intended; in real life each element or criterion need not be applied.

Case Illustration

For our first illustration we will select a policy that is immediately related to a direct practice issue. Let us explore what might generally be considered a knotty problem, both for policy and for direct service practice: the participation of birthparents in the adoption process for their child. Let's assume that we are employed as a program coordinator in a typical private child welfare agency providing adoption and foster care services for children. Conventional practice has been that one or both of the birthparents (i.e., the biological mother and/or father) are assisted in making a decision for a permanent plan for the child at the earliest reasonable opportunity. Aside from making the personal decision regarding adoption, the birthparent is generally limited to the role of a provider of information who might assist in making an appropriate placement. The actual adoption plan and placement is seen as the responsibility of the agency and its staff. However, our agency example, Child Services, Inc., has had a policy in place for two years providing that the birthparent is both encouraged and expected to participate in the planning for the care of the child to as great a degree as possible. The Board of Directors has inquired into the functioning of this policy and you have been given the task of providing an analysis of the "birthparents' participation policy."

Child Services, Inc. is a rather small, sectarian, nonprofit agency that places an average of ten or twelve children in adoption monthly and is a member of the local United Fund. You will recall that the adoption policy was established by the Board just a couple of years ago, with limited concern expressed. As a first step, you decide to look at the agency's *Adoption Manual* in order to find documentation of the policy. (For purposes of discussion, please note that the birthparent is referred to in the singular and as the feminine "she"; the infant is referred to as "he." In actual practice, agencies may give more effort or recognition to inclusion of both birthparents and, in fact, this matter would certainly be a factor in your analysis, as we shall see.)

The Policy Problem and/or Policy Goals

The policy statement. The first set of activities for the analysis is to make it clear to yourself and to those with whom you wish to communicate your policy analysis, just what, in fact, is the policy problem, the policy issue or policy goal or objective under study. That is, we may begin with a concern, or an issue, a felt difficulty or something thought to be a policy problem. However, in order to give focus to our analysis and to "check out" whether we match in our focus with those with or to whom we must communicate our analysis, we must begin with a clean, clear, and uncluttered statement of the focus of the analysis. If we are lucky, there may be a policy goal, or more specifically, a policy objective (taken from an annual plan or an administrative manual, for example), that will help us in obtaining this specificity. Budget proposals, annual program plans, staff manuals, contractual agreements, policy directives and the like are all potential statement sources that can give focus to our definition of policy goals and objectives. These statements are often clues to the underlying principles (policies) that will hopefully be achieved by the policies or directives.

It must be stressed, however, that there are also times when it is advantageous to organizations to give low visibility to their policies or preferences, and the analyst may have to use the documents noted above or other sources to confirm what the policy actually is. For example, during periods of tight financial resources, an agency may actually not publicize the availability of certain services for a client group. Or a particular agency may not, as a matter of policy, actually desire to interact or cooperate with another community agency for some particular reason, but that policy is not apt to be openly stated.

Included in the task of identifying the policy statement is the determination of the policy's foundation or source and the location of legitimacy (the right to exist or take action). This legitimacy might be found in articles of incorporation, bylaws, board minutes, personnel policies, statutes, or administrative rules. Establishing or determining the legitimacy of a policy is a logical early step in any systematic analysis.

At times the analyst is not blessed with a given policy goal or objective, explicit or implied. Sometimes we begin only with a concern, an issue, or a problem. Nevertheless, our first essential task is to "carve out" or "chisel out" a clear and uncluttered conceptualization of what the subject of analysis shall be. For example, in an organizational policy having to do with staff functioning, it would not be helpful to begin our analysis by saying that staff are unhappy. It would be much more helpful if we could (appropriately) say that staff are dissatisfied with a particular set of events, such as the amount of time spent in group staffing of agency clients. An even more helpful focus would be, for example, that staff prefer to spend less time in group assessment and treatment planning of individual clients. A greater level of specificity would be that staff prefer to adjust agency procedure so that less time would be allocated to group assessment and treatment planning subsequent to initiation of the original service plan. The statement should be developed to give focus and direction to the kinds of data to be collected for the analysis and to clarify for all that the effort will, in fact, be focused upon the item of shared concern. In other words, the original policy analysis activity — stating the problem or policy clearly — not only gives focus and direction to subsequent analytic activity but is also a way of communicating and checking out shared meanings and understandings.

In summary, you should be able to state clearly and succinctly, preferably in one sentence, the proposed or existing policy under study. To do this, you need to identify the policy mandate, the guiding principle, the current operational reality, or the desired policy state that concerns you. The source and locus of legitimacy must also be made clear. This clarification must come first if the analysis is to proceed on solid ground.

Case Example

The policy reads, in part, as follows:

> Adoption is an experience which is done with the birthparent and not to her. The agency has a great deal of respect for this expectant parent and her commitment to life itself and her child in particular. The agency sees adoption as an opportunity for the birthparent to experience a great deal of personal growth. The opportunity to grow is enhanced by an atmosphere of openness. This openness enables the expectant parent to anticipate some of the grief and loss experience. . . . It is expected that the worker and the birthparent will together develop a particular contract for how the adoption will occur. . . . Finally, the agency recognizes that the experience of giving birth to a child and releasing him for adoption is a lifelong experience. The agency will continue to be available to the birthparent over the subsequent years and will make every effort possible to provide support. . . .

> The putative father has long been neglected in adoption planning. . . . Child Services, Inc. recognizes that pregnancy and adoption are very significant events in the lives of fathers. Therefore, the worker should make every effort to involve the father in the decision-making process.

The *Manual* contains many procedural provisions and guidelines, of course, such as the means for encouraging involvement of the biological mother and special methods of publishing notice for the putative father. Furthermore, many suggestions of sound professional practice are also interspersed such as the compatibility of the policy with the development of a helping relationship characterized by trust. Thus, having established the source and the wording of the policy, we have taken the first step in our analysis and identified the policy statement. As we noted in our earlier discussion, we are not always blessed with a policy as a given; in this instance, we had an already established policy as a point of departure. Had we not been given this policy to begin our analysis, our first step would probably have been to give more shape or specificity to the issue of birthparents' rights, or more study about some felt difficulty of the presumed need for a priori contracting by birthparents in making adoptive plans, or to translate certain treatment principles into policy. In summary, *we need to begin with problem definition.*

Contemporary issues. Having set forth the policy or problem statement, it is helpful to determine whether there are other related or ancillary issues currently impinging on the policy under study. For example, in the illustration noted above regarding group staffings of client assessments and treatment planning, there may be peripheral issues related to certification requirements for third-party insurance reimbursement, or contractual requirements from one of the fund-

ing sources. These are just some of the possible factors also impinging upon the problem and upon the statement of the problem.

Contemporary issues

Now we need to explore what some of the ancillary issues
are in our case illustration. What is the general mood in the
community toward unwanted pregnancies and birthparents
placing children for adoption? In other words, how reasonable has the agency's expectation been that biological mothers
would not only allow, but actually encourage, prolonged or
extensive participation in adoption planning? This question
needs to be considered. Another possibility is the question of
the likelihood of biological fathers being willing to go against
what are probably long-standing community norms and volun-
tarily participate in planning. Can you think of other contemporary issues that might play a part in such a situation in your
agency or your community?

Historical antecedents. Another concern should be determining
whether any historical "baggage" is being brought to the problem
or the policy. We sometimes inherit theories or procedures that explain
why we do things the way we do; at other times our behavior reflects
a rejection of the past and its procedures. In our illustration of group
staffings, it could be that it was physically easier and therefore logical in the past for staff to get together when the agency was functioning entirely at one location, whereas today its staff operate out
of a number of outreach centers. Or group staffings may have necessarily been more frequent prior to the creation and availability of
case services managers who are now charged with coordinating case
services for clients. These are just some examples of the necessity of
considering the relevance of historical antecedents to the current policy
situation.

Historical antecedents

Let's consider what some of the historical baggage might be that comes with this policy. The first thing that comes to mind is the community attitudes that have existed over the years regarding pregnancies out of wedlock, the propensity toward managing the whole matter in a shroud of secrecy, the leaving the details to "professional discretion," and the presumption of few rights being allocable to the birthparents aside from the consent for release. The process was generally viewed as the birthparent "giving up" the child. Given these community values, there were probably few choices for the birthparents or for the agency's adoption workers that would have encouraged or even tolerated extensive participation and involvement.

The analyst would also need to look to historical events within the agency or the community that might have a bearing on the policy. In this case example, we have a hypothetical situation; let's play it out a little. A major factor in the policy's initiation is that a staff member recognized the need in the past and developed a support group for parents who had released their children for adoption. This then led to communications and visits with a similar agency experiencing similar concerns for that client group, which led to the introduction of outside information from others' experiences.

Exploration of this issue would likely also turn up such matters as public debate revolving around the local school district concerning the number of school-age pregnancies or the number of students dropping out of high school. Another possibility might be a local issue surrounding concern that parent training be provided to adolescents and/or young adults. Certainly a likely candidate for a recent historical issue could be community debate concerning sex education in the school system and how this might be related to the increase in unwanted pregnancies.

Yet another avenue might be a current or recent discussion in the community around pregnancies that occur in the later child-bearing years and the issue of whether expectant parents have the right or responsibility to plan for the future of their unborn child in their own way.

Targets of concern. Another important task is to be able to specify, early on, who or what the target of concern is. The target of the policy concern or the policy statement should be clear in the mind of the analyst so that all subsequent analytic activities are brought to bear in terms of impact upon that target or object. And, of course, in real life the target could be multifaced and multifaceted. In our group staff example we might find the target to be clients who are receiving less than the desired amounts of direct services; or the target might be the work patterns of certain staff who give greatest priority to team interaction and group decision processes; or the target might be alteration of contractual terms with the funding source, such as adjusting expectations regarding the amount of direct services to be provided as opposed to allowances for collateral activity on behalf of clients. In any event, it is very important to determine early on who or what the target or intended beneficiary of the remedy might be. Here it is sometimes helpful and instructive to distinguish the *target* system from the *client* system. The target may be seen as that group or individual *in whom* change is being sought. The client system may be seen as that group or individual *on whose behalf* change is being sought (see Pincus and Minahan, 1973). Obviously, these individuals or groups may or may not necessarily be one and the same. In our group staffing example, the client system in one instance might be those receiving agency services and the target system the staff members stressing group interaction; in another instance, the client system might be the funding source served by the policy change and the target system might be selected staff who provide particular services in a diagnostic or treatment team. These determinations will depend primarily upon the concern or issue and how the analyst casts the analysis, especially the problem, or policy goal or objective statement. And these statements, and how they are cast, are sometimes dependent upon one's view of the world at that particular moment in time.

Another approach to the target of policy action is to look at the desired outcome of the policy in terms of the effects upon system maintenance, system control, or system change, or any mixture of the three. In our example, does continued group staffing of cases essentially provide a holding operation for clients (i.e., system maintenance), a continued source of required labor for staff (i.e., system control), or does it provide for continual evolution of the needs of clients, the needs of staff, and the needs of the agency (i.e., system change)? Put simply, the goal of the policy may be seen as a service system condition as well as a client condition.

Whether the target of the policy is a service system or a client group or individual, it is also instructive early in the analysis to make some estimate of the efficiency of coverage of the target by the policy. That is, we need to get some idea of the extent to which the target is "covered by the policy," both in the aggregate (i.e., to what extent is the whole target covered) and individually (i.e., to what extent each target element is adequately serviced by the policy). This gives us an early notion of the power of the policy in terms of its achieving its intended effects and the extent of its currently being problematic.

Targets of concern

Generally speaking, the target of the policy is the newborn infant, with the agency acting in the capacity of advocate for the child. More specifically, and on an immediate level, the target is the birthparent, whose full and enlightened participation in the process is thereby solicited. From our discussion of types of systems in social services it could be suggested that the child is the client system (the system on whose behalf action is undertaken) and the birthparent is the target system (the system in which behavioral change is being sought). The policy also allows for expansion of the target by providing particular emphasis upon reaching out to and including the biological father of the child. We could also speculate at this point in our analysis and consider the desired and potential outcomes upon the target. To be sure, we see a birthparent who is likely to feel helpless, vulnerable, perhaps full of guilt, and leery of trusting. The policy is aimed at alleviating these feelings. An obvious possibility for accomplishing the desired outcome is to enlist the cooperation of the birthparent-as-client, using interviewing and other casework techniques that obtain the greatest amount of preplacement information. Achieving the desired outcome depends greatly on the theoretical perspectives upon which the policy is founded.

Explicit or implicit theories. It is also helpful to take an early look at how one has cast the problem or the policy goal statement and speculate about what theoretical point of view is expressed by the issue as formulated. As the reader is no doubt aware, the theory underlying the formulation of the problem is likely to dictate or delimit the subsequent analytic methods selected, the analysis of data, and the resultant solution or recommendation. Theories bring with them a limited set of conceptualizations and values which put boundaries around what is seen and considered. For example, it would serve us well in our group staffing example to consider how we tend to operationalize the notion of efficiencies. We could see "efficiency" as bringing the whole range of professional resources of staff to bear upon the assessment or treatment of the client, on the one hand, or as the minimal allocation of professional time to assessment in the interest of delivering more direct services given the available professional staff time. Or we may tend to operate on some implicit theory that group staffing of assessment and treatment planning also serves other goals of staff orientation and staff development, wherein various staff members pass on or share in their expertise. These are just some illustrations.

These theoretical conceptualizations may be explicitly stated at the outset as guiding the problem statement and the policy analysis or they may be stated as conjecture for possible theoretical alternatives. At any rate, it benefits the analyst to bring these theoretical conceptualizations to mind and explicate them as much as possible, if for no other reason than to keep the analyst "honest" or to fore-warn the person or agency to whom the analysis is communicated that these are the possible considerations.

And finally, as with theories, it is well to think "up front" about what values are being expressed in the problem or goal formulation. However, we have reserved for the next chapter the discussion of value considerations as our sixth major set of analytic activities.

Explicit or implicit theories

Some speculation about and/or identification of the theoretical foundations of the policy under analysis can give clues to the incentives for the policy's existence. Increased inclusion of the birthparent may be founded upon the hypothesis that the birthparent's active participation in the adoption process is more likely to result in a successful and functional separation process for that parent. Another (and not necessarily separate) possible explanation is that fuller participation will bring about more successful placements as a result of obtaining the most complete information rather than making decisions under less clear conditions. The theoretical explanation may be founded upon more fundamental values (which we will discuss below), such as fundamental client rights to self-determination by providing policies that support that value. Releasing a child for adoption may be viewed as an act of love by the birthparent, rather than an act of abandonment, and should (according to the theory) be supported in a manner that encourages the birthparent's full and active participation in the adoption process.

Topography of the policy system. Systems thinking has taught us the value of mapping the characteristics of living systems. This concept, mapping the topography of a system, gives us some leads that help to give shape to the policy definition. For example, we can identify implied boundary characteristics, such as what subsystems are included in the definition of the problem, the policy, and/or the system. For purposes of analysis, it is crucial to be aware of the fact that we can arbitrarily and logically determine at this point which subsystems or elements we might choose to include in the definition of "the system" and, therefore, what elements will be subjected to the analysis. This, then, gets us immediately to the questions of the nature and form of the boundaries that give shape to the "policy system" we have selected. For example, what *does* give shape to the boundaries—the origins of sponsorship or legitimacy, auspices, legal status (e.g., charter or bylaws), funding, geographic service area? A review of these characteristics begins to draw conceptual boundaries around the policy system so we know what we are focusing on. It also leads to an early assessment of the policy system's functioning, such as the openness or closedness, or permeability, of the policy system's boundaries, a fundamental measuring stick of system functioning of any kind. More will be said about this later in the discussion of system functioning.

Topography of the policy system

This policy obviously expands the typical boundaries beyond the office space of the adoption worker. As the biological mother is more fully involved, this is likely to mean that those in whom she confides and with whom she converses are more likely to be involved in the decision process. Furthermore, the explicit reference in the policy to the putative father broadens the service system boundaries and introduces more actors.

By inference, this would seem to place agency birthparents and the agency itself more into contact and interaction with the community in which service is provided. The more the recipients of service participate, the more open the agency to inputs; its boundaries become more and more semipermeable to information and values from the community (i.e., broader system) in which it is located.

Summary. It is essential to begin with a clarification of the problem to be studied and/or the goals to be pursued. This is best done by identifying any relevant policy statements and associated issues, keeping in mind the targets or objects of policy and the likely participants.

Criteria for Review or Choice

Now the plot thickens. When we get to the matter of selecting criteria that will give us guides for what to review in our analysis or what criteria to employ in making our selections, we come to a myriad of possibilities. An important point to keep in mind is that criteria themselves are "little policies." That is, criteria for what to review or criteria for guiding principles in making choices are themselves policies in the sense that they are human creations that express preferences, theoretical points of view, priorities, or other manifestations of what we value. For our purposes here, however, we need to select a minimum set of criteria for review or choice as suggested by the characteristics that seem germane to policy analysis at the small-scale level. The policy analyst operating at the small-scale level can, of course, add any criteria that appear to be particularly germane to the policy under study; they are not preordained. The criteria for analysis are merely part of the tool kit, and we decide what tools we need. Nevertheless, a certain core of criteria have served others well and we will include these in our inventory of elements for small-scale policy analysis.

Criteria for Review or Choice

For our case illustration we will use the criteria provided in our earlier discussion. The reader is only reminded that the criteria selected are not cast in stone but are, rather, to be selected by the analyst.

Adequacy, effectiveness, and efficiency. There is hardly a policy that in some way does not demand at least a cursory review of its adequacy (i.e., the extent to which the goal is achieved when the policy is carried out), its effectiveness (i.e., the relationship between its goal and the selected means employed) and its efficiency (i.e., the degree to which the means employed are maximized with the use of the minimum amount of resources). These three criteria should generally be considered in any analysis.

Adequacy, effectiveness, and efficiency

One could first ask, "To what extent does this policy actually accomplish the desired effect of achieving fuller participation of birthparents?" Is there really a reaching out by the worker to the mother or father or does the effort by staff, as mandated in the policy and its attendant guidelines, tend to be perfunctory or routine? What evidence is there that there has been any change in the pattern of participation by birthparents? If that information is not available, the policy analyst not only needs to devise means for obtaining it, but the regular development of such data may even be one of the resultant recommendations of the policy analysis effort.

Another approach is to study whether the policy of participation has, in itself, actually had some bearing on increased participation of birthparents or whether some other policy or staff behavior has, in fact, had that cause-and-effect impact. Here we tend to pursue the question of actual effectiveness, since the desired effect needs to be established in terms of the specific means employed.

We also need to arrive at some estimation of the efficiencies obtained by the policy. In this policy we may want to look at the amount of time and effort needed by staff to obtain the desired level of participation. This is not to say that there is some pre-established level of "efficient" versus "not efficient" participation. Rather, it forces the analysis to make visible the extent to which the means employed in pursuit of a policy goal are maximized with a minimum use of the resources available. This helps to establish some of the "costs" of the policy, thereby flushing out the more detailed criteria of cost for subsequent policy decision making.

Equity, equality, and fairness. Next on the list are questions of equity (i.e., whether situations in similar circumstances are dealt with similarly), equality (i.e., whether persons, groups, or situations are dealt with in the same manner), and fairness (i.e., whether persons or situations are dealt with equivocally as a result of the policy). These three criteria speak generally to the overriding criterion of social justice.

Equity, equality, and fairness

Generally speaking, any policy that opens up the boundaries to participation in the decision process could be considered egalitarian, be it in decisions around one's own direct services or the administrative policies of an agency. That is, the client, participant, or recipient of services is then seen as having some identifiable rights and privileges that place him or her in a relatively egalitarian position in relation to the provider of service. In the birthparents' participation policy we find the biological parents meeting in group interviews with the adoptive parents to share information. The birthparent and the adoption worker each have unique roles to play in this planning process. Policies achieving participation of the receiver of services may not necessarily result in equity (people in similar circumstances may not be treated in a similar fashion), since there is no way of telling how different applications of the policy are distributed. However, the principle of client individualization is more likely to occur when birthparent participation is implemented uniformly and consistently, in which case equity is at least a reasonable possibility. Furthermore, birthparents are more likely to be treated fairly, and not equivocally, when they are active participants in contracting for their participation in adoption planning and in contributing to the process along the way.

Individualism and the work ethic. Given the prevailing American ethos of rugged individualism and the Protestant Ethic to which most of us have been socialized, we must generally consider the impact of the policy upon these factors. While these criteria are frequently in the forefront when income maintenance policies and programs are under review, in a more general sense they apply to many other circumstances and, like it or not, should be considered. For example, even in our illustration of the situation surrounding a policy of group staffings, questions having to do with individual freedoms and prerogatives of professional disciplines quickly arise. And the question of what the impact of providing services will be upon the incentives of individuals to take initiatives of any kind (not just those related to producing income), generally surfaces in some form or another and must be dealt with in policy analysis. These questions must be anticipated in analyzing social welfare policy, regardless of how the analyst personally feels about emphasis on such matters as individualism and the work ethic.

Individualism and the work ethic

As mentioned above, the policy seems to be in concert with the American ethos of individualism, given that people are assisted in the policy of "planning for themselves." On the face of it, the policy of birthparents' participation reinforces or enhances individualism and the agency is thereby supporting the maintenance of community mores. On the other hand, given the departure from unilateral professional discretion that the policy also suggests, there would (again, on the face of it) seem to be less individual discretion allowable for the agency's adoption workers. It is important here, however, to distinguish between democratic methods of social treatment through proper professional and technical judgment exercised by professionals as a matter of social contract, and unilateral manipulation. Adoptive applicants have an opportunity to reject the requirement of their participation. At any rate, the policy of birthparent participation would appear to place these different factors in reasonable perspective and balance.

There appears to be no relation to the prevailing social mores regarding the work ethic in this policy, though one could probably stretch the imagination for this or any other criterion should it seem appropriate to the particular policy under scrutiny.

Impact on rights and statuses. According to David Gil (1970; 1976), it is well to consider the effects of any particular policy in terms of its impact upon individual, group, or organizational rights and statuses. Such consideration not only entails the questions of equity and fairness, but also the political feasibility or practicality of a policy's prospects. Policy can impact one's position in a social system (that is, upon the status associated with a position) or upon the commensurate rewards, perquisites, prerogatives, and privileges of those statuses. For example, policy on staffing of cases can affect individual or disciplinary perquisites or prerogatives, and thereby enhance or hinder the viability of a particular policy.

Impact on rights and statuses

The birthparent participation policy formalizes client rights and statuses. Even if the principles underlying the policy were already embodied in workers' attitudes and practices without the policy, the policy formalizes such rights and statuses. The clients' entitlement to expect certain kinds of behaviors is safeguarded by written policy, as are the workers' methods and procedures in bringing the intended policy effects about. That is, both parties in the helping relationship are given explicit directions and the associated protections in the event that the approach provided by the policy is called into question. Furthermore, the relative statuses of the two parties in the relationship have now become more formalized, without suggesting that the helping relationship has become any more

---

or less sensitive, accepting, nonjudgmental or growth producing.

Identity and self-determination. The reader may recall from our earlier discussion of Kelley's (1975) two "subcriteria" that the impact of a policy upon individual or group identity and self-determination is important. While we will discuss the value aspects of policy analysis in more detail later on, it would be well to include these two criteria as part of the "main frame" of our model for analysis in social welfare policy inasmuch as they are so central to codes of ethics for various helping professionals.

Identity and self-determination

We have, in effect, already touched upon the criteria of identity and self-determination, to some extent. Self-determination is of the very essence in this particular policy. Identity is fostered in that the client is forced to articulate personal choices, as opposed to leaving them to unilateral professional discretion. Emphasizing self-determination and identity would no doubt lead the birthparents to be confronted by their own values and priorities and enhance their ability to be confronted by their own decision criteria surrounding adoptive release and placement. Presumably, this would produce a more lasting and stable problem resolution for both the child and the birthparents.

Eligibility. Eligibility is a criterion that often articulates a number of other explicit and implicit criteria. The criterion of eligibility often relates to the desired state or condition of the target group as a result of the policy; it sometimes relates to the client or target group(s)' level of need; and eligibility criteria almost always relate in some way to the level of financial or other available resources and the political feasibility of a given policy. Nowhere are these aspects of eligibility so visible as in income maintenance policies and programs. However, eligibility also plays a complicated role in small-scale policy systems in such areas as arriving at service system goals relative to financial and personnel resources or to the presence and activity of various interest groups. Living examples can especially be found in the drive towards deinstitutionalization and its relation to the demands upon community mental health systems. Eligibility criteria variously speak to collective treatment goals of client population, to diminishing resources during a period of increasing demands, and to the contests and conflicts between and among various interest groups competing for the range of residential care, partial day care, outpatient and emergency services.

Eligibility

We can only speculate from this example that eligibility is not a consideration in application or implementation of this particular policy. Presuming that the client was otherwise eligible for this agency's services, or this service in particular, the policy under analysis does not affect nor is it affected by the question of eligibility. However, there may be a question of this in some states, for example, regarding the rights of a *minor* child birthparent in an adoptive decision process.

Feedback. An important characteristic of living systems is that devices and channels exist which provide for information that guide the system toward corrective action based upon its output activities (feedback). Feedback is an important aspect of policy systems. Consequently, it is beneficial to have in one's basic tool kit or model for analysis some assessment of the extent to which feedback devices are built into or are an integral part of the policy itself. A modern example of a built-in feedback device in social welfare policy is "sunset legislation," through which policies and/or programs are automatically terminated, pending a reading of the monitoring information and the systematic feedback built into the policy review and discussion process. Another example is the setting of objectives and/or policy priorities for time-limited periods, thereby automatically requiring some process of feedback evaluation. It is well to determine the extent to which feedback devices have been built in or have been working to perform the functions of monitoring, evaluating, and/or controlling for desired policy outcomes. Sometimes agencies or action groups are able to monitor the outcomes of their processes by building in, through policy, routine feedback from their consumers (clients, patients, students, customers, etc). Some action systems employ or designate positions whose responsibility is to primarily deal with both positive and negative feedback of the system (community relations specialists, ombudsmen, delegates, etc.).

Feedback

On the one hand, the policy would seem to allow for corrective feedback to enter into the client-worker problem-solving relationship since both parties would presumably be active participants in the release and adoption processes. On the other hand, there does not appear to be any provision built into the policy itself that allows for a monitoring of the effectiveness of the policy, individually or in the aggregate, across all of the agency's clientele. We might think that birthparents' participation is effective, appropriate, or that it works; but nothing in the policy assures us that there is a built-in monitoring of its processes or ultimate effects. Procedures would have to be developed to correct this deficiency.

Summary. These, then, are some of the essential criteria for reviewing social welfare policy and guiding us in making alternative policy choices. The reader can expand upon the list when certain criteria are particularly germane to one's own situation. However, the criteria presented here are viewed as both generic and useful guides.

System Functioning

The assessment of system functioning focuses on *how* an existing or actual policy is currently functioning, on speculations about the probable functioning of a proposed policy, or on the current functioning of a policy action process engaged in pursuing policy development. In this area of policy analysis it is particularly important to be mindful of whether the subject of analysis is policy content or policy process.

Here we might look at the quality of fit between administrative or organizational structure and stated or implied policy goals. Another likely candidate for inspection is the fit between the actual program design (e.g., centralization versus decentralization or direct service provision versus purchase of service) and policy goals. Other characteristics of system functioning can be assessed, such as the patterns of interaction between and among essential elements, perhaps between client, target, and action systems or interest groups in the case of policy process analysis, or between various program policies and provisions in the case of policy content analysis.

System Functioning

Here we will have to use our creative license as we introduce hypothetical factors into our analysis, using the elements of our outline now to be provided. Some clues to our direction will be to look at how or whether the program's design would encourage or deter realization of the policy goal of birthparent participation. Another direction is to look at the actual patterns of interaction among or between those who participate in the planning and placement decisions.

Some characteristics of subsystem interaction to look for are:

The extent of openness (or closedness) of system boundaries as a consequence of the policy or the policy process. This, of course, has to do with the system's ability to interact and communicate with its environment; the policy should enhance the healthy permeability of system boundaries and interaction.

State of system boundaries

A first place to look is the state of boundaries that exist between system elements, in this case between either of the birthparents and the other; or between either of the birthparents and the agency worker. Are the patterns of interaction any more or less permeable as a result of the policy? For example, there is a tendency to exclude the biological father from planning in adoptions. Many issues in the birthparents' relationship often go unresolved in common practice surrounding adoption planning. The policy analyst would do well to determine the effects of this policy on the boundaries between the birthparents.

The patterns of communication. This is expressed in terms of such phenomena as the presence of "filterers" (spokespersons or interpreters of policy or group positions) or of "gatekeepers" (intake workers, referral and information agencies, planning councils, review boards and the like). Filterers and gatekeepers play particularly powerful and pivotal roles in human systems.

Systems of human communication often have key persons, positions, or events that serve as important channels or nodes in the conveyance of messages, principles or values. It is important to the analysis to determine these channels and nodes. Furthermore, it is also necessary to recognize that communication may be either unilateral or bilateral. The direction and source of communication is also an important determination in the analysis of policy.

Patterns of communication

The impact upon communication is fairly obvious in the reference just made to the two birthparents. The policy mandates an increase in bilateral communication between birthparents and agency personnel. The policy also reduces, to some extent, the unilateral gatekeeping power of the caseworker. The nature of the participation policy requires both client and worker feedback and, perhaps, some other outside observational assessment mechanisms (e.g., frequency of appointments, more reports of client preferences as opposed to worker assumptions of client preferences).

The effect of the policy or the policy process upon tension, variety, and entropy. This is the tendency toward disorder or inability to do work in the policy system. That is, not only should the question of whether such tension, variety, or entropy are present be raised but also whether these characteristics are functional *or* dysfunctional. There is a common tendency to see such characteristics automatically as being negative, unwanted or dysfunctional, but this is not necessarily the case in human policy environments. For example, tension-producing action sometimes brings issues to the fore for examination or resolution; variety sometimes generates creative interchange;

and entropy may sometimes provide a desirable slowing down of circular generative processes that are getting out of hand.

Tension, variety, and entropy

Our earlier discussion suggested that policies or procedures that generate tension for a system are generally seen as "bad," whereas the introduction of variety sometimes generates new and creative interchange among or between system components. Surely, variety in perceptions and preferences is at least more likely to occur in more democratic or participatory decision-making environments. The introduction of a new participant in the process, the birthparent, adds variety. It might be axiomatically stated that, the more new information is introduced into the system, short of overload, the greater the system's ability to do work. The principle of client participation generates more problem-solving resources. In this case, "doing work" is arriving at a problem resolution. Consequently, entropy (the tendency toward disorder and inability to do work) is reduced by the policy since significant actors are involved in doing the essential decision work.

The existence of interface constraints in the policy system. Any adjustment in current arrangements runs the risk of placing components or elements of a system into conflict or competition with one another as the system's resources (both tangible and intangible) are even modestly redistributed. The task of the analyst here is to identify the quality or nature of new interaction now generated at the interface of any two or more components in terms of what constraints are now the "new baggage" of the substantive policy or policy process. These interface constraints are especially apparent in such examples as the clash between competing ideologies or philosophies, limited and fixed resources such as low-income housing properties and industrial development needs, or where people have to learn new ways of doing things, such as new professional disciplines mandated into interaction.

Interface constraints

Another perspective is that, as the current policy adds more information to the decision system, it might also be presumed that each of the parties is confronted with more criteria with which to plan and make ultimate recommendations and decisions. While more information presumably leads to more enlightened decisions, it also introduces more variables and reduces the *probabilities* of total agreement in perceptions and judgments. Thus, the policy increases the likelihood of the birthparents not being in concert — between themselves or with the staff worker. This would appear to be one of the costs of democratizing the process and it will be discussed further. At this point, we can at least say that the birthparents' participation policy may generate more confusion or disagreement in the adoption placement process since more people are now participating in the decision processes (assuming that the policy is being implemented to the fullest intention of the Board of Directors).

The extent to which feedback devices are working. This is determined by effective monitoring, evaluating, and controlling system action in concert with the policy goals. The key question here has to do with the manner in which the policy system manages both positive and negative feedback. For example, is the agency structured such that service outputs can be monitored, as with, for instance, the number of dropouts, recidivists, "successes," returnees, etc.? Is the policy process or the policy's implementation structured to evaluate the nature of its inputs (e.g., type and frequency of particular problems or referrals) or its outcomes (e.g., success or achievement rates, attainment of contractual goals, or treatment plans, etc.)?

A key consideration here is what the output (frequency of events) and outcome (actual achievements) *criteria* are, who sets them, and by whose standards. If the analyst is looking at "what is working," then it is imperative to determine by what criteria and standards of measurement that answer is evaluated.

Functioning of feedback devices

A key question here is how the system is handling both positive and negative feedback in birthparents' participation. That is, do we have any measures or estimates of the extent to which the policy affects birthparents' participation such as dropout rates, and the rate of "no-shows" for appointments, or the incidence of voluntary call-backs, and referrals by former agency clients? Are there any monitoring systems in place, such as client feedback evaluation opportunities during or subsequent to receiving services? These questions need to be answered for such systems installed for this analysis and for future policy analyses. We would need to determine the extent to which clients, individually and collectively, feel they have had adequate opportunity for meaningful participation, or the extent to which they feel they have obtained their contractual goals or treatment plans. This information would properly be obtained from *both* the clients and the agency staff.

The extent to which the existing policy, proposed policy, or the policy process enhances the system's ability to allow for dynamic adaptation. The analyst must assess the impact or potential of the policy or the process to enable the system to be more adaptive and self-corrective. Some clues to this characteristic might be found in policy characteristics of automatic review mandates, the range of representativeness in clientele or decision makers involved, or the flexibility of available change mechanisms, whether such changes be available through legislation, ordinance, rules, guideline development or consensus development. The analyst needs to determine whether the agency uses the feedback information, in either planned or serendipitous ways, to make appropriate adjustments in the policy itself or the procedures or guidelines associated with the policy. This is often the function in "sunset laws," or even the principle behind zero-based budgeting, when installed properly. These techniques, used appropriately, generate ongoing formative evaluations so that the system is ready at the point of renewal to justify continuance or adjustments based upon systematic use of feedback.

Impact on agency's dynamic adaptation

Evidence of dynamic adaptation might be found in the extent to which staff orientation or training has been altered as a result of experience with the policy of parental participation. Another possibility is the extent to which procedures have been routinized for the inclusion of biological fathers in the process, or the extent to which biological mothers have resultantly been built in as members of the placement-planning team.

The location and nature of authority, influence, and leadership in the organization or the policy action system. This has to do with how much power the policy will have—how much scope, salience, clout, or attraction will be present in support of the policy's initiation or implementation. Some questions here have to do with the extent to which such authority, influence, and leadership is formal or informal, centralized or decentralized, and whether the policy has the necessary legitimation (the recognized right to be acted upon), support, or sanction (the attendant and requisite rewards and punishments). These characteristics must not only be assessed in their current contexts but retrospectively in order to gain an adequate perspective.

Authority, influence and leadership

Every policy that is fundamentally meaningful has some aspect of power that keeps it in place. The board authorized the birth-parent policy and is accountable for it. Internally, one might also observe the extent to which the agency's administrative leadership, in the persons of the executive director, program heads, coordinators, or other significant actors, give leadership in pursuing the policy goal. For clues, one might note how often and in what manner the policy arises during orientation of new workers, in staff meeting discussions, and whether its enforcement leaves a paper trail by way of consent forms signed by birthparents, interoffice memos, or the like. Put another way, one might observe whether the policy, given its legitimacy from the board, is also associated with its necessary sanctions (i.e., rewards and/or punishments). Are new staff assisted in developing effective techniques for involving birthparents or is such involvement valued by staff in discussions? Answers to these questions offer clues.

The existence and nature of resistance to change. This entails not only an assessment of resistance to change implied by the policy but also the assessment of resources (e.g., money, supportive and ancillary policies, people power, or technology) needed to maximize, optimize, or "satisfice" the policy goals. This also requires an assessment of the opposing issues, forces, or liabilities that might give resistance to or mitigate against change.

Resistance to change

The task here is to determine if resistance to the change created by the policy of participation exists and, if so, what form the resistance takes. The more obvious methods are tuning in on staff complaints regarding, for example, the inconvenience of including birthparents and looking at the differences in frequency or duration of appointments with clients. Some less obvious possibilities could be changes in the use of collateral contacts (such as the birthparents' family) as opposed to direct client contacts, changes in the rates of home visits or appointments out of the office where staff reach out to the birthparents, and so forth.

These are some of the criteria to explore in the area of policy system functioning. An important point to remember here is that the analyst uses these criteria not merely as a shopping list but as reminders and mind-teasers. Also, the analyst should move through the criteria with a retrospective view concerning historical antecedents and use creative speculation regarding the anticipated consequences of the policy being studied.

Major Strategies

This group of analytic activities consists of determining the major strategies or approaches taken by the policy option and the associated tactics employed in pursuing the policy goal. While the assessment of system functioning focuses on how matters are working, the determination of feasibility focuses on how matters might work in the context of the policy under study. This section of the analysis moves us into considering what major approach or strategy the policy itself provides in achieving the desired effect, and what organizational strategies are employed in moving the policy ahead. The first has to do with the style or philosophy of the policy, the second with the means of implementation.

Major Strategies

From a general perspective, we could say that the policy of birthparents' participation employed the strategy of democratic participation in order to bring about inclusion of birthparents in the adoption planning, release, and placement process.

Three strategic elements that appear in many grand-scale analytic models are (1) the delivery mechanisms selected, (2) the mode of finance, and (3) the types of benefits to be provided. These elements can be directly translated to the small-scale policy analysis via three basic questions:

What overall approach is most appropriate or effective in achieving the policy goal? What come to mind here are grand-scale strategy questions such as (a) whether the policy will allow for a sequential or incremental as opposed to radical change (b) whether the policy development and/or implementation process shall be broadly participatory or limited to a selected number of decision makers; and (c) whether the process will occur through formal (e.g., board or legislated action) or informal procedures. These three considerations give broad parameters to the policy analysis.

Overall approaches

Given the legitimization provided by board action, the agency chose to use a formal approach to achieve birthparents' participation. We could also say that the change was incremental; no standards or performance goals were set in which certain "ideal" levels of participation were established. Professional discretion was left intact and staff pursuit of the goal was presumed. Consequently, we have a mixture of approaches here—a formalized statement of a desired condition with implementation left to less routine and more discretionary staff judgments on a case-by-case basis.

What resources shall be allocated to the policy or the policy process? The fundamental question here has to do with the level of effort and amount of resources to be allocated and spent on the development, installation, and enforcement of the existing or proposed policy, or in managing the policy process. Some obvious "costing" approaches are of value here such as needs assessments, cost/benefit or benefit/cost analyses, and determination of Pareto optima. However, in looking at the small-scale policy analysis environment, our focus here is more on the "soft" or sociopolitical costs of the policy under study.

Resources allocated

By inference, this is a costly policy because, in the short term, it would likely consume more staff time. Presumably, in the long term, it would constitute a wise use of staff resources inasmuch as more appropriate and successful placement decisions would arise and individual clients would experience growth at a time of important decision making. Other cost indices that relate to this particular strategy might include the cost to the agency's public relations—whether the policy would incur more favor or disfavor with the client group it serves and with the community in which the agency is located. In this sense, the policy's approach must be seen as having political costs and, while these considerations may not necessarily be primary determinants, they should be weighed in the analysis.

What types of benefits will accrue to the client and target groups as a result of the policy or the policy process? This question encourages one to look at the tangible or intangible and the direct or indirect benefits anticipated. While outcomes of service and reduction in citizen need are obvious possibilities, the effects on organizational interaction, staff morale, public satisfaction or confidence, and future positioning are also reasonable benefits to include in the analysis. While issues of adequacy, efficiency, and effectiveness are also reasonable and commonly pursued benefits, these softer benefits are generally not part of the explicated goals of grand-scale social welfare policy which are so important for social action on the small-scale level.

Benefits

As already mentioned, the adoptive child-as-client, and the birthparent-as-target, would both presumably benefit from the policy's anticipatory effects. On the worker side, some staff may resent the question that the policy raises regarding their ability to make good judgments and decisions "in the best interests" of the child and the birthparent without extensive participation. A completely different view, however, would be that the benefits accruing to staff as a result of this policy strategy would be found in the assurances that staff are provided with policy support behind their goal of helping clients to make proper decisions. In effect, this policy strategy produces the benefit of enabling staff to achieve the mandates of their professional code of ethics. Consequently, individual and organizational goals are served and supported by the policy.

Summary. It is important to grasp the overall thrust of a policy. Some clues are the strategies and tactics employed, the level of resources devoted to support the policy and the basic benefits to be obtained by the client group as a result of the policy.

Feasibility

As with the determination of major strategies, the assessment of feasibility also has to do with *how* or *whether* a policy goal *might* be achieved. In fact, some of the criteria of feasibility, such as cost and political power, are directly related to and virtually inseparable from such matters as system functioning or major strategies. Nevertheless, it is helpful in the analysis to give particular visibility to issues of feasibility, even at the expense of some redundancy.

Following are some generic considerations.

Legality. Social welfare policies obviously have to be consistent with legislated and judicial mandates and must coexist with other administrative directives. Such policy is made in legislative, judicial, and administrative arenas and its analysis must take both the opportunities and constraints of those arenas into consideration. These three areas of policy generation and support were discussed in detail in chapter 1. In summary, it can be said that the analyst is advised to consider the legislated, judicial, and administrative bases (and alternatives) of the proposed policy. Here the analyst might look at the extent to which the policy is founded on any person's or group's right to take action and/or the statutory or customary support behind such actions. Also, the reader is reminded that these bases of support may very well be small-scale and local in origin, such as local ordinances or board or commission resolutions, the rules of court agencies, or the rule-making behavior of administrative agencies at any level of government or the position of any voluntary agency.

Legality

The policy not only has legal foundation (to the extent that identities are not inappropriately disclosed as a result of it) but, in some states, actual attempts to undertake meaningful measures to include the putative fathers (e.g., locating fathers through newspaper advertising) are a legal requirement. Furthermore, most courts would require assurances that the decision for release was obtained with complete knowledge and consent of the appropriate parties involved. Consequently, the policy would appear to be in concert with both legislative and judicial expectations.

Resource requirements and availability. We have already discussed the issue of resource requirements to some extent in considering current functioning of the policy system. Nevertheless, the issue is still fair game when it comes to thinking of demands placed upon finances, space, personnel, time, power, status, prestige, credibility, and so forth. These resource attributes are all of value to social welfare systems and must be considered in the future context when it comes to assessing feasibility.

The notion of cost, itself, requires a special note in that we often tend to think of cost primarily in economic terms. Yet, many of us are well aware of the fact that cost is also political and social or, more

likely, a mix of political, social, psychological, and economic considerations. An important set of questions in the analysis of social
welfare policy (and a set of questions that may more likely be answered
at the small-scale level) has to do with *who* sets the criteria of cost,
the *appropriateness* of the criteria in determining cost for the particular issue under analysis, and *how* or *under what conditions* cost will
be determined and/or evaluated.

Resource requirements and availability

Cost is always a consideration in social services inasmuch as
social agencies are chartered to serve the public good with
social resources. This is true of both publicly and privately supported programs. There is no question that this policy will
require additional staff time, though the demands of the policy
could be incorporated into staff approaches to the provision
of service. Additional equipment or space would not be
required. For the birthparents-as-client, there would presumably
be a cost incurred by the demands upon personal time required
for increased participation. For the agency, additional visibility would be given to the agency programs in the community, which would have to be weighed as a cost or a benefit.
In any event, it helps to be reminded that besides the criteria
of costs, equally important is the question of who sets those
criteria. The policy decision examined here impacts upon staff,
clientele, the agency as a whole, and perhaps other components in the community. It is important to consider whether
the policymaker (in this case the board of Child Services, Inc.)
has the interests of each of the affected social components in
mind and has the legitimate authority to unilaterally affect each
of those components.

Power and influence. Power has been defined by Polsby
(1963) as the ability of one actor to do something that specifies the

probability of future events for another actor. When power (which is an attribute of social actors) is exercised, it is called influence. Feasibility considerations require assessment of whether the power and influence requirements associated with maintaining or installing a particular policy are adequate and appropriate or whether issues of power and influence must be dealt with a priori. A tendency for the policy analyst, however, is to think of power on the grand scale or in terms of the more obvious play of influence and to overlook the small-scale level, where power and influence may not be explicit or obvious. The future of any given policy is dependent upon the distribution of power in the policy's environment. The subtleties of power and influence are generally not dramatic, as evidenced by the ability of individuals and groups to meet policy with passive aggressive resistance, for example, or (on the other hand) the ability of policy leaders to lead, at times, with charismatic leadership styles or to capitalize on a trust that has been established over time. That is, only infrequently does the policy process generate headlines and overt struggles. The processes of power and influence are generally subtle.

Power and influence

The birthparents' participation policy has clearly provided for a fundamental shift in power to the birthparent in the adoption-planning process. This is not to say that the birthparent has become a controlling factor, but her influence has increased markedly. We also need to look at whether the board, the agency's administrative structure, and the technology and competence of the staff can assure delivery of the policy goals. Surely the board has the power (legitimate authority) to mandate such a policy. The adequacy of the administrative structure might be manifested in proper procedures for supervision of staff in regard to the policy. Administrative influence might also be observed in the extent to which administrative staff provide leadership in giving visibility to the participatory philosophy inherent in the birthparent policy in other areas of the agency. The staff, of course, exercise the ultimate power in their influence on the working relationship with the birthparent-as-client; the direct service worker enters at "the point where the shoe hits the pavement." This is where the real power of policy is observed and exercised – or subverted. The staff must have the necessary social treatment skills to ensure maximized client participation as well as the necessary orientation for such participation.

Rationality. All policies and their analyses must satisfy someone's understanding of rationality. That is, the statement of conclusions and/or recommendations must have some logical link (preferably seen in the connections between a philosophy and a theory) to the original problem statement and the methodology used in gathering the information and arriving at the conclusions or recommendations. To be believable, the analysis must use conventional understanding and conventional means. This is not to say that policy analysis cannot be innovative; rather, the actual *use* of the policy analysis rests heavily on normative conventions. When the analyst goes beyond those conventions, he or she must be aware of that fact.

Rationality

Earlier we considered the theoretical foundations of the policy under analysis. However, while a policy may be theoretically sound, it may not necessarily be rational in terms of its practicality, logistics, or workability. The birthparents' participation policy does not appear unreasonably cumbersome; thus, staff can implement it. That is, here is a point at which practice theory can immediately be translated into workable practice.

Environmental impact. Policies certainly have impact on their internal and external environments in regard to such issues as resource requirements and various costs. However, there are other impact issues that are more indirect and less tangible. Here we might consider the long-term effects or precedent-setting potential of a particular policy's continuation or introduction. We might look at the implications of a particular type of departure from the past in a given policy and see risks resulting in long-range benefits; or, we may see negative implications for the future, such as a reactionary return to an old form.

Environmental impact

A test of a policy's impact on its environment might be, at the agency level, to observe the increased rates of birthparent participation within the agency. Another test at the agency level might be the extent to which the policy's impact is evident in workers' outreach efforts to clients, such as increased numbers of home visits or less reliance upon collateral contacts for information. Another test of impact could be to observe the manifestations of the participatory philosophy in other agency programs and some considerations regarding whether that policy approach might be appropriate to other program areas.

At the community level, the analyst could establish indices of community impact. In this agency, the birthparent support group has gone beyond their own personal needs and is taking interest in national adoptive issues, legislation, and trends. Other avenues for analysis exist, such as the relationship between increased client participation and new referrals made to the agency by satisfied former birthparent clientele. Another example might be the extent to which the agency is viewed by the community at large or by funding sources as being "open" or "cooperative."

Newly perceived self-interests. Finally, in regard to feasibility, we return to the concept introduced in chapter 3 concerning the role of perceived self-interest in the play of policy. It was Gil's contention, you will recall, that a newly perceived self-interest on the part of influential actors holds promise for bringing about policy change. Hence, self-interest is of vital importance as a feasibility consideration in analyzing social welfare policy. These perceptions may generate or free up necessary resources, reduce resistances to either maintenance or change, or become powerful assets in other social process ways.

Newly perceived self-interests

As we discussed earlier, an important dynamic for policy change (or policy maintenance for that matter) is the extent to which significant policy actors perceive that their individual or collective self-interests may be served by pursuit of the policy goal. For the birthparent clients, the policy provides for a more open system in which the clients become less providers of information and more decision makers in matters important to their own lives. For the workers, the policy provides support legitimated by board action for pursuit of practice goals that are consistent with professional ethics relating to client self-determination. For the agency, the mandates and expectations of law and the judiciary are integrated with agency practice. Consequently, the policy relates to the self-interest of a number of significant actors in the policy field.

Summary

This chapter has introduced the elements of a model for small-scale social welfare policy analysis. We considered the determination of the policy problem or goals as the first set of activities in policy analysis. Next, we looked at the matter of setting the criteria for reviewing and choice taking; then at determination of the major strategic approaches to maintaining or installing a policy (or the manner in which policy is pursued). We ended with a discussion of various considerations in determining a policy's feasibility.

The first step is to define or delineate the particular problem or specific policy to be analyzed, with an emphasis on determining its base of legitimacy. The second step is to focus on the generic criteria to be used in the analysis, particularly regarding clients and targets. The third is a focus on the organizational, administrative, or environmental functioning of the policy system and the interaction of system components. This is followed by a forth focus on two levels: the major policy strategy selected and the actual policy implemented. The fifth area of focus is the elements that constitute feasibility in achieving problem resolution or attaining the policy goal.

Summary

This case illustration has been an attempt to walk through the application of criteria set forth in the discussion and outline of content elements for small-scale policy analysis. We have organized our discussion around the major analytic tasks provided above. In chapter 5 we will give more attention to the task of assessing congruence with desired values since we wish to give special attention to that analytic responsibility.

The reader is again reminded that the job of the analyst is not to religiously grind through the outline or its elements, as in going to the market with a shopping list and leaving with undesirable merchandise. Rather, the outline is provided as a reminder to look, to pick and choose, and to make decisions along the way. In this illustration, we have attempted to apply each criterion — running the risk at some points of being pedantic or conjuring up absurd examples. But a model is only a tool, and the analyst should use it as it applies to a given situation.

A summary outline of the elements in content analysis follows. In chapter 5 we will treat the sixth major area of policy analysis activity — the assessment of congruence between the policy under study and the desired values of the analyst or the analyst's sponsor.

Content Elements for Analyzing Small-Scale Policy (An Outline)

1. *The Policy Problem and/or Policy Goals.* A focus on the definition or delineation of the particular problem or the specific policy that is to be analyzed. Identification should include, at the outset, a written account of the source or location of the policy in terms of its base(s) of legitimacy and its location(s).

    a. The policy statement
    b. Contemporary issues
    c. Historical antecedents
    d. Targets of concern
        (1) Client and target subsystems
        (2) System maintenance, control, or change
        (3) Efficiency in coverage
    e. Explicit or implicit theories
    f. Topography of the policy system

2. *Criteria for Review or Choice.* A focus on the generic criteria to be used in the analysis, particularly with regard to the clients and targets affected by the policy.

    a. Adequacy, effectiveness, and efficiency
    b. Equity, equality, and fairness
    c. Individualism and the work ethic
    d. Impact on rights and statuses
    e. Identity and self-determination
    f. Eligibility
    g. Feedback

3. *System Functioning.* A focus on the organizational, administrative, or environmental functioning of the policy system and the interaction of components in that system.

    a. State of system boundaries
    b. Patterns of communication

   c. Tension, variety, and entropy
   d. Interface constraints
   e. Functioning of feedback devices
   f. Dynamic adaptation
   g. Authority, influence, and leadership
   h. Resistance to change

4. *Major Strategies.* A focus on two levels. First is the major policy strategy selected in the particular policy option(s) taken; second is the particular strategies employed in implementation of the policy itself.

   a. Overall approaches
   b. Resources allocated
   c. Types of benefits for clients and targets

5. *Feasibility.* A focus on the elements that help achieve resolution of the problem or attainment of the policy goal.

   a. Legality
      (1) Legislative
      (2) Judicial
      (3) Administrative
   b. Resource requirements and availability
   c. Power and influence
   d. Rationality
   e. Environmental impact
   f. Newly perceived self-interests

6. *Congruence with Desired Values.* See Value Elements for Analyzing for Small-Scale Policy (An Outline).

Note: Recommendations may follow, where appropriate.

Case Illustrations

In the pages that follow, three case illustrations are provided that apply the outline, "Content Elements for Analysis of Small-Scale Policy." The first case example, entitled "Multiple Mandates of Confidentiality," concerns a policy that affects all human service agencies. The particular focus on confidentiality is given to the many forces impinging upon an agency and its staff in carrying out confidentiality policy. The second case example, entitled "Utilization Monitoring of Provisions of Care," relates to a variety of policy situations involving the contracting and purchase of services. The third case, entitled "Integrated Policy for the Downtown Mall," focuses more on factors external to an agency that relate to content analysis elements.

Case 1: Multiple Mandates of Confidentiality

In this case illustration we will examine a policy that no doubt cuts across all agencies providing social services—confidentiality of client information. Our perspective in the analysis will be to examine the policy in a multiprogram agency and particularly to focus on the diverse or multiple sources and mandates for the confidentiality policy.

While it appears that all codes of ethics in the helping professions include a commitment to confidentiality, the operationalization of this principle is less than automatic when one is confronted by diverse pieces of federal and state legislation legitimizing the policy of confidentiality. That is, there are significant differences in the many pieces of legislation governing confidentiality. Furthemore, confidentiality as a principle frequently runs head on into accountability to funding agencies or support sources. Consequently, maintaining confidentiality in the social services setting is hardly a pro forma assurance, regardless of individual professional commitments to ethical behavior. In our analysis, we will focus on the multiple sources and mandates of confidentiality and give special attention to the interface constraints between confidentiality and accountability.

The agency, Community Services, Inc., is a typical multiprogram private child and family service agency located in a large city. Community Services, Inc. (CSI) is a member of a statewide federation of such agencies and offers programs in family counseling, child welfare services, case management and training services for the developmentally disabled, and community consultation. Its sources of funding are varied, with support from the United Fund, third party payment from various insurance carriers and Title XX, contracts with the county community mental health board as a contractual provider, fees directly paid by clients, and a few other sources. The agency is organized around three main program units; client records are not shared from unit to unit. Only in the case of adoptions would a state agency see the client record. While the county's community mental health director is technically the holder of the record for clients for whom services are provided under mental health funding, client files are held at CSI. The agency is very much integrated into its community by virtue of its variety of programs and their associated funding sources.

1. The Policy Problem and/or Policy Goals

Generally speaking, the universal policy goal of confidentiality is to assure recipients of services that their associations with the provider of services will be maintained in secrecy insofar as the law allows (i.e., excluding felonious behavior or potential harm to others). <u>Confidentiality is also viewed as one of many vehicles for sound social treatment</u>. A variety of policy problems occur when confidentiality is violated: for the individual, loss of security and privacy; for the agency, loss of integrity; and for the community, a loss of trust. To a great extent, loss of confidentiality by the providers of service removes that agency as a viable option for services by those who value the provision of services with a safeguarded right to privacy.

a. The policy statement

The confidentiality policy at CSI is simply stated.

Community Services, Inc. shall respect and attempt to safeguard the rights of clients to confidential treatment of information exchanged, to privacy in their relationship with the agency, and to rights of redress. (*CSI Manual,* p. 2)

While the confidentiality policy is a strong statement of values, it should be noted that the statement does equivocate to some extent in the sense that only the "attempt" to safeguard is assured.

This wording would appear realistic, given the variety of legal and judicial sources that bear on the matter of confidentiality. Each piece of legislation has its own administrative rules and, in some cases, exceptions. It would be improper for the agency to generalize in a cavalier manner regarding this policy.

The primary foundation of confidentiality in policy is provided in the U.S. Constitution, Article IV, which provides for "the right of people to be secure in their persons, houses, papers, and effects" and that this right "shall not be violated." In the state in which CSI is located, its various programs also have a variety of legitimating sources in state law for the confidentiality policy. The child protective services program has its source in the Child Protection Law. Both the foster care program and the adoption program have separate provisions in the Child Care Act. The programs for the developmentally disabled relate especially to provisions in the Social Welfare Code, the Mental Health Code and the state law for mandatory special education. Each program is bound by the provisions of the state's Freedom of Information Act. At the federal level, the agency policy and practice is bound by the Education for All Handicapped Children Act, the Freedom of Information Act, and the Family Rights to Privacy Act. No doubt this sounds familiar to many readers. On the one hand, we are assured in our hypothetical policy analysis that the policy under study guarantees legitimatization; on the other hand, we are reminded that there are likely to be many confusing and/or competing provisions. Added to the mandate for maintenance of confidentiality is the heavy demand for accountability—the requirement that each agency provide adequate and timely information to its sources of support, attesting to the fact that funds are used appropriately.

b. Contemporary issues

While confidentiality of client communications has long been a cornerstone of social work practice, confidentiality and privacy, strangely enough, are relatively recent preoccupations of modern America, arising perhaps out of its emphasis in the civil rights area. Invasion of privacy has loomed larger in recent years, in part due to the explosion in information technology, but perhaps (sadly enough) partly due to the erosion of commitments to confidentiality by providers of services in a variety of fields.

In our hypothetical case illustration, recent events in the community involving child abuse situations that, on the surface, appear to have been unreported by professionals to the state protective services agency, have renewed local debate on confidentiality practices in the social services. Also, the recent death of an elderly woman who lived alone and refused social services has engendered heated debate over whether agency workers have a responsibility to inform "proper authorities" when someone presumably in need refuses services.

c. Historical antecedents

As noted above, we have the two-pronged historical background behind confidentiality: the long-established commitment to confidentiality held by social workers and other human service workers; and the more recent emphasis arising out of the civil rights movement. More recent events in the judicial system across the country add another thread wherein the competing interests of recipients of public services (e.g., parties to a contested divorce, or natural and adoptive parents) each have claims to information provided or obtained in the course of the provision of social services.

d. Targets of concern

The targets of concern in confidentiality policies are generally limited to the providers of services — the caseworkers, clerical staff, and administrators who represent the agency in community situations. Hence, the policy may be said to perform system control as opposed to system maintenance or system change functions. The policy provides a mandate primarily for the providers of services. Our policy analysis, then, should ensure that each of the provider groups has been adequately oriented and supervised with respect to the policy. Do new staff receive adequate orientation, not only to the letter of the policy, but to the spirit and function of the principle of confidentiality? Do administrative staff have proper procedures in place, such as security and availability of files, proper and effective client release of information procedures, and the like? Does the board of directors have a workable hearing procedure when grievances or alleged violations of the policy take place?

There is no uniform provision in each of the relevant statutes regarding the question of privileged communication of social service personnel. The child abuse legislation, for example, mandates reporting by social workers of suspected child abuse, but not of adult abuse under the adult protective service legislation. The law in our hypothetical situation grants immunity for breach of confidentiality in reporting suspected child abuse. Other pieces of legislation do not provide for privileged communication by social workers, but some protection is afforded some categories of licensed psychologists and psychiatrists.

While the identity of the targets of the policy might be clear, the identity of the client systems (i.e., those systems on whose behalf change or services are sought) is not quite so clear. This is perhaps due to the variety of legislation that legitimates confidentiality practices in the various programs. We see the rights of parents, the rights of children, the rights of the public to know how and even, in some instances, to whom some services are provided. Our analysis here, then, would necessarily have to focus on the manner and extent to which the legal and ethical confidentiality provisions are satisfied by internal policy and procedure. For example, in order to meet the expectations of the mental health code and mental health funding sources, we could examine the materials and procedures of informing clientele, at first contact with the agency, exactly what their rights are in the area of confidentiality and what clients might do in situations where they have concerns about confidentiality practices. Here we would need to examine procedures and determine how the policy is communicated and/or explained, how "informed consent" for the release of information is determined and by whom, what forms were developed and how adequate they are and undertake some "policy audit" of these practices and materials. These types of procedures and materials would likely need to be reviewed for each of the agency's programs, in regard to each relevant piece of legislation, and for each funding source.

e. Explicit or implicit theories

The explicit theoretical basis of the policy arises out of the constitutional provision that citizens have a right to privacy in their persons and their papers, by essentially providing that this fundamental right shall be protected in the policies and practices of all forms of social interaction.

The implicit social treatment theories are related more to the presumed beneficial effects of the trust relationship between the provider and receiver of social services necessary for effective help to be given. Inherent in the confidentiality principle, the rights of the individual or group are protected while, at the same time, the helping relationship is built upon the assumption that the recipient of services is free to disclose any and all information thought to be pertinent to problem resolution. The provider may give assurances that disclosure of that information will not occur. As noted above, however, these complete assurances cannot always be guaranteed, as, for example, in the case of suspected child abuse or of information regarding impending harm to another citizen. Consequently, a theory of sound social practice is frequently in conflict with socio-legal expectations.

The analyst will need to determine, then, the extent to which staff are well informed about the reality and the management of this dilemma. The policy analysis can be helpful in identifying any existing disparities, and can be beneficial in developing remedial materials or procedures for staff and clientele.

f. Topography of the policy

The map of system components and system interaction is rather crowded and complex in the case of confidentiality. Given the variety and nature of the legislation that legitimizes the policy, as well as the various funding sources involved, we can see many organizational actors in the field. Some examples are the local and state departments of social services pertaining to child protection, adoptive care and Title XX reporting, or financing requirements; and the local and state mental health requirements regarding recipients' rights and information system reporting. Since much case activity involves the participation of more than one agency or provider of services, there are a myriad of individual and organizational actors, not to mention the clients and the agency staff themselves.

In terms of policy analysis, it would be helpful to determine whether interagency agreements or understandings are in place with each of the above funding components or other contractual partners regarding procedures and expectations in the management of client information. This would require review of contract provisions, for example, regarding the right to data, or review of forms providing release of client information, with appropriate safeguards for all parties with whom the agency interacts. These are just some of the possibilities.

2. Criteria for Review or Choice
In this section of the analysis we will have to be creative in determining the basic criteria for review of this particular policy. Nevertheless, the fundamental criteria give us some guidance.

a. Adequacy, effectiveness and efficiency
In regard to adequacy of the policy, we want to determine adequacy in terms of the extent to which the policy assures confidentiality for individual clients and how adequately it provides guidance to those individuals who administer it. We also want to determine adequacy from the point of view of the policy's aggregate effects on clientele and providers of services. Some indicators for the analysis are individual client feedback, for example, via systematic feedback from both clients and staff upon termination of services at the agency. Another approach would be to observe or otherwise study the attitudes and behavior of clients at the point of intake to determine their reactions to front-

end procedures and information regarding confidentiality. Concerning the aggregate effects upon adequacy, the policy analyst might observe the number and nature of recipient complaints pertaining to confidentiality matters and/or obtain staff comments regarding problems in administering the policy as it might affect, for example, the timely flow of information or the quality of helping relationships.

The assessment of the policy's effectiveness should be based upon the extent to which the policy achieves the desired effects of client trust, privacy, and confidence in the context of the agency's information management procedures. Again, this would have to be done by gathering the views of clients and staff alike.

The question of efficiency might be addressed in the analysis by the extent or degree to which both client and staff efforts are allocated to pursuit of the policy goal and in the policy's administration. Some indicators might be the extent to which services were or were not provided in a timely manner as a result of the policy's implementation. In this case, CSI has had some complaints from clients, agency staff, or other agencies regarding cooperative services not being able to be provided in a timely manner as a result of the policy. While some agencies have tried to deal with this problem by asking clientele to sign blanket a priori release of information approvals, this is not legal under some statutes and rules and, furthermore, the approach is not consistent with the principles underlying confidentiality. The analyst may need to determine very specifically whether the problem exists only in certain programs of the agency, only under certain emergency conditions, or whether it is a manifestation of differential administration of the policy by different staff members; the latter are some possible avenues for inquiry.

b. Equity, equality, and fairness

The uniformity and consistency of policy implementation would, in the main, be more assured by having standardized procedures for client release of information in place. The analyst should see whether such procedures as well as forms and staff training are in place. Equality of application might be observed by examination of the different staff's practices surrounding the policy. The issue of fairness could be pursued by determining how the agency's own information regarding particular clients is handled in the other agencies with which CSI cooperates. Some indices of equity, equality, and fairness could be obtained, or at least clues given, by examination of any standards review for certification or accreditation undertaken by the agency, since most guidelines or requirements for standards reviews by certifying or accrediting agencies would likely include confidentiality provisions.

c. Individualism and the work ethic

The confidentiality policy would likely foster and support attitudes regarding individualism existing in the community and/or manifested by the client. After all, properly administered, the policy provides for protection of very private information that individuals might reveal to a limited number of people. Thus, there seems to be no implication for this policy in regard to the work ethic.

d. Impact on rights and statuses

The large number of statutes, administrative rules, and guidelines surrounding the issue of confidentiality give ample evidence that client rights and agency responsibilities have been codified to a great degree. This growth in legislation and regulations has led to new statuses ascribed to the client population and has given agencies the responsibility of specifically ensuring the protection of privacy; the policy cannot be taken for granted. The analyst needs to confirm this formalization of rights and responsibilities through observation of the management of client records, conveyance of management data, and by listening to verbal manifestations of commitments to the policy.

e. Identity and self-determination

The policy of confidentiality in information provided about clients and services is bound to impact favorably upon the self-image of clients since their individual prerogatives are not subsumed under unilateral procedures by agency staff or faceless organizational procedures. However, some of this positive impact upon self-concept and identity fostered by the confidentiality policy may be reduced by the manner in which the agency administers the policy, how individual staff workers apply the policy, or how the agency transmits information to other agencies. The client has a right to know, and needs reassurance, that the policy is strictly carried out at all levels. Otherwise, its beneficial effects are undermined.

f. Eligibility

Eligibility is not a question, generally speaking, for this policy since it is universally applied to all of the agency's clientele. However, it should be noted that clients do, in a sense, disqualify some information for protection, depending upon the particular legislation and the particular information. For example, the agency does not technically need to formally obtain release of information on each incident of information-sharing with other mental health funded agencies in a mental health funded client situation. (This technicality exists because of the state attorney general's ruling that the county's mental health director is the "holder of the record.") However, the worker is not precluded from explaining to the client the reasons for sharing information, the conditions and time limitations placed upon sharing that information, and so forth. Furthermore, the worker cannot unilaterally declare *all* information to be eligible for confidential treatment inasmuch as information regarding commitment of a felony, for example, is exempt from coverage. In some states, minors cannot expect complete confidentiality in all situations requesting services (e.g., seeking information regarding family planning or contraceptives) though, at this writing, the status of this legal principle is now being debated.

g. Feedback

This particular policy enjoys some aspects of an automatic, built-in feedback device inasmuch as clients can refuse to grant permission to share certain types of information. The policy analyst could, then, have some clues as to the extent to which confidentiality is felt by clients to be assured. Presumably, a high rate of refusals, generally speaking, could be indicative of the clientele's lack of faith in the agency's or worker's implementation of the policy. In situations wherein signed releases are required to be completed by clients prior to release of information, an auditing of those materials in case records would be useful in the policy analysis.

3. System Functioning

We have up to this point actually been assessing system functioning but, in this section, we will force our analysis to look more directly at the operational, organizational, or administrative structures pertaining to achievement of the policy goal.

a. State of system boundaries

Here we need to look at the permeability of system boundaries pertaining to the policy. From one perspective, the boundaries must be impermeable: the strictest of privacy must be maintained and no information shall pass over the agency system's boundaries without explicit client permission. From another perspective, client information, for purposive uses to which the client agrees, must be free to be moved about: the confidentiality system's boundaries must be semipermeable in this regard. Furthermore, the procedures for implementing the confidentiality policy must not be so inflexible that a client's refusal to share information does not unnecessarily preclude the provision of appropriate services. The policy analyst would do well, then, to concentrate upon the extent to which the policy and its implementation shape or condition the boundaries that exist between clients and staff, or between agencies. Subsequently, the analyst must make some judgments about the appropriateness of those boundary conditions.

b. Patterns of communication

The nature of confidentiality policy and the maintenance of privacy gets to the very heart of communications and communication patterning. In the administration of this policy, however, we appear to have two types of communication patterns. One could be characterized as the flow of information pertaining directly to individual clients for the purposes of case management or case services management. The other would relate more to reporting and providing information about clients in the aggregate to funding or sponsoring groups. One could almost say that for every dollar that comes in, a report element goes back out.

Communication, then, could be said to be bilateral in either instance. Ironically, confidentiality generates a bilateral flow of communication, as opposed to the stereotyped image of the secret unilateral flow of information. Thus, in a real sense, confidentiality tends to open the flow of communication. The task for the policy analyst is to determine whether the information patterns indicate that the information is provided along proper channels, from the right sources, to the right destinations, and in a timely manner—all with the client's proper consent. Where that consent requires implicit or explicit permissions, it is the job of the analyst to determine the means whereby the essential principles of the policy are honored.

c. Tension, variety, and entropy

We said in chapter 4 that information gives order and predictability to a system; and the confidentiality policy, with its attendant rules and guidelines, gives order and predictability to a system. Hence, while a surface view may suggest that more paperwork and rules contribute to disorder, the policy would appear to promise more order, less entropy, and the ability for the system to work more effectively. While the overload of paperwork (e.g., written and explicit releases of information) would appear to produce tension in the workplace, especially when action needs to take place, tension is actually reduced for the client who, presumably, is informed of what is happening by the mandates of sharing information with and about him or her. The task for the policy analyst is to determine the realities of actual and perceived tension and to establish whether, in fact, the policy actually fosters the reduction of disorder in the service system.

d. Interface constraints

In CSI, each program requires its own release of information prior to such a release to other program units in the same agency. Though not unusual, this is not a common practice in agencies of this size. While this requirement places agency components into competition, so to speak, it nonetheless ensures a greater emphasis upon the agency's commitment to the policy. Our analysis should confirm or challenge the necessity of this practice since, generally speaking, a client may reasonably be presumed to provide information to an agency and not a program or a person. The agency may be said to have ownership over the operation of the service, not its professional or clerical personnel.

e. Functioning of feedback devices

As noted earlier, it is helpful to have built-in monitoring provisions in the policy or in its rules or guidelines. Requiring written and signed releases of information provides an automatic monitoring device since releases are available through a review of agency records. The analyst would need to establish the existence and location of those releases. Another task is to determine the expressed satisfaction or dissatisfaction of clientele with the functioning of the policy, perhaps through such means as client feedback instruments during and subsequent to receiving services.

f. Dynamic adaptation

Here the analyst needs to determine whether the agency has in place a designee person, office, group or committee with the authority to make adjustments as a result of feedback concerning the policy. In the case of CSI, the recipient rights officer is the conduit for such information and that person has a direct line of communication to the executive director.

g. Authority, influence, and leadership

As was just mentioned, the recipient rights officer has the authority to hear complaints and make recommendations directly to the executive director. The executive director, in turn, exercises leadership by being a good listener and by developing consensus in a model of shared decision making with administrative staff. Consequently, once policy is made, it is generally widely supported. The task of the analyst here is to be assured that the consensus model of leadership does not adversely affect, or somehow benignly squelch, negative feedback from clientele. Given that assurance, the policy would appear to have broad support, with appropriate leadership given by the influence elements within the agency.

h. Resistance to change

There is no question that the codification and specification now required in confidentiality procedures places the professional worker into a situation of less discretion. Considering that social workers (and others) have held commitments to confidentiality predating the surge of emphasis in this area, they are apt to show some resistance to policy implementation. The analyst should not be alarmed if such resistance is evident but, rather, should consider the extent to which it mitigates achievement of the policy goal.

4. Major Strategies

At this point we need to consider the strategic approach used by the agency in achieving the policy goal and in implementing the policy itself.

a. Overall approaches

As the overall approach to helping clients feel a sense of trust and confidence in the agency and its staff, the policy puts the matter to a stiff test. In choosing the vehicle of confidentiality, the agency asks the client to take a high risk—to share meaningful secrets about his or her personal life—with people who he or she likely has never before known. On the other side, the agency stakes its own reputation on the presumption that it can deliver on its promises (which, by the way, is reason enough for the agency and its staff not to make false and unlimited promises about its ability to maintain secrecy at all costs and in all circumstances).

In terms of organizational approaches, the agency has taken the most conservative of approaches and has formalized the movement of information about clients from one program to another, even within that same agency. As the CSI policy statement indicates, the agency has even noted in its written policy manual that persons thought to be aggrieved have a right to redress. Consequently, the agency has not only made a commitment to deliver on the promise of the policy, but has provided assurances that, lacking such delivery, the client will be assured the right to redress. The analyst would do well to examine those redress procedures to see that they function adequately and have been used properly.

b. Resources allocated

Except for computing the prorated amount of time spent by the recipient rights officer and by agency staff in completing client release forms, informing clients regarding the agency policy, and managing the grievance procedure, it would be difficult to determine the cost of implementation of this policy. However, one may conclude that a very large amount of staff resources have been committed, both formally and informally, to the implementation of this policy. One obvious and proper cost is found in orientation and training of staff to implement the policy. The analyst would have to establish some kind of "soft" criteria of cost, such as anecdotes or estimates of time that could be required to comply with policy expectations. In one sense, the analyst could compute an estimate of the opportunity costs (the costs foregone by not taking action) in not complying with the legislative and funding requirements associated with maintaining confidentiality. However, this would appear to be a purely academic exercise since the practice is mandatory.

c. Types of benefits for clients and targets

The most obvious benefit accrued to the client group as a result of the policy is the freedom to share relevant information in the interest of problem solving. The client is reasonably assured that sensitive personal information can be shared with agency staff for the purpose of obtaining help or some service without being embarrassed or having disclosed such information to unauthorized persons. For the staff-member-as-target, the policy gives a guide for action and gives legitimization, provided by law, by the courts and by the CSI board of directors, to a central value held by the workers' professional association. Here we have a mixture of mutually supportive self-interests.

5. Feasibility

In this section of our analysis we will examine the aspects of the policy that are likely to make the policy goal achievable, given the policy as provided.

a. Legality

As noted earlier, with this particular policy we have legitimacy in constitutional, legislative, and judicial law as well as roots in the ethics of the professional association. There are perhaps very few policies that enjoy such legitimacy and sanction. In some respects, the administrative rules arising out of much of the legislation give more specificity for direction (e.g., the mental health code and its recipient rights requirements) than any other new policy governing agency relationships with its clientele.

b. Resource requirements and availability

The accountability side of information management is likely to require more resources than the actual provision of confidentiality assurances. That is, the record-keeping and auditing of confidentiality procedures, and the reporting of the information obtained on aggregate client activity, are likely to be more costly in terms of personnel and equipment than the implementation of confidentiality itself. To be sure, the maintenance of confidentiality is not trivial. However, the development and maintenance of confidentiality, itself, is an integral part of the helping relationship, such that it would be impractical to factor out the confidentiality element.

One aspect of determining resource availability is to examine the extent to which staff have been properly oriented and trained in carrying out the technical aspects of maintenance of confidentiality. Training incurs a cost and the analyst would do well to prorate that cost over the appropriate caseload of the agency to get an estimate of confidentiality's share in the costs per units of service in the agency.

c. Power and influence

Clearly, the power is with the client in this policy because the Constitution, state and federal legislatures, the courts and administrative agencies are there to ensure the client's rights. Thinking in terms of feasibility, we can look to the administrative structure to implement and maintain the policy, and we can conclude whether or not the structural arrangements are adequate to carry out the various mandates. The mandates are not in question; the organizational and procedural arrangements for carrying them out are.   *mandates*

An avenue for our analysis might be to identify the locations of influence in the policy system and determine whether those individuals or those loci are, in fact, supportive of the various expectations for confidentiality. Some possibilities are the executive director, program heads, the recipient rights officer, those who audit for certification standards, licensing authorities and, of course, key staff workers.

d. Rationality

The policy is rational in the sense that it comes with the support and sanction of a variety of powerful legitimating sources, and is consistent with basic American values. Furthermore, the policy is consistent with social treatment theories and, therefore, represents both sound administrative practice as well as a proper principle in social practice.

e. Environmental impact

The agency policy concerning confidentiality would likely not have a significant or outstanding impact on wider community practices since the policy's underlying principles are so much in concert with those of the rest of society at this time. Also, strict adherence to the principles of the policy could mitigate the growing abuse in the area of automated data retrieval systems, data banks, management information systems, and the like. In that sense, the confidentiality policy could help to sustain countervailing values opposing the rise in the management of information for its own sake rather than for the sake of those who provide and use social services.

The impact on the agency itself should also be considered when analyzing the policy. Communications could surely be said to be more formal and routine as a result of the policy. The effects of this phenomenon should not automatically be assumed to be negative; rather, they should be identified descriptively by the analyst prior to making evaluative judgments.

f. Newly perceived self-interests

As noted before, policies are partly accepted and/or sustained by the perceptions held by key actors that self-interests (of individuals or the groups they represent) can be served; there appears to be something in this policy for everyone. For clientele, increased assurances are provided that their constitutional and statutory rights are to be protected in the process of receiving services. The professional providers are reassured that their code of ethics has the support of law and the board under which they serve. Administrative officers of the agency can be assured that they administer a policy that has the support of the board, the staff and the clientele; they are not placed in a compromising position. In fact, the policy analyst would do well to frequently ask whether deviations from guidelines and procedures compromise the interests of any of these groups or components in the policy system. That question will provide a useful foil for breaking into the analysis at various points.

Summary

In Case 1 we examined the multiple mandates of a confidentiality policy in a private, multiprogram child and family service agency.

Here and there we noted the policy's contingent ramifications with the expectations of accountability. Many suggestions for exploration were provided. However, the real-life analyst must rely on his or her own creativity and intimate knowledge of the inner workings of the actual policy system. The model given here merely serves as a tickler, a guide, and must be augmented by professional experience, knowledge, and sensitivity.

Case 2: Utilization Monitoring of Provisions of Care

Our next case illustration involves a policy piloted by the state which mandates utilization reviews for Medicaid to be conducted by the local county offices. This policy illustration could analogously be played out in a number of similar situations. Given the expanding use of purchase of services by state and private funding sources through contracting, and given the push to install more responsibility and accountability at the local level, this policy allows us to explore a number of issues simultaneously. The issues embodied in this illustration go beyond Medicaid or federal/state/local relationships and are likely found in many intergovernmental and interagency (either private or public) contractual relationships.

Our case illustration is driven by a broader policy — the federal mandate that each state administering the Medicaid program must maintain statewide surveillance and have a utilization control program for Medicaid usage. In our case illustration, the State Department of Social Services (SDSS) has decided, through a pilot program, to employ a policy strategy requiring that the county offices of the SDSS shall monitor and provide safeguards for the appropriateness and quality of all reimbursed services by means of a postpayment review process. This strategy, which we will call the Service Monitoring Policy, has been inserted in agreements between one half of the local county offices and the state funding agency. For purposes of illustration, we will focus only on those aspects of the Service Monitoring Policy (SMP) that pertain to prescription drug purchases. Given the extensive relationship between pharmacotherapy and deinstitutionalization, this policy exploration has other obvious associations with many current policy concerns of human services workers.

1. The Policy Problem and/or Policy Goals

On the face of it, this policy addresses the two-pronged problem of inappropriate service being provided to citizens and the inefficient use of financial and medical resources. Put another way, policy goals have to do with getting appropriate services to those who are eligible and in need at an expenditure level commensurate with the level of service needed and provided.

A corollary problem and goal here would appear to be the concern over the massive levels of government involved in service provision and interest in shifting more responsibility and accountability for the delivery of services to local levels of government.

✗   *a. The Policy Statement*

The policy statement, legitimated by federal Medicaid regulations under the Social Security Act, Title XIX, is taken from the SDSS Service Monitoring Manual, as follows:

> The purpose of the Service Monitoring Program and Policy is to safeguard against unnecessary or inappropriate use of Medicaid services and against excess payments . . . and to assess the quality of these services. . . . The local agency shall establish a post-payment review process whose purpose is, among other things, to allow for correction of misutilization practices of recipients and providers.

A reading of the section of the manual pertaining to prescription drug purchases would lead us to conclude that the policy essentially has a negative thrust, pertaining primarily to cost containment and misutilization. However, a review of the entire document would appear to give a balanced emphasis to the dangers of the problem for the state's citizens, inasmuch as there are obvious implications for individuals in overutilization of drugs without appropriate supervision, as well as other community issues in improper management of drug prescriptions and purchases.

b. Contemporary issues

There are many issues embedded in the question of control of the distribution of and payment for prescription drugs (and many other health care procedures, for that matter) through public programs. Health professionals in the service system (in this case, the state) have expressed concern regarding misuse of the Medicaid provisions concerning prescription drugs. There is a belief that some clients are harming their health by overuse of certain drugs (even to the end result of fostering addiction or complicating health problems). Authorities have some suspicion of criminal behavior, with reports that drug purchases by Medicaid clients have been made for profit. Certain drugs have been singled out as being especially subject to misuse or abuse.

Another issue, as one might expect, is that any attempt to control the management of a medical procedure, including the prescription and/or administration of drugs, runs the risk of the provider agency coming into conflict with the client's personal physician or clinic. Thus, we hear the cry of "governmental interference in medicine." (This, of course, could as well apply to the "intrusion" of any social agency into the professional relationship, not only in health care but in other areas as well, e.g., client-attorney, tenant-landlord).

Then, of course, we have the issue of cost control. Public welfare programs of an income maintenance nature, whether by cash or in-kind devices, tend to be under constant scrutiny for cost control.

Finally, we have the whole cart of baggage associated with any suggestion of "drug abuse" and all the attendant fears. While misuse of a prescription drug provision may have nothing at all to do with drug abuse per se, the two issues become intertwined and provide a political backdrop for the policy analyst to take into consideration.

c. Historical antecedents

Medicare and Medicaid provisions of the Social Security Act have been in existence for approximately twenty years and, as is well known, the expenditure levels have increased geometrically—as have charges of abuse of the system. These realities tend to belie the fact that the program has tremendous value to a great many citizens in need.

The program has seen, along with other "quality assurance" and surveillance thrusts in public welfare, a shift in accountability from the federal government, down through the states, to the local levels of government. This appears to be the point at which we are now engaged with this policy. In this situation, the state is obligated to control the utilization of services with post-payment reviews and that task has been delegated to the local levels.

d. Targets of concern

(1) *Client and target subsystems.* In the policy system under study, it is difficult to separate the client system from the target system. In theory, the clients (i.e., the component on whose behalf action is taken) are those eligible citizens who are current or potential beneficiaries of the prescription drug provisions of the program. The targets (i.e., those in whom behavior change is being sought) would presumably be the providers of service, in this case dispensers of prescription drugs. On the one hand, we find the reality of over one-half of the dollar outlays for Medicaid actually going to health care providers, not to the client group, which suggests some confusion in the identity of the client group. On the other hand, the client/recipient group (not the target group) would appear to be the group in whom change is being sought. (Perhaps this lack of role identity gives rise to some of the confusion that exists in the program.) We might conclude that the client system in this policy is either the aggregate citizen group called "Medicaid recipients," or even the law-abiding provider groups, while the target system is really a subsystem of abusers within each client and target system.

(2) *System maintenance, control, or change.* From an over-all perspective, the policy is one of system control in the sense that it attempts to reduce the overuse and misuse of drugs under the medical assistance program and to reduce overall or, at least, unnecessary costs. From a systems change perspective, the policy is aimed at altering the behavior patterns of clients and providers that pertain to a particular client's health status.

(3) *Efficiency in coverage.* The policy would appear to have considerable power due to its ability to cover the entire state and the entire range of both recipients and providers. However, other issues in efficiency, discussed later, rest on the ability to adequately implement the policy.

e. Explicit or implicit theories

A prevailing implicit theory in this policy approach would appear to be that clients need an external control mechanism to help force them to reduce their drug use and change their behavior. However, another view that could be implied by the policy is that professional judgments and intentions of providers may not always be taken at face value.

Another theoretical explanation is that the policy supports a more basic premise—that all public welfare programs exist only as residual programs whose fundamental goal is to help the client achieve independence as soon as and using as few resources as possible. This premise is contrary to the reality that a certain number of Medicaid recipients will require ongoing care. For some citizens, no amount of control will provide support at a level or in a manner that will effect independent client functioning.

Yet another theory might be that, given the positive political value attached to public opinion that there is sound cost containment in any public welfare program, the policy would, on the whole, be beneficial to the entire SDSS, its county programs and, ultimately, to all recipients of public welfare benefits. The strategy would presumably foster public confidence and wider acceptance in this and other public welfare programs. Furthermore, some professional providers themselves suggest that some clients/patients tend to overuse the system and, as providers, they feel impotent in attempting to create their own unilateral restrictions when, technically, "official" provisions are available. Ironically, these groups support any policy that provides legitimacy outside of their own professional discretion.

f. Topography of the policy

The map of the policy system is, of course, heavily populated and complex. There are the various levels of government agencies with obligations and interests, from the federal down to the local levels. Then we have a large number and variety of professional associations and provider groups, contracting agencies, client advocate groups, citizen tax abatement movements and their associated groups, welfare watchdogs, and so forth. Given the formal and complex nature of intergovernmental obligations and expectations, the auditing apparatus itself is demanding, especially since the policy involves extensive amounts of funding, encompasses one-half of the entire state and its counties, and evolves around the very salient issues of accountability and appropriate medical care.

2. Criteria for Review or Choice

In this section we will select the core criteria that will be routinely applied to our policy.

a. Adequacy, effectiveness and efficiency

Aggregate adequacy is not a concern in this policy, since the entire state population of service recipients and their providers are presumably covered. However, the ability of the policy to provide for adequate coverage is very difficult to determine in our analysis. The adequacy of appropriate and sufficient coverage is a highly individualized matter for the recipient and, of course, adequacy is a subjective matter when left to the individual discretion of those who prescribe drugs. In our analysis, it would be necessary to review any studies available on the relationship between different medical conditions and average quantities or dosages. Again, since only normative conditions would become apparent, only aggregate adequacy in coverage would be estimated, however, and only approximations would be suggested for individual accuracy.

The effectiveness of the policy might be determined by samplings of error rates in inappropriately filled prescriptions, the number or nature of alleged or proven fraudulent charges, self-reports from the client population on whether the policy achieves its desired effects, or other means. The analyst should consider field studies involving clients and providers as well as reviews of secondary data in the analysis since the policy's implementation leaves so much to judgment and the partly political application of the criteria.

The question of efficiency might be approached by making comparisons on a benefit/cost basis of the alleged or presumed rate of inappropriate use of particular drugs compared to the frequency of client complaints or appeals, or the costs incurred in follow-up investigations. The latter approach could also be based on some sampling approach to gather data. The client feedback approach is fraught with considerable danger, however, because of the reliance on a clientele that is vocal, articulate, mobile, and willing and able to register their concerns. However, this could be overcome in part by an outreach program not only to clients but to others significant in their lives.

b. Equity, equality, and fairness
It is difficult to determine equity (i.e., that persons in similar circumstances are treated similarly) in the absence of a thorough familiarity with standards and guidelines used to implement the policy. Standards delineate the policy objectives in the course of implementation; guidelines provide some clues as to whether those standards are being properly adhered to by the means selected. The analyst would have to become familiar with those guidelines and obtain some evidence that they were systematically applied in the field in order to make any inferences regarding equity. Furthermore, the question of equity runs straight into the matter of individualization in treatment and the prescription of drugs. Therefore, the question is not so easily resolved.

Equality is more likely to be assured, but only if the policy is administered uniformly and consistently throughout the state. The analyst could make some inference regarding equality in application if the guidelines are clear and widely published. Another technique might be to determine whether adequate inservice training has been provided to the staff who administer the service and/or conduct postpayment reviews. Yet another approach of value for the analyst might be to determine whether reports of alleged misuse or abuse occur disproportionately throughout the state.

Fairness, wherein persons are not thought to be dealt with equivocally as a result of the policy, could be determined by such measures as studying the nature of grievances and complaints or, perhaps, determining the extent to which persons had been allowed particular benefits, only to have those benefits removed without apparent cause in the record. (Again, this would depend on a vocal and articulate group.) In the latter instance, criteria for "just cause" would have to be established and applied case by case, in at least an adequate sample.

c. Individualism and the work ethic

The policy would appear contrary to the American ethic of individualism since it does not presume that the individual has the right to make his or her own decision regarding treatment involving prescription drugs funded by Medicaid. However, in the case of prescription drugs and other aspects of medical care, this appears not so much contrary to the ethic of individualism, but, rather, a reliance upon the American belief that decisions regarding drug and medical care use should be left to those thought to be particularly qualified.

Also, with outside funding comes strings—an axiom in grant-in-aid programs of any kind. The grant would appear to obviate individualism in this case.

The work ethic would not appear to be directly related. However, illogically, any association with a public welfare program of any kind tends to call in sociopolitical commentaries about the virtues and habits of recipients and their willingness to work. No doubt this will cloud the receipt and interpretation of the policy analysis; this tendency emphasizes the care with which this kind of an analysis must be conducted and reported. This policy provides a prime example of the mixture of political and moral values inherent in policy choices.

d. Impact on rights and statuses

From the perspective of the client group, they are given no choice as to whether they wish to participate in the policy pilot. Consequently, their rights appear to be constrained, if not violated. While the responsibility for accountability continues to be left with the state, according to federal regulations, the state's utilization review policy shifts more of the implementation responsibility onto the local providers of Medicaid provisions (in this case, dispensers of drugs). Yet there do not appear to be any commensurate rights allocated to the localities as a result of a shift in those responsibilities. In fact, the localities actually take on more of the role of a regulatory agency. For purposes of policy analysis, the analyst could simultaneously focus on two levels. The first level could be a search and identification of what new rights or entitlements the locality and the local agency might now have due to a shift in responsibility. The second level would be a determination of the extent to which the local provider agency and its staff are ready and able to undertake the new regulatory function. This may entail plans for staff development, for example.

e. Identity and self-determination

The policy suggests far less opportunity for self-determination, since the recipient of prescription drugs would undoubtedly enjoy less autonomy in utilization as a result of closer scrutiny by the provider agency. Prescription drug purchases under Medicaid (as well as visits to physicians and other treatments) will now be monitored at the county office level. Furthermore, there is likely to be a reduced incidence of clients taking the initiative to seek voluntary or preventative medical care since the propensity on the part of the monitoring agency will be to discourage such use of the medical care system. Consequently, the criteria for "success" will differ for the client components and the provider components in the use of the medical care system.

f. Eligibility

All Supplemental Security Income (SSI) recipients, Aid to Dependent Children (ADC) recipients, and others on General Assistance are eligible for benefits and are, therefore, encompassed under the policy in the pilot area. All counties and all recipients so covered in the state will be covered by the policy; therefore, the policy may be said to have universal applicability in that regard. This has tremendous implications for criteria of feasibility, which will be discussed later.

g. Feedback

Feedback is built into the policy in the sense that, as a monitoring device itself, the policy assumes that deviations from the desired policy goal of reducing misuse will be identified and corrected by the local regulatory activities. The very nature of the policy is permeated with the feedback and corrective-information features of the regulatory intent, from the federal level, to the states, and (in the case of the state in our example), down to the local county level. Printouts showing clients' physician visits, drug usage, and emergency room use will be maintained in the state central office and will be shared with the local offices. A requirement of client authorization by means of a voucher form obtained before going to a physician or before getting a prescription filled or refilled provides for immediate engagement with the information system and for automatic corrective feedback.

3. System Functioning

At this point in our analysis we need to focus more on the organizational, administrative, and environmental functioning of the policy system.

a. State of system boundaries

The policy results in much tighter or relatively imperme-able boundaries in providing access to prescription drugs and physician visits. The boundaries allowing for interaction have been tightened by reduced discretion of the client group and by a more active "filtering" role by the local monitoring agency. The mechanism of requiring prior authorization through a voucher has served as the primary vehicle to tighten these boundaries, and the local monitoring requirement has, at least until proven otherwise by the pilot, sealed the gatekeeping function. Given that many of the eligible clientele also have, on the whole, limited transportation options available to them, access to the system is further limited by the voucher requirement. Given that few staff workers in the counties "cross the boundaries" by making home visits, access to the system is further constrained. This fact may run contrary to the overarching policy goal of providing appropriate service to those citizens who are in need. The policy, then, could possibly achieve an unintended effect; thus, systematic monitoring of this aspect of the policy should be developed via the analytic process.

b. Patterns of communication

On the one hand, it could be said that communication between recipients and their physicians would be reduced since, presumably, the requirement of a voucher for a physician's visit would constrain contact between patient and physician. On the other hand, if clients actually do obtain prescription drugs without their physician's assistance, then adequate communication would not appear to be occurring. In fact, it could even be argued that those clients who actually experience a medical condition needing pharmacotherapy would have a propensity to contact and communicate more fully with their physicians. Again, however, this requires an aggressive and articulate person and also presumes the availability of a physician with a propensity to listen.

The increased caseload activity required by prior voucher authorization is likely to create tension in the client-caseworker relationship as the caseworker's ability to handle an increased caseload is strained. This, of course, also has implications for the analyst in terms of feasibility.

c. Tension, variety, and entropy

Tension in the overall system is likely to be created by increased demands upon the client to pursue necessary services, for the casework providers, for the monitoring group, and for the pharmacists and physicians who will need to keep a paper trail of their transactions for the pilot project. Some clients may choose (or be forced) to start paying some of their physician and prescription bills themselves because of their inability to come to the local office to obtain a voucher or their inability to communicate their needs adequately; this could result in a reduction in their spendable incomes in other necessary areas of their budgets and create additional unwanted and unintended tensions.

Due to lack of information and/or preparation about project billings under the pilot policy, some providers may provide services to clients without having the necessary vouchers and, therefore, not receive authorization or Medicaid reimbursement. This could not only create tension between the provider and the service and monitoring agency, but also between the client and all elements of the system.

Presumably, however, there would be less variety and more uniformity within the counties participating in the pilot and this would be an important outcome criterion in the policy evaluation. Also, if one could argue for more efficiency in the overall system as a result of the policy, one could also demonstrate that the policy enables the system to do more work and provide more overall benefits, and prove that the policy did not foster entropy in the system.

d. Interface constraints

The point of greatest constraint between the various components of the system would likely fall upon the client and any component with which the client interacts. In other words, the client would feel the more negative effects of the policy in terms of relations with providers (caseworkers, pharmacists, or physicians). While caseworkers, pharmacists, and physicians would also be likely to feel the negative effects of this policy in their client relations (assuming that the resource pool will *not* increase while the client pool *will*), there will be other clients with whom these providers will have the opportunity to interact. Thus, providers may remain active participants in the system while the client group may not.

e. Functioning of feedback devices

Thinking in organizational terms, we would have to look at the timeliness, accuracy, and utility of the data reported to the central state office *and* as it flows back to the local agency responsible for monitoring. The monitoring data not only needs to be obtained and exchanged between each level but plans are needed for corrective action in ways that both appropriately meet client needs and properly distribute agency resources. We should also look at the effectiveness of the communications between the monitoring agency, the clients and the providers potentially affected by any adjustment in service provision.

f. Dynamic adaptation

The utilization monitoring policy could effect dynamic adaptation of the system to the extent that the feedback on client need, client utilization, and inappropriate provider distribution of services is used to adjust agency practices. Dynamic adaptation, the organization's ability to appropriately adjust forms of organization, could be a beneficial outcome of the policy. The analysis should search for ways in which the corrective feedback could lead to automatic organizational adjustments, such as incentive systems for providers who provide timely reports to the monitoring agency.

g. Authority, influence, and leadership

The policy maintains a hierarchical patterning of authority (i.e., the right to take action) in that each level is accountable to the next *higher* governmental level. However, while the power of authority over the next *lower* level tends to be the same for each level, the power of influence differs. Defining influence as the actual exercise of power, influence behavior is necessarily constantly exercised by the local county agency in order to meet its responsibilities. The higher the level, the less demanded in the way of affirmative influence action, which is entirely the point of passing on responsibility to the lower levels of government.

This allocation of influence also affords an opportunity for the local monitoring agency to provide leadership in its own county by the way it sets the tone for exercising its responsibility. The policy analyst would do well to examine the procedures used to implement the policy, since clues to the nature of those procedures will be found here. For example, the analysis could determine whether the procedures or guidelines encourage proper and appropriate distribution of services to those entitled to them; on the other hand, the leadership of the monitoring agency may instead be characterized by negative or exclusionary gatekeeping behavior that discourages service utilization. In either event, the monitoring agency's style of leadership sets the tone for the overall system's orientation to providing services, and the analysis should bring this to light.

h. Resistance to change

The change here is primarily in the shift to the governmental level that now becomes the locus of responsibility. While there might be some resentment regarding the new responsibility, there is little likelihood that significant resistance will be manifested since the sanctions for the local level would be too severe. Both the client population and the monitoring agency would suffer due to reduced funding. This is characteristic of "quality assurance" programs that focus on cost controls.

4. Major Strategies

Here we will examine the overall policy approach taken to achieve the policy goal as well as the means of implementation used to support that strategy.

a. Overall approaches

The key policy option has been taken by the State Department of Social Services in its decision to transfer the task of monitoring to the local county level. Except for whatever monitoring devices that the state decides to employ, the implementation strategies are found at the local level. The policy analyst would be well advised to review the features of the state-local contract for the program (or the guidelines published in lieu of such a contract) to determine the local implementation options. Some possibilities might be deviations allowed in error rates or ranges allowed in maximum allowable reimbursements.

b. Resources allocated

Here we need to look at the hard-cost criteria, such as the dollar value of benefits appropriately and inappropriately provided or the full-time staff equivalents necessary for policy implementation. Softer criteria should also be examined in terms of resources to be allocated, such as any potential alteration in the quality of the relationships between clients/patients and their providers of medical care, or the potential impact upon the relationships between the monitoring agency and the medical care providers. These changes will affect the functioning of the entire delivery system and, consequently, can be expressed as a cost. Will the system relationships become any more or less cooperative or contentious? The tighter the monitoring, the more contentiousness is likely in system interrelationships; this is a cost in policy implementation that analysis should make visible.

c. Types of benefits for clients and targets

For the client group, the policy goal is presumably to conserve the financial resources in such a way that benefits will be delivered to those who have proper entitlement. Also, an additional major client benefit here is intervention in any process wherein any one person in the client group has become involved in the illegal or medically inappropriate use of prescription drugs. For the provider group (i.e., pharmacists and physicians) the benefits would presumably center around assurances that, given adherence to the monitoring policy requirements, reimbursement will be forthcoming with minimal delays on the part of the monitoring agency.

5. Feasibility
In this section we will focus upon the factors that particularly bring about policy goal attainment.

a. Legality
It is clear that the policy has sufficient legitimacy. The benefits available, assuming the client and provider have met all requirements, are provided by federal law; the requirement of monitoring is established by federal rules and published in the *Federal Register*. There is nothing in the federal rules or the statute itself that precludes the states from passing the monitoring tasks down to the local level; the states are still left with ultimate accountability. There do not appear to be any implications for the judicial aspects of legality in this particular policy.

b. Resource requirements and availability
Implementation of the policy requires massive amounts of increased staff time, both clerical and professional, as well as extensive expansion of the computerized management information system. Voucher authorizations would require systematic review; so too with authorizations for payment. Each of these elements would have to be integrated with monitoring procedures in the expanded management information system. To be sure, the analyst would have to integrate whatever has been done in the way of costing-out these increased resource requirements.

Also, we should not overlook the increase in resource expenditures necessitated on the part of the client group. Inasmuch as the policy would presumably require more frequent trips to the provider of prescriptions, and perhaps more costs for medical reviews, we will have to explore these and other costs to the client effected by the mandatory utilization review policy.

c. Power and influence

Clearly power, in the form of legitimate authority through statute and rule, emanates from the federal level and moves down to the local level in this particular policy. The state has been able to exercise influence in shaping the implementation of the policy by making the discretionary decision to place the task of implementation at the local level. It has been feasible to mandate the policy of service monitoring from the highest level, given the leverage of the grant-in-aid device. It appears quite feasible to implement the policy of monitoring utilization at the local level, given appropriate and sufficient resources in staff and logistical supports.

d. Rationality

The most forceful argument for the rationality of the policy resides in the use of the local level of government to implement what is, ultimately, a federal goal. This is reasonable, given the history of success in placing responsibility for broad social goals in the hands of those who are nearest to the people and place where those goals will ultimately be achieved. Alternately, it would be unreasonable and irrational to expect a federal workforce to be established to carry out the monitoring tasks.

From the perspective of the state, the policy is rational in that the state's legitimate power over its county offices is being used properly. However, there is some risk that, given insufficient clarity in implementation guidelines or insufficient financial resources, the policy might not be rational. Were these insufficiencies to occur, there might be no uniformity or consistency in implementation from county to county and the state's obligation to provide services equitably would be undermined.

e. Environmental impact

Since public opinion generally favors restrictions on virtually any public welfare program, successful implementation of the pilot policy would curry public favor; conversely, failure in its implementation could further erode public confidence. The policy poses certain risks in this regard since, given the state of the economy, with reduced levels of public funding, and the danger of not having enough staff resources for implementation, the policy leaves much to chance.

The policy could also erode the client group's confidence in the local SDSS offices. Local control in this policy instance means carrying out the regulatory function without preempting the state's prerogative of setting the goals and the guidelines. Except for the actual review of the particulars through staff investigations, local control essentially consists of making recommendations and giving advice to the applicant or client. The applicant/client must provide proof that his or her health needs warrant a drug prescription and that physician visits are not excessive. Consequently, the client may begin to see the county staff as less a provider of services and more a gatekeeper for state resources.

f. Newly perceived self-interests

There appear to be no self-interests for the client or the local office in this pilot policy. It is primarily the self-interest of the SDSS that appears to be served. The mandates of the federal statute and the federal guidelines would be served in either event, i.e., monitoring by the state or the local agency.

Summary

In this case illustration we have used our guide to analyze the pilot policy initiated by the State Department of Social Services requiring that mandatory reviews of all Medicaid provisions be conducted by local offices of the department. This illustration is not unlike many situations involving interagency relationships, public or private, in which contractual relationships with another agency require analysis of the obligations incurred in each provision.

While our application in this illustration has dutifully marched through each part of our "Content Elements for Analyzing Small-

Scale Policy" outline, actual application need not include such compulsive recognition of each detail. The outline serves as an inventory, so to speak, of elements in the warehouse. At the risk of stretching the reader's imagination here and there, we have attempted to apply each element of the outline for purposes of illustration and to stimulate thinking.

Case 3: Integrated Policy for the Downtown Mall

In this illustration of the analysis of policy content we will select a policy issue that touches upon a situation with which many individual citizens, communities, and service agencies struggle. The situation involves the "problem" of what goes on in gathering places in central cities. In the case at hand we will look at what is to be done about the "mall people." We will continue with this problem and policy analysis in Case 6 (regarding the values elements in analysis) and in Case 8 (regarding the process elements).

In our case illustration we find that the community of Rapid River is attempting to deal with the issue of constant complaints from business people, the police, and the general citizenry about the number of "vagrants" congregating around the downtown mall and frequenting the mall's shops. Complaints are also received from the citizens who frequent the mall and from many social agency personnel who work with them. Many "mall people" feel that they are often victimized or portrayed as second class citizens and undesirables in the community. They claim that what is considered by some business people as "loafing" or "loitering" is nothing more than harmless recreational window shopping and that what some shoppers call "harassment" is often a gesture of friendliness. While the police have on record instances of assault or theft, including shoplifting in the mall area, some of which are attributed to the "mall people," many such reports are unfounded.

This policy analysis example will be seen from the perspective of Frances LaRose, city commissioner of Rapid Falls. She has received the whole range of complaints and inquiries concerning the issue and is seen as a commissioner who is understanding of human resource issues in the community.

1. The Policy Problem and/or Policy Goals

A general view of the problem might be that there is a dispute over the ownership of and entitlement to the resources of the community, in this case the downtown mall. The mall is comprised of pedestrian walkways on a closed thoroughfare, enclosed arcades on various levels, a variety of shops, a hotel, and meeting rooms. It was built and is jointly funded by a combination of private enterprise and city revenue and is perceived as a community treasure.

The problem may be cast in terms of "who has access to those facilities and under what conditions?" This approach to the problem takes into consideration conflicts between what are perceived to be the rights of some individual citizens—business people or "mall people"—and the rights of the community as a whole. Another conceptualization of the problem might be that the city has not adequately provided support services for all elements of the community using the downtown mall facility. Inherent in the latter conceptualization is some question of whether the city or other units of government, or even the private sector, is responsible for the problem's resolution.

a. The policy statement

In this situation we do not have the luxury of beginning with a policy statement from which to proceed with our analysis. At this point we can only speculate about what our policy might be inferred to be, or what policy we might assume to be desirable. Lacking any analysis it would be difficult to issue a final policy position. However, given what we all might know about these types of situations, we could perhaps suggest a few policy *principles* that might be suitable or reasonable. We will use the following policy statement, proposed by Commissioner LaRose, as a heuristic approach just to get the analysis process going.

It is the policy of the City of Rapid River that all citizens of the community shall have equal access to all public facilities associated with the Downtown Mall; that the civil rights of no citizen of the community will be violated by any policy or procedure related to any activity of any public or private group while associated with the Downtown Mall; and that all ordinances of the city and laws of the State and Federal governments shall be observed insofar as those ordinances and laws pertain to conduct of citizens on the Mall.

Commissioner LaRose begins, then, with principles that would appear to advance the rights and responsibilities of city government, honoring the rights of all parties involved, and simultaneously acknowledging the responsibilities of all of the community's citizenry.

b. Contemporary issues

One basic issue involves the control of a valuable resource in the community and concerns the distribution of that resource. There are no doubt differences within the community about the various purposes to be served by the mall—commerce, recreation, aesthetics, housing, entertainment, and so forth. A related matter is the extent to which the public is responsible for supporting and encouraging the success of free enterprise, and the public good to be served by that support; another is the role of city government in regulating how individuals use leisure time and/or choose to relate to other citizens in the community.

From a social welfare services perspective, there are other issues related to the identity and needs of the mall people. First is the question of who the mall people actually are. Commissioner LaRose finds that a large number of the controversial citizens are persons who had been treated for mental illness in the state hospital located in the city and who are not functioning at an optimal level within the limits of their handicap. In other words, these are the "deinstitutionalized" found in so many communities. However, there are many other groups involved.

Some of the mall people are adolescents, many of whom are enrolled in school programs but who regularly skip school; others are school youth conducting legitimate business after school. Another group is comprised of men residing in a large "half-way house" recently located in the city by the state Department of Prisons, all of whom participate to varying degrees in job-training programs in the community. Another group is comprised of developmentally disabled adults who work at a sheltered work-shop in the downtown area, shop at the mall, use mall restau-rants, and congregate at the many bus stops in the mall area. Yet another group is comprised of senior citizens who use the mall as a place to meet friends. For many of these groups, the central issue evolves around the question of whether an adequate system of supports is in place. A related question is the extent to which various agencies are responsible for the provision of those supports and the level of resources to be made available for such a system.

c. Historical antecedents

One obvious bit of historical information has to do with the shift in emphasis from institutionalization to community care for the mentally ill and the developmentally disabled. To some extent, this is also true of correctional programs for criminal offenders. Coupled with this are years of neglect of programming outside of schools for young people and, except for a few "senior centers," nothing for independent and mobile senior citizens.

An overlay for this problem is the recent rash of hostilities occurring around the state toward the development of group homes for former patients of state institutional programs. The recent cutbacks in state services in all areas of government finance have led to reductions in institutional programming; dollars have not followed those citizens into the local communities to pro-vide the financial support needed for community programming. Program planners and government decision makers have found, on the one hand, that the general citizenry is not willing to finance services at the same levels as in recent years. On the other hand, demands are made on government agencies to "do something."

d. Targets of concern

On the face of it, the targets of concern expressed in the problem statement would appear to be the mall people in general, and the groups noted above, in particular. In this instance those groups are cast more or less in the role of pariahs. However, the policy proposed by Commissioner LaRose suggests that all elements of the community should be the targets of the concern. That is, we see in the policy a concern for the rights and responsibilities of all citizens involved. This perspective, should it be viable in its political context, should allow for a democratic or generally impartial approach to problem resolution. Nevertheless, the arbitrary assignment of identity of who the targets actually are is a crucial element in giving direction and a philosophy to the policy analysis.

e. Explicit or implicit theories

The general stance of the business community — that government should intervene — supports a theory that government is the proper regulatory instrument to manage interrelationships of the city's citizens, at least in the area of central-city commerce. This posture rests on the assumption that the rights of all parties are easily definable and distributable. An opposite view might be that publicly supported facilities should routinely be made available for broad public use. This would not necessarily include indiscriminate use of those facilities, however. Implicit in Commissioner LaRose's policy is a classical democratic theory of government — that all people should have equal rights until and/or unless laws are violated. In essence, part of the policy task here is to come to some clear statement of agreement on a viable set of policy principles for the situation. This, perhaps, is a situation in which the opinion of a city attorney or other arbiter could give direction to subsequent action and policy analysis.

f. Topography of the policy

In drawing our "map" of the components of this living policy system, we have already located a number of people actively engaged in the issue, ranging from merchants to various groups among the mall people. A number of state agencies and their local counterparts are also suggested, such as public welfare, mental health, corrections, senior services, and the schools. The city transportation system and the location of its bus stops are also implicated, as are the police, operators of residential care facilities providing homes to many of the mall people, and no doubt, the local Chamber of Commerce as well as various professional associations with an interest in the issue.

In a physical context, it might be said that our mapping of the issue involves only the central city, and the mall in particular. However, the fact that the central city is the only logical place for so many people to congregate is also evidence of the absence of appropriate programs or other alternatives elsewhere in the city or in nearby communities. It also suggests that adequate resources are not being devoted to helping many citizens who find themselves in the role of "mall people." Such resources might appropriately be directed to assisting citizens in obtaining the skills, resources, or supports necessary to function in a personally satisfying way in the community.

2. Criteria for Review or Choice

This section of our analysis will focus on the basic criteria for policy review.

a. Adequacy, effectiveness, and efficiency

From a perspective of aggregate adequacy, the current approach to the problem is not adequate. That is, rights and responsibilities are not clear to a sufficient number of elements in the policy system. From a perspective of individual adequacy, the current approach does not provide sufficient protection for any particular individual. Merchants and individual shoppers alike do not feel adequately served or protected. On the other hand, should each individual's and group's right and responsibility (implied in Commissioner LaRose's proposed policy) be made clear, the remaining question of adequacy would appear to lie only in the area of regulation and enforcement. The commissioner's proposal implies uniform enforcement.

The policy implied in current community behavior is obviously not effective as there appears to be an insufficient connection between the goal of open and unrestricted participation or cooperation and the means of regulating behavior. Presumably, the proposed policy makes a direct connection between the means and the end, achieved by integrating principles of citizens' rights to public facilities with the enforcement of ordinances. The efficiency of the proposed policy would remain to be seen in the level of effort and resources needed to achieve the goal; the current approach is obviously neither effective nor efficient.

If the mall people are to be treated equitably by all citizens of the community, however, some will have to be provided with the skills to function within normative expectations. Service agencies in the community will need to target such skill development as appropriate routines when waiting for and riding the bus, methods of properly greeting others in public places, and appropriate behavior in the various shops. Providing people with specific social skills will increase their opportunities for equitable treatment; the social agencies have an opportunity and a responsibility to provide supports to help people obtain those skills. It would also be beneficial if efforts were made to provide some public education for merchants and other people who use the mall, helping them understand the nature of the problem and the purpose of efforts to deal with the problem.

b. Equity, equality, and fairness

We do not have adequate information at this point in our analysis about whether any particular group within the mall people are not treated similarly in similar circumstances (the question of equity); we do know, however, that the mall people, taken as a whole, are treated differentially compared to other citizens.

All citizens on the mall are treated equitably in the sense that there are no flagrant restrictions imposed upon any group wishing access to the mall. However, the principle of fairness is certainly lacking at the present time and would likely be remedied in the commissioner's proposed policy. However, that policy would need to be backed up by other community supportive services, such as crisis intervention or a downtown day treatment or day activity center.

c. Individualism and the work ethic

The repeated allegations of vagrancy and loitering by some people connected with the mall suggest that a judgment is being made that mall peoples' time would be better spent in more gainful activities. This theme is often heard, in spite of the fact that many of the developmentally disabled adults actually are engaged in daily sheltered workshop activities, many of the senior citizens frequenting the mall have properly retired from employment, and many of the youths and persons receiving aftercare are unable to obtain employment. Expectations regarding the work ethic appear to be either unrealistic or a misguided analysis of the real problem.

d. Impact on rights and statuses

The commissioner's proposal appears, if enforced, to assure the realization of rights of all elements in the community and would likely accord a higher, though appropriate, status to the mall people. Properly enforced, the policy would protect the rights of the merchants and shoppers on the mall, while at the same time not imposing any unfair or improper status for the "mall people."

e. Identity

The proposed policy would hopefully enhance the self-image of mall people while, at the same time, not reflect negatively on the character of others in the community. The focus on the principle of citizens' rights in the proposed policy obviously has a direct connection to the principle of self-determination. Discussion of this element will be continued in Case 6, regarding the value elements of analysis of this problem.

f. Eligibility

There is no eligibility criteria, per se, associated with this issue, though one could reasonably suggest that there is actually some sort of "admissions" requirement to the mall and its facilities. Issues associated with eligibility are more likely to emerge when and if the agencies having responsibility. for various individuals or groups within the mall population develop supportive programs, such as day treatment, an activity center, social skills training, and crisis intervention services. At that point, there will likely be turf and domain issues regarding agencies and programs, along with the associated competition for resources. These matters will be examined in detail in Case 8 in our analysis of the process elements of policy analysis.

g. Feedback

The feedback device built into the current approach is obviously in place, as evidenced by the outcries from the community, though the self-corrective nature of that feedback is unquestionably ineffective. A self-corrective feedback measure is built into Commissioner LaRose's proposed policy statement. This is true to the extent that the principles of citizens' rights to equal access and the protection of civil rights (i.e., of "mall people" and merchants alike) are monitored and corrected through the enforcement included in the statement. Consequently, the proposed policy has promise of including its own mechanism for monitoring and control, a desirable feature of social policy. However, we are again reminded of the importance of supportive community social service to be made available to all elements associated with the mall if that self-corrective expectation is to be realized.

3. System Functioning

This section of our analysis will focus on current or potential system functioning under the proposed policy. For this policy issue we will give particular attention to matters of design of programs offering support to various elements in the system.

a. Openness or closedness of system boundaries

The boundaries of actual and symbolic access to the mall are effectively restricted for all elements of the system at the current time. Merchants, mall people, and other citizens do not feel free to use the resources and exercise their basic rights. The proposed or potential policy would at least give shape to those boundaries by opening up opportunities for participation and collaboration.

b. Patterns of communication

Patterns of communication in one sense may be said to be unilateral, with some elements of the community telling others that they are "undesirables." There is an absence of dialogue. Social service agencies could play a key role in bringing about bilateral communication and in opening up the closed intrasystem boundaries now existing between and among elements. Public education would perform a particularly significant function in this regard, as would any agency efforts at enhancing individual mall people's functioning.

An important activity, then, would be to identify key modes and channels of communication. Individual "mall people" who play leadership roles in the various groups could be very helpful, as could certain active and influential merchants in the Downtown Merchant's Association, the news media, and certain individuals associated with planning and funding agencies. The city manager's office could perhaps play a key role as communication coordinator or convenor, particularly with a city commissioner playing an active role.

c. Tension, variety, and entropy

The present situation is not able to tolerate the variety of inputs (i.e., behaviors or attitudes) contributing to the mall environment. This has resulted in tension and increased entropy, or a decrease in the community's ability to function effectively. The proposed policy would provide for more order and predictability and, consequently, less entropy as well as the inclusion of more variety in the mall area. However, the systemic tension will likely continue in the absence of supportive measures and services. While variety may be increased and disorder decreased by a firm enforcement and protection of a citizens' rights approach to policy, without these service supports tension may in fact be increased by such an approach.

d. Interface constraints

Interface constraints exist to the extent that various elements are placed into competition or conflict with one another. In this situation the clash appears to be over both resources and ideology. From a resource perspective, the mall is a resource and elements are in competition over its control. From an ideological perspective, the clash is over the purposes for which the mall will be used, e.g., a center of commerce, a recreational area, a meeting place, or a bus terminal. Both the resource issues and the ideological issues will have to be negotiated more fully and openly by various elements in the community if resolution is to be obtained. Current policy does not provide that channel. The proposed policy, while it would support and be compatible with efforts to resolve these clashes, will not in itself provide the resolution.

e. Functioning of feedback devices

As noted above, automatic or built-in feedback devices are useful to provide monitoring of policy effectiveness. Those feedback devices are now manifested in complaints to the police, referrals to the existing mental health crisis services, occasional referrals to adult protective services—all on an ad hoc basis for specific problem intervention. The proposed policy would suggest more police enforcement but not other, more service-oriented monitoring and corrective adjustment efforts.

f. Dynamic adaptation

There is currently no office, agency, person, or group with the authority or responsibility to adjust arrangements in the system to make the proposed policy workable. Possible solutions could be appointment of an ombudsman on site at the mall or increased Police Department foot patrols schooled in human relations. However, these efforts would not likely provide system-wide adaptation but rather, only individual problem resolution. Given the diverse nature of elements having controlling and vested interests in mall activities, adaptive efforts would likely have to be made by a variety of agencies and offices, perhaps all coordinated by a central office, such as that of the city manager, or a social agency under contract.

g. Authority, influence, and leadership

Leadership is lacking in present problem resolution and will likely have to come from representatives of key interest groups. The proposed policy will provide legitimacy if leadership efforts are centered on certification and protection of rights. Authority to take other actions will likely have to be a result of jointly arrived at community agreements. However, the sanction and legitimacy afforded that process by the proposed rights-oriented policy would give impetus to these cooperative efforts. Those agencies and individuals having access to such legitimacy and leadership would have to play active roles in exerting their influence on the policy process.

h. Resistance to change

There will be great resistance to change in the absence of viable alternatives that address all elements. Lacking any change in supports provided to the mall people or changes in any behaviors that are seen as undesirable, merchants will likely continue to press for restrictive solutions. Without supportive programs and services, the mall people will have no other choices in their search for a "community space."

Other users of the mall are also resistant to change. Continued dissatisfaction will perhaps result in shoppers moving their business and entertainment activities to the suburbs or other outlying areas. Continued participation in mall activities will probably be determined in large part by the ability of the mall people and the merchants to come to successful resolution of the problem. In effect, the continued participation of the general public in mall affairs will also be greatly determined by the success of the human service agencies in providing the kinds of supportive services that will resolve this conflict.

4. Major Strategies
This section will consider the overall strategic approaches that have been and might otherwise be taken for problem resolution.

a. Overall approaches
In the existing circumstances, there is no apparent overall approach to problem resolution, other than one group implying that another group must be removed from the system. However, this approach does not represent the strategic choice of any significant number of people.

The overall approach of the proposed policy is one of strict control of rights-violating behavior and enforcement of the city ordinances and other pertinent laws. Hence, the approach is essentially legalistic and regulatory. This approach, as noted above, is likely to succeed only if complementary supportive services are provided. Such supports would likely be educational (e.g., public education of merchants and the general citizenry) and interventive (e.g., day treatment services, a downtown activity alternative program, or crisis services for acting-out persons).

b. Resources allocated
Currently, no extraordinary resources are allocated. The proposed policy would require assignment of more foot patrol officers to the mall and/or more squad car patrols. More enforcement would also require court or administrative actions by appropriate agencies. The additional human service agencies' support programs suggested above would require extensive financial resources. However, given the cost of doing nothing and the ultimate cost

to the community incurred by tension in the mall area, some level of outlay would have to be seriously considered.

c. Types of benefits for clients and targets

In this instance, the "client" (i.e., that element on whose behalf action is taken) and the "target" (that element who is the object of action) may be considered one and the same. Policy change and interventive efforts would be aimed at all of the citizen elements noted above and benefits would presumably accrue to each of those elements. The desired result of the policy would be for all citizens to be free to frequent the mall area and all merchants assured that their efforts for community development and success are supported. The various strategies would be targeted for each of the population elements.

5. Feasibility

This section will consider aspects of the policy that are likely to make problem resolution achievable.

a. Legality

The current situation tends toward exclusion of mall people from the mall area and has no legitimacy in legislative, judicial, or administrative policy. The proposed policy would have legitimacy in constitutional law, state and federal statutes, and local ordinance. Also, courts have clarified some requirements of access to public facilities and have prohibited discriminatory service to citizens in public places. The rights of citizens on public properties adjoining the Mall are less clear and depend on very particular circumstances. At any rate, the legal foundations of relationships are not essentially at odds in this issue. The issues evolve more around exercise of rights and role expectations of various citizens.

b. Resource requirements and availability

As noted above, resources will be needed for additional enforcement and for supports provided by human service agencies. The relative size of the public safety budget, for foot patrols in particular, would have to be examined. Past efforts to develop the foot patrol concept in the community have looked to community development block grants as the funding source. However, other needs are competing for those funds. In the service area, the move to community care and "deinstitutionalization" has led to the transfer of some state dollars heretofore allocated to hospital inpatient care into community mental health budgets. However, recent state funding problems have strained existing programs and led to cutbacks in service areas, particularly in outpatient counseling services for the less severely impaired. Nonetheless, mental health funds represent a possible source of support for new programming, as do adult protective services funds through the state Department of Social Services, given the frequent incidences of abuse reported on the mall. The correctional system has not generally allocated large amounts of financial resources or staff to support prison-based community placement programs. While the local court programs could be of assistance in developing supportive programs for correctional half-way house residents, state prison officials would have to lend their own support to the local effort.

c. Power and influence

The authority of the law gives a great deal of sanction to the proposed policy, but its power is essentially to be found in its impetus for other efforts to be undertaken. The reality of legal sanction would appear to give more power to the mall people than at present but leadership, rather than raw power, is needed to achieve the policy goal. Influence will have to be exercised by the Merchant's Association, the executives and boards of the major funding sources (e.g., corrections, mental health, and public welfare) and by the city commission and/or the city manager's office.

d. Rationality

The proposed policy is rational in the sense that it rests upon generally accepted and legitimate means of resolving problems involving citizens' rights. Its practicality will be enhanced by meshing the regulatory and enforcement strategy with a public education and supportive services strategy; the rationality of the policy theroretically stands alone without these additional measures.

e. Environmental impact

The quality of the Downtown Mall environment at the present time is one of tension and, at various points, hostility and fear. The proposed policy would perhaps lessen some realistic fears and suggest that individuals and businesses would receive adequate protections. However, tensions or hostilities would not likely be eased by the proposed policy alone.

f. Newly perceived self-interests

The commissioner's proposed policy will succeed if individuals, groups, and businesses are able to expand their range of perceived self- or group-interests served by the policy. A strategy of cooperation and accommodation by business people in the mall area, providing that such efforts are successful, would presumably return more business activity to the mall area. The Merchants' Association and such groups as the Community Economic Development Corporation are likely to see this possibility, but may need some assistance in realizing it. State funding agencies may be helped to see the economies of supporting successful, community-based efforts as alternatives to public disenchantment to community care strategies. This scenario would likely mean more strains on institutional budgets. A key element in subjecting the proposed policy to useful analysis will be Commissioner LaRose's efforts (or the efforts of her policy analysts) to bring these newly perceived self-interests to light.

Summary

In Case 3 we have examined the threat of exclusion of mall people from the downtown mall and considered a proposed policy offered by a city commissioner, Frances LaRose. We have also considered what complementary approaches to problem resolution might be necessary in the commissioner's proposed approach to the problem. Case 6 will take a more detailed look at the values aspects of the proposed policy and Case 8 will analyze the process elements in this hypothetical case illustration.

5

Value Elements for Small-Scale Policy Analysis

This chapter will continue the discussion of the essential elements of a model for small-scale policy analysis, giving special attention to the sixth element—assessing congruence with desired values. The first content elements, already discussed, are (1) identifying the policy problem or policy goals, (2) setting the criteria for review or choice, (3) assessing system functioning, (4) determining major strategies, and (5) determining feasibility. As with chapter 4, we will present an outline; its focus will be values. That outline, entitled "Value Elements for Analyzing Small-Scale Policy," follows the end of the narrative portion of this chapter.

Values are particularly central in the practice of social work and other human service professions. Values pertain to desires, wants, or priorities, while ethics pertain more to the behaviors necessary to attain those preferences. However, as Levy (1979b) points out, these distinctly different elements become merged in professional practice. That is, the professional person cannot easily separate values from ethics. Nevertheless, values may be seen as the *principles of means* and ethics, the *principles of ends*. For some the values and ethics of their professional orientation may provide the driving force for their commitment to social welfare in general and social welfare policy analysis in particular. In this chapter, we will focus primarily on the values aspects inasmuch as our purpose here is to examine the substantive content of policy, rather than how we are to behave ethically in our practice.

For the professions as a whole, values are integrating forces that become part of some professions' charters, as evidenced in professional codes of ethics. Consequently, any model for social welfare policy analysis must give explicit attention to the value element in order to be consistent with the profession's mandates and meet the professional responsibility owed to the clientele being served.

This chapter is organized around three content areas. The first is a brief review of those central values considered generic to social work practice, particularly as they relate to policy analysis. The second is a detailed discussion regarding the necessity of a set of values that are consistent with the general system approach or theory of social processes. In the third section, special attention is given to sexism, classism, racism, poverty, and ageism as these issues pertain to policy analysis.

As with chapter 4, we will introduce a detailed case example throughout the narrative for illustrative purposes. Once again, the reader is reminded that not every element need be "covered" in an actual analysis; rather, the application is provided in the chapter in order to illustrate the points made in the narrative. Our illustration begins here.

Case Illustration

In the case illustration in chapter 4, we explored the policy of Child Services, Inc. that both encourages and expects birthparents in adoption situations to participate in planning for the care of the newborn child to as great a degree as possible. We considered a number of elements in our analysis of that policy situation that had value implications. However, we will now give our attention to those elements for a *values* analysis. Again, the reader is reminded that application of each values element in our narrative is meant for illustrative purposes; an exhaustive application of each element may not be necessary or appropriate to all policy situations.

Generic Values

Many in the field have attempted to put forth lists of values thought to be generic to social work practice, perhaps in an effort to develop a consensus definition of the core ethos that glues us together and guides our choices for action. We have already included specific references to two of those values in chapter 4, identity maintenance and self-determination, which were included in the content model for policy analysis. We will use these concepts as our starting point.

Generic Values

Here we will focus on the core values to be considered in the birthparents' participation policy.

Identity

As noted earlier, if the substance of the analysis is to be its social welfare nature, we must consider the impact of the policy upon the self-image of the beneficiary or target of the policy. A fundamental value element in our model must be that we give explicit attention to the impact of social welfare activity on the self-image of people and their need and right to human dignity: this must be our first consideration. In practical terms, the analysis must take into consideration the policy's impact upon individual, group, or organizational feelings of self-worth and identity. The analysis must assess the actual or probable outcomes of the policy with respect to these "human rights."

Identity

Our analysis leads us to conclude that the policy of birthparents' participation in adoption processes provides a formalization of rights and status for the birthparent that legitimizes and supports optimum participation. In terms of a person's identity, this policy would appear to foster and support a client's perception of him- or herself as a person of worth who not only has a right to participate but is someone who can make meaningful contributions to the problem-solving process. The birthparent enters the policy process as a team member, a role that both contributes to the policy goal of achieving the best possible arrangement for the newborn child and, at the same time, incorporates a professional value for social practice.

Self-Determination

Again, as noted, for social welfare analysis we must consider the impact of the policy upon the right of citizens to a voice in the determination of those policies that vitally affect them. This is not to say that everyone is involved to the fullest in every policy decision affecting their lives. Nonetheless, the *rights* of citizens must be explicitly reviewed and considered, and these rights must be honored in the policy and, of course, in the policy analysis. Whether these same rights of self-determination will be honored equally in the subsequent decisions arising out of the analysis is, of course, another matter. However, the analyst has an ethical obligation, in the analysis itself, to consider the value element of self-determination of client and target groups.

Self-Determination

The policy directs the agency to move away from the traditional practice of casting the birthparent into the "giving up the child" role and the associated task of providing a formal release in a timely manner. Rather, the policy allows for the birthparent to be a continuous decision-making participant. By fostering birthparent participation during the process, the birthparent's right to self-determination is protected while, at the same time, the birthparent is utilized as a resource in achieving the policy goal.

There are a number of other possible values which could be included in our model. Reamer suggests that "values considered central to the profession . . . (are) . . . individual worth and dignity, self-determination, adequate living conditions, and acceptance by and respect of others" (Reamer, 1982, p. 10). Lewis includes "justice, security, knowledge, beauty and self-respect . . . (and) . . . liberty and opportunity, income and health, education and esthetic satisfaction, and self-respect for all persons" (Lewis, 1982, p. 141). Although making particular reference to ethics, Lewis also suggests combating unfair discrimination, providing equal opportunity, and assuring citizen participation in decisions affecting their lives (Lewis, 1982, pp. 99-100). In a discussion of ethical dilemmas, Reamer (1983) refers to four principles to be applied as criteria for distributing scarce resources—equality, need, contribution, and compensation. Some of these suggestions are good examples of the close relationship between values and ethics confronted by professionals.

Perhaps the most concise but inclusive list of value considerations is offered by Felix Biestek in *The Casework Relationship* (1957). While this book spoke ostensibly only to the practice of social casework, Biestek's enumeration of central principles (i.e., values) provides a suitable basic list. In addition to the notions of self-identity and self-determination, we can borrow three additional principles from Biestek: confidentiality, individualization, and the nonjudgmental attitude. These principles also exemplify the merging of values and ethics that occurs in professional practice suggested by Levy, noted above.

Confidentiality

A citizen's right to confidentiality in personal matters is a central and recurrent theme in our society. Numerous federal and state statutes and their attendant regulations address the issue of privacy and confidentiality of information. Surely the analysis of policy should consider this value. In practical terms, this does not merely refer to whether or how personal or organizational records are "kept secret." The issue of confidentiality also plays itself out in more subtle ways, such as the maintenance of security around unique identifier numbers in management information systems, for example, or in how people are, de facto, required to make personal or organizational "secrets" known, such as family history. A common example is the requirement of financial disclosure, often not even necessary, though required as a matter of routine.

Confidentiality

Since the birthparent is not coerced into disclosure of any sensitive information as a precondition of participation, the maintenance of confidentiality is not endangered by the policy. However, the prospective adoptive parents are, in a sense, coerced since they are placed in a "take it or leave it" situation. They can accept the policy or not continue in the adoptive process. The analyst should also be aware that the implementation of the policy is likely to include many more people and relationships during the adoption planning process, thereby making confidentiality more difficult to maintain. This is not to say that the agency or its casework staff would in any way relax their own confidentiality commitments or procedures, but it does mean that staff would have to be all the more vigilant in assuring protection of confidentiality.

Individualization

Individualization refers to the need for individuals (or groups or organizations) to be treated in terms of their unique nature, needs and qualities. Individualization may be seen as the opposite of stereotyping and the playing out of discrimination and prejudice. It can be manifested by giving consideration in policy analysis to the value of self-identity, but it relates particularly to the dangers of invidious distinctions and biased policy. In practice, then, policy analysis should consider the impact of a policy on individualization—the recognition of the unique nature of potentially affected individuals, groups, or organizations.

Individualization

Individualization, a principle providing that the unique nature of the individual will be respected, is very much assured by the commitment to maintain client identity. However, the analyst should be reminded that the policy of both encouraging and expecting birthparents' participation does *not* mean unilateral or irresponsible decision making. Consequently, individualization has its limits in this situation, perhaps suggesting individual preferences and meanings within the rather circumscribed context of the birthparents' role in planning and the rights of the other parties in the adoptive process.

Nonjudgmental Attitude

The nonjudgmental attitude is more of a quality desired in the policy analyst than a quality sought after in the analysis itself. Surely, all education is a political act, as Freire (1972) has reminded us, and policy analysis unquestionably has a heavy educative function. To be sure, the pursuit of any set of values is a judgmental, political act in itself. This fact notwithstanding, the policy analysis should still give attention to both the judgmental nature of the analysis itself and the extent to which a given policy, in its net effect, makes unfair or improper judgments about the clients or targets of the policy. For example, a policy may make unwarranted assumptions about the competence of individuals or groups (as is often the case in policies affecting handicapped citizens). A notable example in our social welfare history has been the presumption, embodied in some income maintenance policies, that people who are out of money are somehow also out of morality or other socially desirable characteristics.

Nonjudgmental Attitude

The birthparent participation policy would appear to give tacit and implicit support to the value of holding a nonjudgmental attitude toward the client or client group. After all, the policy provides for a movement away from the very judgmental notion that adoption is a "giving up" rather than a "planning for." Consequently, the meta-message of acceptance of the client is embodied in the policy.

These, then, might be seen as core values in social welfare policy analysis. However, one shortcoming of relying only on this set of values is that, taken together, they are lacking in any organizing theoretical framework consistent with the mission of social welfare institutions. Social practice needs a coherent set of values, ethics, and theories in order to guide practitioners' actions. Systems thinking offers an additional set of values and is also consistent with those values already discussed. Hence, systems thinking offers the additional asset of having both a theoretical base and a philosophical foundation.

Frameworks as the Source of Values

As was noted in chapter 2, frameworks are constructions that embody both a philosophy or a world view as well as a theoretical/technical conceptualization of how things work. Social work as a profession has often been in search of such a combination of philosophy and theory.

It is hard to say when social work began or what its operating framework was. Early evidence may be found in the person of the pharaohs' "vissier," who, as the official doer of good works, functioned out of a philosophy of personal self-interest and a theory of the building of heavenly credits for the pharaoh. We can also see the Christian concept of charity and the Jewish tradition of *tzedakah* as undoubtedly linked to the original framework of social work practice. However, the professionalization of social work is commonly seen as having its "first stage" roots somewhere in the middle of the nineteenth century and is characterized by the persons and behavior of the "friendly visitors." The philosophy underpinning the friendly visitor era was, perhaps, that of "noblesse oblige" and the theory was one of the utility of moral persuasion and exhortation in bringing about individual change. Paternalistic liberalism was an added ingredient.

A second stage in the development of social work practice might be found in the Progressive Era, in the persons of social reformers such as Jane Addams, who primarily operated out of a democratic philosophy of popular participation and a theory of the power and utility of change through legislation. The legislative approach of the Progressive Era, coupled with the values underlying social work practice at the time, provided a natural fit for the application of values to policy analysis in bringing about social welfare change.

Social work practice moved into a new era or a third stage in the 1920s, emphasizing individualism in its philosophical orientation. Social work practice of that time rested primarily upon Freudian theory or neo-Freudian theoretical orientations, which subsequently flourished. That emphasis—upon the individual as the locus and vehicle for problem and change—has undergone considerable adjustment, as evidenced by the social work field's general concurrence with the social welfare "revolution" of the 1960s and its relatively new attention to the social structure as the locus and potential for problem and change. Various philosophical orientations and theoretical explanations emerged during the 1960s, not the least of which has come to be called "systems thinking" or "systems theory."

The Many Faces of Systems Approaches

Systems thinking offers a set of values that are worth considering in any human systems analysis. However, there are so many views of what systems thinking actually is that these underlying values are often overlooked. For our purposes here, it is extremely important to be aware of which conceptualization we might accept.

Systems thinking runs from a set of concepts that suggest isomorphisms (i.e., similarities in structures and processes) among all levels of living things, to various conceptualizations of the interrelatedness of social structures and processes, to the far end of the continuum with mechanistic models of what is and what ought to be. The emphasis upon isomorphic qualities of levels of human functioning (i.e., individuals, groups, organizations and communities) might be seen in the original work of von Bertalanffy (1968), James Miller (1978), David Easton (1965), and Walter Buckley (1967). A prevailing emphasis upon the interrelatedness of social structure and events enjoys great popularity in the literature and is exemplified in social work by Pincus and Minahan (1973) or Anderson and Carter (1974). The more mechanistic views have been exploited by state and federal government agencies, particularly the Department of Defense, and have been characterized and critiqued by Ida Hoos (1972). Whatever the emphasis, however, there is a widely held view that systems thinking, being a grand-level framework, tends to be conservatizing. Perhaps because of the emphasis placed upon mapping and description and its strange terminology, systems thinking has not received recognition for the human values that it embodies.

Values for Human System Realities

If one examines the basic principles underlying human systems thinking, it is impossible not to recognize the value base upon which this perspective rests. Indeed, systems thinking offers a set of humanistic values that one might even consider "radical" in that they offer a departure from conventional ways of seeing things. "Radical" conceptions of the world generally assert that social problems are caused by inequitable social structures; that social structures are determined by economic factors; that social institutions are developed and supported to maintain the existing inequitable structure (or to ameliorate such effects—a common criticism of social work); and that social change can come about only through dialectical means (Keefe, 1978).

We would argue here that the basic tenets of systems thinking not only provide an adequate world view but offer an additional set of values for consideration in effective and realistic social welfare policy analysis. Five core concepts of system thinking are particularly relevant for our purposes: (1) indeterminateness, (2) multifinality, (3) nonsummativity, (4) morphogenesis, and (5) stochastic processes.

Values for Human System Realities

In our birthparents' participation policy, the practice theory would likely be something to the effect that participatory methods of social treatment are more effective in problem solving. Such participation assumes development of more adequate information, greater consensus, and greater commitment to the decisions made. This theoretical foundation is consistent with the values reviewed above. Consequently, we find that theory and values in this case appear to be compatible.

In this section we will focus on the particular values underlying the policy that especially pertain to human or socio-cultural systems.

Indeterminateness

A classic concept of social thought is a *determinate* view that the end processes of social action are very much determined and preordained by social structure and social processes. For example, much of our Western preoccupation and enchantment with technology leads us to believe that all problems can be solved. Our faith in progress leads us to conclude that those matters that are not now in hand do, in fact, have a solution and much of our social process is merely aimed at discovering the answer.

Rather, the policy analysis could proceed instead around the concept of *in*determinateness, which recognizes that the end states of social processes are determined and altered *in process*. This, of course, is consistent with a Hegelian view of the evolution of ideas in which each idea (thesis) generates its opposite (antithesis), out of which is formed a new idea (synthesis). This recognition of the dialectical nature of social process helps the policy analyst recognize the reality of unintended effects of a given policy and reduces some of the dangers inherent in positivistic approaches to assessment, review, and analysis. The concept of indeterminateness radicalizes the analysis in the sense that end states are not seen as being fixed, linear and/or simplistic.

Indeterminateness

The policy seems to imply a faith in the systems principle of indeterminateness, that the end states of social problem solving are actually determined in process, i.e., they are not predetermined. By expanding the pool of actors and decision makers through the active inclusion of the birthparent, the reality of indeterminateness is given the opportunity to operate. The policy allows for the end state to be determined in process in that the motives and role of the birthparent are not delimited at the outset, and the plan for the newborn is developed in process with even more information and more actors than is traditionally the case.

Multifinality

A corollary to indeterminateness is the notion of multifinality, the concept that original conditions can result in multiple end state conditions. This is in contrast to common linear Western thinking that prior states end in clearly predictable and fixed probabilities. That lineation is seen in the crude stereotypical thinking, for example, that "kids coming from across the tracks all end up the same," or "once a _____, always a _____," or "the policy is this way because that's the way it has to be done," or "we've always done things this way, that's why!" Multifinality is evident in many human system realities. The obverse condition is *equifinality*, the notion that differing origins can arrive through social process at similar end states. The implication for social welfare policy analysis is that we can avoid the traps of simplistic positivism and recognize the reality of different policies possibly achieving similar results, on the one hand, or similar policies achieving different results, on the other. While these notions seem like common sense, social practice does not give overwhelming evidence of our thinking in such "radical" terms.

Multifinality

The policy tends to support the notion that a variety of end states can arise out of similar conditions. Contrary to the presumption that the problem is simply to plan for an "unwanted child that is to be given up," the policy allows for the similar initial state (pregnancy and impending birth) to be seen as an opportunity for a variety of end states. *(alternatives)*

Nonsummativity

Traditional views of social process and structure are additive or summative, whereas a view of human nature embodied in system thinking is that the social organization is *non*summative. That is, a classic view of human organization holds that the whole is *nothing other than* the sum of its parts. A human systems view, instead, assumes that human aggregations are nonsummative, or that the whole is *greater than* the sum of its parts. Consequently, any adequate model for policy analysis recognizes the qualities that emerge when collective policy action occurs; this is the real meaning of "holism." The notion of nonsummativity is manifested in the concept of treating the "whole person," by the recognition of the unique character of some groups "as group," and by the alleged "personality" of some organizations or associations; a "national character" is even attributed to many nations. Policy analysis must take these emergent holistic qualities into consideration in reviewing feasibility, for example.

Nonsummativity

The notion that the whole is something more than the sum of its parts is also suggested by this policy approach since the policy fosters the development of a *holistic* approach to adoption planning. That is, the worker does not see each actor separately and "add up the pieces," so to speak. Rather, the birthparent and the potential adoptive parents are active group participants during and around appropriate events in the planning process. Holistic approaches to problem solving may be said to be nonsummative since they view process and outcomes as something greater than the sum of the observable parts.

Morphogenesis

The notion of morphogenesis (i.e., the recognition that human systems have the capacity to alter forms and processes) has frequently been observed in operation by social work practitioners. This concept, a recognition of the coexistent ability of human systems to maintain stability and also provide system change and/or elaboration, is a radical valuing of systems in that it rejects the more mechanistic notion of system equilibrium. Social workers have long held that individuals or groups are not only affected by their environment but have an effect upon it, and that this process continues over time. This humanistic view of the reciprocal interaction of person-in-environment requires the policy analyst to acknowledge and account for the constant dialectic between system components and their environments, which brings about new emergent qualities through human processes. Such qualities have been observed as being "serendipitous" outcomes of new system purposes, structures, processes, and outcomes and can, at times, be attributable to the play of policy principles.

Morphogenesis

Morphogenesis is a human systems principle that holds that human systems have the ability to change forms in process.

While individual human systems do not manifest any structural or sociopsychological change as a result of the policy (though such change may come about), the change appears to be organizational. The policy allows for a fundamental change in the nature of the interaction of key components in the system by a radical redefinition of the role of birthparent. To that extent, the policy may be said to allow or provide for the morphogenetic nature of human systems—that an organization has within it the resources to fundamentally change its forms.

Stochastic Processes

At the same time that human systems are nonsummative (i.e., comprised of more than the sum of their parts) and morphogenetic (able to change their forms), other forces are at work, i.e., a stochastic ordering or sequencing of *probabilities* (not certitudes) is also at play. That is, an inherent lawfulness exists in the ordering or sequencing of social events. This lawfulness is the real measure of the power of policy—the ability of policy to relate to the range of human values *while at the same time* giving predictability to a human system. The primary function of any social policy is to give order and predictability, and to tell living systems what is preferred, expected, or desired. A well-developed social policy gives order and predictability (stochasticism) while simultaneously honoring the other values desirable in that policy.

Stochastic Processes

Policy has been said to create a stochastic phenomenon in organizations; that is, that policy creates a certain lawfulness or predictability to the sequencing of future events. In one sense, this is true for the birthparents' participation policy since it mandates the right to such participation. Presumably, as the birthparent becomes involved, more information is added to the decision process and, consequently, the potential outcome is more likely to be known—or at least to be more predictable. However, this analysis could also yield another conclusion: that participation of the birthparent makes future events even more improbable, or less predictable. The inclusion of each additional actor, with more decision prerogatives, may be said to produce a greater number of potential outcomes. In this case, the principle of stochastic processes in human systems sheds little light on our analysis except to suggest that even more outcomes are possible with the inclusion of more key actors in the process.

It is argued here that these central system principles provide useful value components for our policy analysis model. However, given the special circumstances or social conditions of certain groups and categories of people in our society, we must include other considerations for the value component of our model.

Discriminatory Factors

As noted in the reference to Lewis, above, some of us value and are in the habit of giving watchful attention to policies and programs that may be discriminatory. Since helping professions have established ethical standards for combating discrimination in our society, they *must* consider issues of discrimination based on gender or sexual orientation, ethnicity or social class, race, economic or handicapping condition, or age in any social welfare policy analysis. Given the insidious and institutionalized nature of the various discriminatory "isms," it is absolutely essential that these factors be routinely considered in our policy analyses. Consequently, the final component of the value element of our model requires that we review the implications of these potentially discriminatory factors.

Discriminatory Factors

The processes of adoption planning and placement have long been seen as primarily "women's work." The biological father has been much less involved in the process and few agencies have made concerted attempts to include him. It is only fairly recently that some states have required systematic attempts to locate and include the biological father.

The professions have largely given the task of providing child welfare services to female workers inasmuch as an overwhelming number of child welfare staff working in the area of adoptions are women. This is, no doubt, a reflection of our societal orientation to the care of children; perhaps the professions merely reflect those values.

The policy also has racial implications. Given the disproportionate rate of adolescent pregnancies and births among the black population, and the greater likelihood of those birthparents to keep their child, agencies are in even more need of staff who can assist this client group in making decisions. To a great extent, this issue highlights a need for increased numbers of black and other minority staff in adoption agencies in general and Child Services, Inc. in particular to ensure that the minority birthparent group is represented adequately.

The staff of Child Services, Inc. must reach out to that group of birthparents and aggressively inform them of the policy and their entitlements to participation. As with many private child placing agencies, Child Services, Inc. has a disproportionately small clientele from lower income groups. Therefore, special efforts must be made to reach such groups.

Summary

This chapter has considered the value elements of our model for social welfare policy analysis. We have reviewed some of the generic value components that should be considered for our analytic model. We have also given special attention to the underlying principles of a human systems view of social process and considered what additional values ought to be made explicit in our model in that regard. Finally, we have observed that any model for social welfare policy analysis must give explicit consideration to the implications of factors such as sexism, classism, racism, poverty, and ageism if our behavior is to be consistent with the code of ethics by which we obtain our fundamental social legitimacy.

The following summary outline for these value elements will be followed by an application of the value elements to the illustrations discussed in cases 2 and 3 in chapter 5.

Value Elements for Analyzing Small-Scale Policy (An Outline)

1. *Generic values.* A focus on the core values that should be considered or reflected in policy content and process.

   a. Identity
   b. Self-determination
   c. Confidentiality
   d. Individualization
   e. Nonjudgmental attitude

2. *Frameworks as the Source of Values.* A focus on the particular values that might be implicit or reflected in the theoretical explanations of the problems as defined or the strategies selected by the policy option(s).

3. *Values in Human System Approaches.* A focus on the particular values underlying human system approaches to the problem or the policy.

   a. Indeterminateness
   b. Multifinality
   c. Nonsummativity
   d. Morphogenesis
   e. Stochastic processes

4. *Discriminatory Factors.* A focus on the implications of the content and the process of policy for issues of discrimination based on

gender or sexual preference, ethnicity or social class, race, economic or handicapping condition, or age.

Case Illustrations

Case 4: Values and Confidentiality

One of the case illustrations in chapter 4, Case 1, provided an analysis of the multiple mandates and demands of confidentiality placed upon Community Services, Inc. This case is a continuation of that policy analysis, with the focus on value elements. As a multiprogram agency, Community Services, Inc. has many sources of support and many controlling statutes and administrative rules governing confidentiality and accountability. The agency constantly has the responsibility for the maintenance of the very central value of confidentiality of client information thrust upon it. The reader will recall that the policy goal is to assure clientele that their associations with the agency will be maintained in secrecy (insofar as the law allows). Furthermore, confidentiality is seen as a necessary element in the provision of effective social treatment. Consequently, the principle of confidentiality and its associated policy serves ethical, professional/technical, and legal purposes.

We will once again use our Value Elements for Analyzing Small-Scale Policy outline in our analysis of Case 4's value elements. The outline will be used as a supplement and a checklist — a supplement to the values considerations already given both explicitly and implicitly in the original analysis of Case 1 and a checklist to serve as a reminder of what might be considered.

1. Generic Values
In this section the central professional values in the code of ethics will be reviewed.

a. Identity
The confidentiality policy provides to some extent for the maintenance and development of the client's sense of identity

in his or her dealings with the agency. This occurs through the policy's underscoring of the rights and prerogatives held by the client as a person in his or her own right and runs counter to the propensity of both public and private agencies to require that forms be filled out and information collected for information's sake. Many organizations providing services to the public do not routinely provide appropriate safeguards (or at least assurances that they will provide safeguards) to protect the confidentiality of the personal information provided and obtained.

An additional right, which contributes to a sense of identity, is the client's right to redress, i.e., grievance, complaint, or appeal. This right not only informs client groups that confidentiality is valued but assures them that there are certain sanctions to guarantee this right. Furthermore, the client is given notice of the right to exercise those sanctions.

b. Self-determination

The policy does not generally speak to the value of client self-determination, per se. Self-determination, the principle wherein the client has and retains the right to make those choices and decisions that vitally affect his or her destiny, is not generally promoted by the principle of confidentiality. However, the principle of confidentiality in an agency's policy could very well encourage a client to articulate thoughts and preferences that otherwise might not be presumed safe to utter. To the extent that the confidentiality policy enables frank and honest expression, self-determination is also enhanced.

The confidentiality policy relates obliquely to the question of self-determination when one looks at the other side of the demand for information—the public's right to know where its social service resources are going. The public does have a right to hold the agency accountable; but it may in part achieve that accountability by a reporting of services activity. However, the policy does not preclude the individual's right to withhold personal information that is not central to the service provided in order for the agency to satisfy the public's competing right to know.

c. Confidentiality

Confidentiality, the principle wherein the client is assured privacy in the communication and maintenance of personal information, is one of the cornerstones of professional service ethics. However, as noted in our analysis of content elements, this assurance does not cover information regarding violations of law or situations wherein harm may be done to oneself or others. Therefore, confidentiality itself has its limitations and constraints. It is very important that each client is *explicitly* informed of the limitations on confidentiality—that client awareness in this area should not be presumed.

Guidelines and procedures for the policy should give special attention to each detail of requirements for "informed consent." Staff should be oriented in such a way that informed consent is uniformly and consistently addressed with each of the agency's clients.

d. Individualization

Individualization is not apparently a consideration in terms of this agency's confidentiality policy. That is, there is nothing in the policy or its implementation procedures that suggests that individualization is either fostered or impeded. As in the case of self-determination, it could be suggested that the confidentiality policy is not inconsistent with the principle of individualization. While assurances of confidentiality do offer some promise that the agency will not treat clients "like any other number," the relationship between the two principles is generally tangential.

e. Nonjudgmental attitude

The confidentiality policy does not completely embrace the concept of judgments not being made by agency staff about a client's behavior. This is true due to the requirements of most rights-to-privacy and confidentiality legislation or rules, which require that law enforcement officials be notified of information obtained regarding felonious behavior. However, it should be stressed that the confidentiality policy does not actually place the professional helper in a compromising or conflicting position. First, as stated above, procedures for providing informed consent should be routinely implemented. Existence of such procedures would forewarn the client regarding limitations on information that can be shared with an expectation of the maintenance of secrecy. Second, the professional helper is able to maintain a nonjudgmental attitude regarding the alleged felonious behavior. That is, the worker need not attach personal value to any behavior reported by the client.

It may be said, then, that the principle of a nonjudgmental attitude is neither supported nor hindered by the confidentiality policy. However, the degree to which the principle and the policy are separate may be somewhat subtle and, while the policy analyst may be clear about that separateness, that clarity should be confirmed with staff in the policy's implementation.

2. Frameworks as the Source of Values
In this section we will search for both the value implications of the theoretical explanation of the problem as defined and the theory behind the policy option selected.

The theory behind the problem would appear to be three-pronged: first, confidentiality is a cornerstone of professional ethics and unequivocally must be honored; second, clients cannot be assisted when secrecy is not assured; and third, the integrity and reputation of the agency cannot be maintained when staff do not protect confidentiality of client information. The appropriateness of the policy to the problem, then, can be seen in both ethical and pragmatic terms.

The strategy for implementation of these policy goals values the constitutional and statutory rights of individual citizens, the legal bases of the social system, and the fundamental rights of individuals as persons.

3. Values in Human System Approaches
The confidentiality policy will now be reviewed with special attention given to principles central to a human systems view of structure and values.

a. Indeterminateness

The confidentiality policy (and its various sources of legitimation) support the notion that the end states of social systems are determined during the life of social interaction. The policy essentially communicates the meta-message that the client is free to provide information concerning the problem or need, and subsequent decisions will be jointly made regarding the distribution or sharing of that information. This broad characterization has its qualifications, of course, as with allegedly felonious behavior; a client is not guaranteed confidentiality when disclosing information regarding felonious acts. At the very least, the confidentiality policy provides that end states will not be predetermined because of a sharing of private and personal information. Indeed, the question of the use of that information is independent of the sharing of that information.

b. Multifinality

The confidentiality policy would appear to have little to do with the principle of multifinality—that similar initial states may produce different end states. However, one could argue that the confidentiality policy does suggest an environment in which all of the information is encouraged to be put "on the table" prior to making any analysis (i.e., diagnosis or assessment) or before deciding what problem resolution steps (e.g., social treatment plan) might be taken. To this extent, there is a relationship between the principle of multifinality and confidentiality.

c. Nonsummativity

The principle of nonsummativity, that the whole is greater than the sum of its parts, is consistent with the confidentiality policy in the sense that individual bits of information are actually meaningless until considered in a holistic context. This leads us to conclude that the policy is not in conflict with this particular principle.

d. Morphogenesis

Inherent in the principle of confidentiality is the notion that, given necessary and sufficient information for problem resolution, the client can not only be helped but can even be the genesis of that helping process. This notion is entirely consistent with the human systems principle of morphogenesis— that human systems have within themselves the ability to change their forms and structures. We sometimes give life or shape to this phenomenon by noting that someone is a "new person" after having shared significant information. While this expression is frequently associated with an individual's confession of guilt or sharing of uncomfortable secrets, its application is far more generic. The confidentiality policy offers that opportunity for growth in human structure.

e. Stochastic processes

The principle of stochastic processes in human systems— that there is a lawfulness inherent in the sequencing of events—is entirely consistent with the confidentiality policy. In fact, it may be said that the principle and assurances of confidentiality, as with much of policy, do themselves create the potential for a probable sequence of events. That probable sequencing is based upon the trust fostered in the client by the professional person and the agency as a result of observable commitment to the policy. As noted previously, policy itself provides for the sequencing of future events; policy makes life more predictable and probabilistic. The policy of confidentiality sets the tone and increases the likelihood of successful treatment by the trust created in the client-worker relationship.

4. Discriminatory Factors

The confidentiality policy does not appear to have any particular implications for issues of sex, class, race or poverty inasmuch as its meaning to client groups and application to service agencies is universal. However, it is very important that we make a conscientious review of potential discriminatory factors to help us guard against our own unwitting participation in institutional "isms."

For example, if there is a differential between the socio-economic class of the recipients and providers of services, we could logically infer that the development of trust is much more difficult than when similar socioeconomic groups share information. In addition, symbols, jargon, and slang that are communicated may not have shared meaning. Therefore, confidentiality is an important element in the development of the necessary trust that is required in shaping this new and/or infrequent relationship. In the same vein, people who are poor or oppressed may feel they are in an untenable position precisely because of the policies or programs of the institutions that are represented by the agency and/or professional service provider. Again, the maintenance of confidentiality is all the more important in the development of a trusting and otherwise positive helping relationship.

Summary

This application of the values outline to Case 4, "Multiple Mandates of Confidentiality," is aimed at giving further explicit consideration to values issues when applying the outline on content elements in policy analysis. Each element of the values outline was considered, not in an attempt to force application of each part, but to provide illustrations for use of the outline in policy analysis. The values outline provides a supplement or an adjunct to value elements actually considered explicitly or implicitly in the earlier analysis of Case 1.

Case 5: Values and Utilization Monitoring

Case 2, involving the State Department of Social Services' policy of mandatory utilization reviews of Medicaid provisions by local county offices, is somewhat more complicated regarding application of the values outline than was our earlier illustration. In this policy we have a mixture and variety of client and target groups. We have tiers of superordinate-subordinate relationships, with controlling administrative rules. Nevertheless, the policy illustration is not unlike many contractual and/or purchase of service situations in which the policy analyst must consider the obligations of each party to the other and play out the implications of contract provision.

Once again, we will attempt to apply each element of our outline, "Values Elements for Analyzing Small-Scale Policy," not simply for the purpose of "covering" each element but to provide illustrations of how the outline might be used. In actual use, some elements of the outline may require extensive application and discussion, while others may be eliminated. In either instance, the outline serves as a checklist for the value elements to be considered.

As the reader will recall, the utilization monitoring of Medicaid provisions policy is one in which the State Department of Social Services (SDSS) exercised its discretionary authority in meeting federal regulations by assigning the responsibility for monitoring to the local county offices. The state established this strategy as a pilot policy in one-half of the state's counties and, for purposes of our analysis, we focused only on those aspects of the Service Monitoring Policy (SMP) that pertain to prescription drug purchases. The policy requires that the county offices of the SDSS monitor and provide safeguards for the appropriateness and quality of all reimbursed services by means of a post-payment review process. This provision exists in the program and funding contracts between SDSS and the one-half of its county offices involved in the pilot.

1. Generic Values

In this section we will focus on the basic set of values requiring consideration in the policy analysis.

a. Identity

Here we can consider the impact of the policy on the self-image or identity of the client group, the target group, and the county agency itself. The reader would likely agree that the primary purpose of a review of values would be to see if the policy or the organizational behavior had implications for ethical commitments to the client group; unquestionably, this is where the first commitment to values must be placed. However, this particular policy, given its triad of components, provides opportunity for a more extended analysis.

The client group—the group on whose behalf the action is taken (in this case, the recipients of services)—would appear to be affected neither more nor less by the policy in the sense that federal regulations require utilization monitoring, regardless of the level of government performing the task. However, the practical reality is that monitoring, given adequate funding and staffing, is likely to be more frequent and perhaps more thorough when carried out at the local level. In terms of client identity, then, the client is cast more in the role of a subject of investigation. He or she becomes less a citizen entitled to a service and, to some extent, more a person whose claim to entitlements must be subject to scrutiny. Aside from the fact that the policy also satisfies the public's need for accountability, the net impact on the client group is likely to be adverse in terms of their feelings of worth and dignity. Much depends, however, on the manner in which the policy is implemented and the nature of the monitoring relationships directly impacting upon the client group.

From another perspective, the analyst could argue that the policy enhances the self-identity of the client group. Being mindful of the fact that the policy goal is to provide safeguards for the appropriateness and quality of all reimbursed services, it could be argued that the policy advocates for the client and implicitly views him or her as a citizen who is entitled to quality medical care. In this sense, the policy has a positive effect upon client identity.

As for the target group—those who are the targets of the action to be taken—we have the providers of services, such as pharmacists who dispense prescription drugs, and the physicians who see the client group and write the prescriptions. By implication, the professional discretionary judgments and ethical and/or administrative practices of that group will, by inference, be called into question. Consequently, aside from the benefit of maintaining public faith in the functioning of the services system, the policy would likely have a negative effect and constitute a challenge to the integrity of the provider target group.

For the local agency, a new role has definitely been established—that of regulator—in addition to the extant role of services facilitator. The proper conduct of this new role by staff and the local agency as a whole will likely require commensurate orientation and training of both field and administrative staff.

b. Self-determination

As with most regulatory policies or rules, the self-determination of the subjects is reduced or constrained. Individual clients *do* retain the right to share in decisions about whether they are to receive services. However, their ability to unilaterally take action on a matter such as getting transportation to the office to obtain a voucher could preclude their ability to exercise self-determination. Our analysis could conclude that the clients are not actually restricted from receiving any benefits to which they were not entitled, but our content analysis has shown that, given the other limitations placed upon people who are poor, the constraints on choice are likely to be compounded.

The professional providers of prescriptions and prescription drugs will, of course, be constrained in the exercise of discretionary judgment. This will be especially true of the prescribing physician; the local agency will not have the authority to overrule medical decisions, but the physician's decisions will be subject to scrutiny, perhaps engendering a caution not previously present. On the more positive side, however, it should be noted that the policy provides that there be a *post-payment* review. This is important to note in that the regulatory arm of the agency will not intrude at the time of the original professional decision nor at the point of the provision of services.

The state's allocation of the monitoring responsibility to the local agency has left little choice for local self-determination regarding this particular provision.

(It should be mentioned that we have not included in this narrow focus in our analysis the constraints on client self-determination caused by the limited number of service providers who are willing to take Medicaid patients. That problem is by no means insignificant and will be discussed later, in Part 4 of this values analysis.)

c. Confidentiality

On the face of it, the policy of utilization monitoring should not impact on the principle of client confidentiality. However, the analysis should caution us that, given more staff actors involved, and given more intrusion into the services relationship, the risks to the maintenance of confidentiality are greater. As a result of the policy, we will have more forays, more investigations, and more people participating in events surrounding the provision of public services to citizens. More information will be collected, stored, recalled, analyzed, and reported, and the agencies involved will need to take additional security precautions.

However, from a technical perspective, the client's rights to confidentiality are not breached by the policy. The funding agency is entitled to this use of information as a condition of providing public social services to its citizens.

d. Individualization

The principle of individualization should not be challenged or threatened as a result of the policy. The client will likely be individually assessed in terms of medical needs by the attending physician and the prescription will be filled appropriately by a pharmacist of choice. Some limits will likely be placed upon the client due to standardization of services available or the constraints engendered by limited fee schedules. However, these features are limitations put in place by the Medicaid program in general and not by the particular provisions of the utilization monitoring policy.

e. Nonjudgmental attitude

The policy does not appear to be a threat to the ethical principle of the maintenance of a nonjudgmental attitude toward the client. The policy mandates a review of the appropriateness and quality of all reimbursed services. It does not suggest that any judgments be made regarding the appropriateness of the motives or behavior of the client as an individual or group.

2. Frameworks as the Source of Values

We can only speculate here on the theory underlying the problem to be resolved or the particular policy strategy employed. Also, we will have to reach further to determine the values implied in the underlying theoretical perspective(s).

Many regulatory provisions have their foundations in the theory that equity is obtained for the citizen entitled to benefits when provisions are uniformly and consistently applied. This assures both the potential recipient and the general public supporting the program that equity is being achieved. A corollary is that programs enjoy continued support when the public is assured that services are provided in an efficient and effective manner and, in the case of monitoring, the agency's efforts at assuring appropriateness and quality of services should develop and maintain public support. Indeed, the client/recipient of services also desires reassurances that services are appropriate and of a sufficient quality.

It would appear that an overriding theory is that government intrusion in the area of medical care is best only after the professional client-provider experience has occurred. This is manifested in the provision that the reviews shall be conducted *after* the point of payment, which suggests respect for the inviolateness of the client-provider relationship.

Another perspective is that those who might work against the policy goals are more likely to be disinclined to do so in the face of an extensive and systematic apparatus for monitoring the policy. In this regard, the theory is that the policy acts as a deterrent to abuse by both recipients and providers of services.

It would appear, then, that the policy is driven by values of equity, efficiency, effectiveness, and respect, which means that to achieve those valued ends a uniform and consistent application of rules, reassurances provided to the public, post-payment review, and systematic monitoring exists.

3. Values in Human System Approaches

This portion of the outline application will focus on the particular human system values underlying the approach to the problem or the policy.

a. Indeterminateness

This policy seems to equivocate regarding the principle of indeterminateness—that the end states of social problem solving are actually determined in process. On the one hand, the indeterminateness principle seems to be reflected in the procedural aspect requiring that monitoring be effected by means of a post-payment review. This would suggest that individual situations and needs are played out in the client-provider relationships, with monitoring and review taking place only after the fact or point of service. On the other hand, the policy seems to say, in effect, that the decision on the appropriateness and quality of services will be made after the fact. By implication, there appears a presumption of only one possible end state (though perhaps a variety of relationships in process). The end state is determined by rules, payment schedules, and the like. The provision of services is not viewed as being an indeterminate phenomenon; rather, the implication is that there is only one "right" way for proper provision of services.

For the policy analyst, this means that the human systems principle of indeterminateness (if it is to be valued by the agency) will itself have to be monitored in the implementation of the utilization monitoring policy. The manner in which this is done will fundamentally affect the nature of the relationships between the agency, the client group, and the provider groups. In a sense, the tone of the policy's implementation may be set by the commitment to the value of indeterminateness. That tone will be reflected in the agency's reasonable flexibility, on the one hand, or rigidity and officiousness, on the other. Given the earlier observations about uniformity, consistency, and equity, the policy sets a difficult task for the agency.

b. Multifinality

Multifinality is the human systems principle that a variety of end states can arise out of similar conditions; the obverse is that of equifinality, that similar beginning states can eventuate in a variety of end states. The utilization monitoring policy, being based upon statute and associated administrative regulations, is more likely not to be compatible with this principle. Statutes, rules and regulations tend to demand specificity and standardization. The definition of beginning states, in this illustration, evolves around determination of eligibility. While there are a variety of conditions relating to need for prescriptions for drugs under Medicaid, the actual identification of eligibility status is specified and does not suggest a commitment to the principle of equifinality. Consistent with this is the fact that the determination of appropriateness of benefits is not a multifinal phenomenon; the range of appropriate benefits is virtually fixed. The space for the introduction of the principle of multifinality might come in the determination of "quality," since that matter is to a greater extent left to a subjective judgment, though no doubt the policy analyst will play a role in developing standards and guidelines for what constitutes "quality."

c. Nonsummativity

The principle of nonsummativity, that the whole is greater than the sum of its parts, appears to be recognized in the policy. This is evident in the recognition that the major elements of the service system in this instance must be included—the client/patient/recipient, the provider(s), and the county agency itself. The clients' needs, the providers' judgments, and the agency's regulatory task must be taken into consideration, *in toto,* for utilization monitoring to effectively take place, since monitoring is not only of the recipient or the provider. Assessment in the review must be based upon a mixture of criteria involving eligibility, appropriateness of services, quality of services, and, no doubt, the appropriateness of the fee level.

d. Morphogenesis

The principle of morphogenesis holds that human systems have the ability to change forms in process. Nothing evident appears in the utilization monitoring policy that enhances the county office's ability to adapt its structures or processes as a result of the policy's implementation. Neither is there any suggestion that the condition or behavior of the client or provider groups would change as a result of the policy. Morphogenesis is neither fostered or hindered by the policy. There could be some suggestion that the coercive effects of the policy might alter the behavior patterns of the few who abuse the availability of the services, but there is no evidence to suggest that this is true.

e. Stochastic processes

This policy is perhaps a prime example of the stochastic nature of social policy — the giving of order and predictability to the ordering or the sequencing of events. In practice, the utilization monitoring policy provides for more predictability for the recipient of physicians' examinations, prescriptions, and the prescription drugs themselves, since notice is given, a priori, that subsequent review will be forthcoming, based upon certain standards. The same holds for the providers of services under the program. The behavior and decisions of the provider become more probabilistic as they become more limited by assurances that decisions will be audited in a post-payment review. Thus, positive or negative post-payment reviews probabilistically affect subsequent behavior and decisions of providers. Consequently, the policy may be presumed to achieve the power desired in most policy — the giving of order and predictability to subsequent events.

4. Discriminatory Factors

This section will examine the potential impact or implications of the policy with respect to characteristics of gender or sexual orientation, ethnicity or social class, race, economic or handicapping conditions, or age. A major implication in this policy is directed at the poor. By definition, persons of low income are eligible for Medicaid provisions of any kind, not just prescription drugs. Experience shows us that not all providers of services in various communities have been willing to participate in the Medicaid program. Some have refused because of the level of the payment schedules; others because of the inconvenience encountered in working with large government agencies; others have refused solely on the basis of ideology. The utilization monitoring policy, regardless of its positive rationale and effects, is likely to place even greater limitations on the pool of willing providers who will make their services available to citizens in economic need. Concurrently, more stress will likely be placed upon the client group.

The policy analyst would do well to study existing demographic profiles of the recipients of services and determine whether there are any differential characteristics based upon sex, age, or race. For example, there may be a disproportionate number of citizens in certain age groups; or a disproportionate representation of persons of certain racial groups receiving certain types of services. While such disproportionate representations, in and of themselves, may not be undesirable, their implications should be studied. The analyst may find that there is a propensity to limit certain kinds of drugs to women, for example (as has been noted in some studies in the area of pharmacotherapy), or that certain patterns tend to appear among client groups living in particular neighborhoods. The policy analyst has an opportunity here to identify institutional, albeit unintentional, sexist or racist effects of either the service system or the policy implementation itself.

Summary

This application of the values outline to the utilization monitoring policy has offered suggestions of what the analyst might focus upon in an actual policy analysis. Again, the actual analysis need not generate information for each and every element of the outline. However, a concerted effort should be made to apply the outline. Each element should at least be considered so as to "tease the mind" of the analyst and assure confrontation with some essential value elements in policy analysis.

Case 6: Values and the Downtown Mall

In Case 3 we examined community concern over the use of the downtown mall, particularly the relationships between the "mall people," merchants, and other visitors to the mall. City Commissioner Frances LaRose had proposed the following policy:

> It is the policy of the City of Rapid River that all citizens of the community shall have equal access to all public facilities associated with the Downtown Mall; that the civil rights of no citizen of the community will be violated by any policy or procedure related to any activity of any public or private group while associated with the Downtown Mall; and that all ordinances of the city and laws of the State and Federal governments shall be observed insofar as those ordinances and laws pertain to conduct of citizens on the Mall.

In addition to the policy proposal provided by Commissioner LaRose, our analysis in Case 3 also considered the complementary approach of providing certain social service supports to some individual mall people and developing a public education program.

This policy problem clearly represents a clash of values concerning the uses of community resources and the determination of what should constitute "appropriate" or "acceptable" behavior in public places. As the reader will recall from Case 3, we actually have two policy strategies under consideration in this analysis. The first is Commissioner LaRose's strategy of regulation and enforcement, aimed at protecting the rights of all elements of the system. The second strategy complements the first and includes providing supportive social services for the mall people and public education efforts for merchants and other downtown visitors. Our analysis will proceed with these two approaches in mind.

1. Generic Values
This section will focus on the basic set of values in our analysis.

a. Identity
The self-image and feelings of self-worth of the mall people are certainly under assault at this time, with some merchants asking for their removal from the mall area and some citizens claiming sole ownership of the downtown mall. Some merchants are losing faith in the city's leadership, feeling that personal invest-

ments of time and resources in the central city have neither been properly acknowledged nor adequately protected. Collectively speaking, the identity of the downtown mall as an attractive place for business and recreation has suffered. Community pride has suffered as many suburban citizens refuse to bring their business to this area.

The commissioner's proposed policy relates to the maintenance of individual dignity and identity in that its legislated rights approach treats all elements of the community equitably. Development of mall peoples' social skills will enhance their self-concepts and identity as more appropriate behavior will likely elicit more rewarding community responses.

b. Self-determination

The opportunities for self-determination by all elements on the mall are constrained under the current circumstances. Some merchants feel their freedom to conduct business is restricted by the behavior of mall people. Some shoppers do not feel comfortable in freely moving about. Many of the mall people feel the pressure of constraints on their movement in the community, the mall situation only being symptomatic of a larger trend.

The proposed policy provides restrictions on all elements. However, that policy strategy is based upon legitimate authority (i.e., statutes and regulations) and not upon the capricious use of authority or power.

c. Confidentiality

Generally speaking, confidentiality is not at issue here. However, if agency services are not provided discreetly, some individuals could be singled out or identified as "agency people," so to speak. Such a practice would not only be dysfunctional from a programmatic perspective, but would violate clients' rights to confidentiality.

d. Individualization

The current situation has led to the labeling of a certain category of city residents as "mall people"; this, in itself, is a loss of individualization. As individual behavior and needs are arbitrarily placed into categories, individualization is threatened. There also exist some stereotyping of and prejudicial attitudes toward some of the mall merchants. Some merchants have been labeled as greedy or uncaring when, in fact, they have made positive efforts to make the mall a favorable environment for all citizens of the community, including the mall people.

The proposed policy would allow for individualization only insofar as individuals have entitlements to legitimate access. The complementary social services strategy, designed to provide skill development commensurate with an individual's needs, would certainly foster individualization.

e. Nonjudgmental Attitude

The present environment provides extensive evidence of judgments being made about the behavior of many peoples and the motivations of others. The proposed policy will permit no prejudgment of individual behavior unless and/or until such time as an ordinance or law had been violated.

2. Frameworks as the Source of Values

The two approaches to the problem, regulation and enforcement on the one hand and supportive services on the other, suggest very different values in problem resolution. The regulatory and enforcement strategy gives the highest value to social control, as does the opportunity to rightfully obtain one's entitlements. This is not to say that social control is necessarily a negative or unwarranted strategy. Nevertheless, the approach assumes that the policy goal can best be achieved through legal management and relational restrictions.

The services strategy values the provision of supports through development of individuals' social skills in such matters as taking the bus, engaging in appropriate behaviors in shops and restaurants, and learning how to properly greet others on the mall. This strategy is also aimed at public education. The fundamental assumption is that individuals are in need of remediation and that community resources should be made available to fill those gaps or meet those deficits.

The two approaches have compatible values, however, thereby suggesting the potential for success. While each is rooted in a different perspective about social behavior, they are complementary policy thrusts.

3. Values in Human System Approaches

This part of our analysis will focus on reviewing human systems principles underlying the approaches to the policy and the problem.

a. Indeterminateness

Both Commissioner LaRose's and the supportive services approach express an indeterminate view of social process. The regulatory and enforcement approach does not suggest a preconceived notion of social relationships and social ends. Rather, the end states of social relationships would be determined in process and, as per the policy, would be handled accordingly should the rights of any one person be violated. The services strategy is also dependent upon the actualities of social process, through such means as assessments of individual needs for supportive services, helping individuals to gain control over life events, and public education.

b. Multifinality

Neither policy approach suggests having uniformity or sameness in the expectations of any element in the downtown mall social system. The multifinality principle — that a variety of end states can arise out of original conditions — is supported. As long as neither merchants nor mall people are stereotyped and unilaterally cast into role expectations, the principle of multifinality will be fostered by the direction of policy in this situation.

c. Nonsummativity

The principle of nonsummativity — that the whole is more than the sum of its parts — could come to fruition in this situation if the various elements are brought together. If the situation is dealt with holistically (as a community problem), the principle of nonsummativity is more likely to be realized. This means that each of the key elements will have to make their own contributions to problem resolution; both the regulatory strategy and the supportive services strategy appear to foster achievement of that goal. This means the ability of *each* element to cope or deal with the problem will be enhanced.

d. Morphogenesis

The principle of morphogenesis, that human systems have the ability to change their own forms in process, is not necessarily enhanced by the two policy strategies. The current situation of labeling and demands for exclusion or restraint would require considerable change in community attitudes. The regulatory and service strategy is aimed primarily at changes in behaviors, rather than attitudes. The supportive services strategy is also aimed primarily at changes in behaviors. However, the community propensity for name calling and/or demands for exclusion and withdrawal could be altered if, over time, those same elements in the community were to witness the positive effects of behavior change. This, of course, is predicated on the assumption that changes in behavior breed changes in attitude; the efficacy of this assumption remains to be seen.

e. Stochastic processes

Both policy strategies suggest a probable alteration in the sequence of subsequent events, to the extent that attempts at behavioral change are successful. Both the Commissioner's regulatory policy approach and the supportive services strategy are intended to narrow the range of probabilities of citizens' behavior with respect to the mall. Each strategy aims at channeling or shaping the types of behavior on the mall, one through control and the other through education and/or training. Each generates more predictability and lawfulness in the sequence of social processes to follow, and each supports the policy goal of making the mall attractive and readily available to all citizens of the community.

4. Discriminatory Factors

This policy problem and its resolution has particular implications for young people, the city's senior citizens, and especially for those who rely upon public welfare, mental health, and correctional services. As was noted in Case 3, the mall people population ranges from school youth to men residing in a correctional "halfway house," to developmentally disabled adults working downtown in a sheltered workshop, to senior citizens, to individuals on aftercare following release from state institutions. While many individuals have client relationships with various human services agencies, many are citizens who are not formally related to any community organizations. Nevertheless, it is clear that the problem is more of a burden for certain age groups in the community, for those in difficult economic conditions, and for many who possess multiple handicaps in coping with society.

The commissioner's proposed policy appears to treat all of these elements equitably. The regulatory and enforcement strategy is a leveling device. The supportive services strategy is, on the other hand, predicated on the primacy of the majority's way of conducting affairs on the mall; ironically, the services approach creates a greater burden for change on the victims, currently perceived by many as those with the problem.

Summary

This case illustration has been a continuation of the discussion begun in Case 3 concerning the conduct of citizens on the downtown mall. Particular attention has been given to the relationship of the policy options to the merchants on the mall and, in particular, to the mall people.

6

Process Elements for Small-Scale Policy Analysis

The task of this chapter is to introduce the elements of a model for policy analysis that pertain to the *process* aspects of policy. Chapter 4 gave attention to the content aspects and chapter 5 to values. It is difficult to separate or select out the substantive content, people processes, and value issues that exist in the play of power. Admittedly, content, values, and process cannot be easily separated in real life but, for purposes of developing our understanding, we must treat them separately here. As we move through the chapter, we will actually be developing an outline, as was done in the earlier chapters.

As in chapters 4 and 5, we will intersperse a case example throughout the narrative of this chapter for illustrative purposes.

Case Illustration

This illustration exemplifies in many respects what occurs in many communities—the actual problems in coordinating interagency efforts in delivering social services. In our case example, twenty-one human service agencies in Valley Falls, a population area of nearly one million, have coalesced to form a Community Case Coordination Team (hereafter referred to as TEAM), which has the stated purpose of "improving the coordination of existing area services to dysfunctional multisystem clients." The coalition is comprised of public and private, voluntary and governmental agencies from a variety of jurisdictions and political boundaries in the immediate geographical area. However, as will be noted in our analysis, the initiative for the policy process arose out of the efforts of five agencies primarily serving a transient, low-income clientele in the Middleside neighborhood.

Major Elements of Process

Having surveyed the essential elements of a few process models in chapter 3, we will now attempt to reduce their number in order to better understand the range and variety of elements playing a part in the process of policy development and implementation. We will approach our discussion of policy process elements by identifying three aspects: (1) milestones, (2) interest group relationships, and (3) process resources. These aspects are extracted and reduced from a number of views of process thinking, most of them noted earlier. Special attention will be given, however, to those explanations of system process that pertain in particular to the policy process at the local or small-scale level.

Milestones embodies such concepts as stages or phases often included in process explanations that emphasize the time dimensions of policy process (the completion of certain crucial tasks). *Interest group relationships* include those concepts included in various models that emphasize the competitive or cooperative interaction of the policy processes actors. *Process resources* include those tangible and intangible assets and liabilities needed and/or held by policy action systems that should be noted in an analysis of policy process.

The Policy and the Problem

The first task is to develop a clear and concise statement which delineates the policy that is under analysis or the problem that is of concern. As with the analysis of content, the analysis of process must proceed from a clear notion of what is to be the focus of concern. (This is not to say, of course, that the focus cannot change during the analysis.)

The Policy and the Problem

This first section will give some shape to the problem generating the policy process and some definition of the policy itself.

The Middleside neighborhood, a densely populated area characterized by a mix of small industries and both multiple-unit and large, single-family, older residential units near the

---

center of the central city, provides the geographical focus for our policy. Middleside is heavily populated by single, indigent street people and a large number of individuals who are products of the move toward deinstitutionalization over the past few years. It became apparent to many of the agencies serving the area that poor interagency communication contributed to underutilization of necessary services for some citizens of the area, while at the same time some clients were using disproportionate amounts of those services. Yet another group of residents were inappropriately using the service system at the expense of those who were very much in need of available support services. As the broad areas of service gaps and duplication became increasingly problematic for the responsible agencies, poor coordination of agency services became more of a threat to needy citizens and clients, as well as an issue for the agencies involved.

The TEAM was originally established by five agencies as an integral part of each agency's program operations. That is, the new interagency coordination policy required each agency to treat interagency coordination as an integral part of its program operations in an effort to "improve the coordination of existing area services to dysfunctional multisystem clients." Until the establishment of the TEAM, no formal mechanism for coordinating services existed. The factors that contributed to that state of affairs included increased agency specialization, increased agency independence, ambiguity in case management responsibilities, differing funding sources, and an atmosphere of growing territoriality and competition. Other problems included a lack of understanding by agency staff of the operating procedures of other agencies, different treatment philosophies, and a lack of available resources for interagency coordination activities. Many of the clientele in the Middleside neighborhood experienced conflicting advice and services from those agencies.

A five-member coalition of agencies, primarily serving or located in Middleside, served as the impetus for this policy process. This group included the emergency room of St. Louis

Hospital, the Valley Falls Police Department, The Salvation Army Mission Center, Transitions Detox Center, and The Bridge, the county mental health program's daytime drop-in center. A staff member from a neighboring county health department, on leave to complete a graduate program in social work and serving a student field-education internship at The Bridge, was assigned to chair the TEAM. She was chosen because she was an older, experienced worker who was known to Valley Falls professionals, having recently been employed by a local family services agency. She was also seen as occupying a neutral position.

Eventually, the original five-member coalition developed a number of more specific goals for other agencies to consider. The TEAM, which utilized the "case conferencing" method of agency interaction, assured all potential participating agencies that no new system would be added nor would any additional steps in service delivery be a requirement of participation. Also, more specific goals were articulated over time: **(1)** to formalize and strengthen existing information networks in interagency communication or coordination; **(2)** to service problematic cases common to two or more member agencies by engaging in case management during regular and scheduled team meetings; **(3)** to determine more specific case management responsibility and procedures for shared management, with ongoing feedback on progress; **(4)** to review referrals of multiproblem clients and formulate appropriate service plans; and **(5)** to influence community policy, planning, and resource development regarding services to dysfunctional multisystem clients by issuing TEAM reports and recommendations to member agency participants.

Milestones in Policy Processes

It is wise to include in your model for analysis some accounting of the temporal and / or developmental aspects of the process of policy. That is, all policy and its analysis should give some consideration to the fact that policy exists within a time dimension. One guide for us here is the emphasis in some models on the notion that policy processes have a life of their own, with certain stages, phases, or tasks being characteristic of particular times in the policy's life cycle. For purposes of analysis it is helpful to think of the *milestones* that are to be achieved over the life of a policy process. Milestones may be thought of as the major developmental tasks, if you will, that must be performed in the process dimension of policy. These milestones must be included in the analysis to determine whether the policy has satisfied requisite developmental tasks, has the necessary ingredients for moving through those tasks, and whether certain major events have occurred (or are likely to occur) to achieve the desired policy effects. Some examples are the establishment of an "initiating set" aimed at taking action, the achievement of sponsorship or legitimation, and the recruitment of significant talent in sufficient numbers to carry out the policy action (see Warren, 1963). Other examples might be the development of key coalitions, or obtaining necessary contractual agreements (to be discussed below). Milestones are the touchstones of policy process, the key steps providing bridges between espoused principles and desired end states. They might also be seen as the seizing of opportunity at appropriate times or points in a policy's history or as filling a policy space in a vacuum of social action.

Charter and legitimacy. Every policy must be founded upon an original agreement or template which makes its presence right and proper. That is, policies must have legitimacy, or the right to be brought into effect. A corollary is that those who enforce or implement policy must have the legitimacy to do so, or the right to take action. There is no question that obtaining a charter or the pursuit and obtaining of legitimacy are, in themselves, process phenomena. (Everything in the human systems world is in some way interrelated.) Nevertheless, no policy can move ahead, or be applied, or stand alone without legitimacy, whether that legitimacy is ascribed at its birth or achieved during its lifetime by the social action of the policy actors.

There are a number of levels and sources of legitimacy for social welfare policy, ranging from constitutional foundations, judicial and legislated rulings, and administrative policy (which may or may not have its foundations in these higher levels). The ultimate legal legitimacy is, of course, constitutional mandate. Organizational (or administrative) policy has its potential for legitimacy in many areas, but its firmest foundation is in the double sanction of both judicial and/or legislated legitimacy supported by broad popular consent. A good example of the latter situation is the self-regulating behavior of day-care center providers who have meaningful input into state licensing laws regulating child day care and, themselves, take adverse action against peers who violate the administrative rules that enforce the statute.

In policy analysis it is well to identify the sources, nature, and effects of chartering and legitimacy if one is to truly understand the context of the policy under analysis. For example, we can look to the existence of judicial orders, legislated authorizations or appropriations, board or committee resolutions, city or county ordinances, contract agreements or requirements, and other manifestations of the right to take action. These are examples of sources of legitimacy.

The existence of a charter (or having legitimacy) is not only a source of power and assurance but a fundamental milestone around which policy action takes place and from which it can proceed. This is best illustrated in the case of administrative rules (i.e., standards or regulations that have the force of law) that are developed subsequent to some enabling legislation. For example, whenever any regulatory legislation is passed by the federal government or virtually any state legislature, that legislation tends to be quite general, indicating the population or enterprise to be protected or limited and the administrative agency responsible for monitoring regulatory activity. The general purpose of the legislation is usually also stated in the statute. However, federal administrative procedures legislation and the administrative procedures acts of virtually every state require a rather detailed and explicit set of routines for an administrative agency to follow in publishing proposed rules (i.e., administrative policy), in receiving and responding to input offered on the part of those affected, and in final legislative review prior to promulgation of the rules. Prior to completion of these required steps, many administrative rules are mere policy without authority (as is the case with many guidelines). Once having fulfilled the requirements (publishing proposed rules, conducting public hearings and legislative review), the rule has the firmest of legitimacy—the force of law. Therefore, the existence of a charter and/or legitimacy constitutes a major milestone that must be considered in the analysis of policy, especially (in this case) when it involves administrative rules arising out of legislated regulatory policy.

Charter and legitimacy

The charter for policy action serving as the original agreement or template may be found in the impetus by the original five agencies to pilot the case coordination idea. Our analysis might even pursue the question of which particular individual(s) in which particular agencies actually came forth with the idea. This set of actors derived their legitimacy first as individuals and next as an action system from the organizations by whom they were employed. In one sense, then, their legitimacy was legislative in that each agency was legally constituted and had as part of its own mission the service activity being pursued by its staff in the Middleside neighborhood. A review of the authority of each of the five agencies reveals a range of sponsorship from public (the Valley Falls Police Department and the Bridge, a county mental health agency) to private (St. Louis Emergency Room, Transitions Detox Center, and the Salvation Army Mission).

The action system's charter to bring about change in the service system itself was legitimated by the agreed-upon responsibility of each team member. The five proponents of the plan, each a member of middle management as program coordinators in the neighborhood, simply requested permission to proceed with the pilot as an experimental project. Each member, in turn, was expected to report back on pilot project experiences to their own administrative head, thereby further legitimating their ongoing activity with the TEAM project.

Action system. In order for social action to take place (i.e., for policy processes to occur) there must be an identifiable set of social actors who can or do actually assume responsibility for pursuing, implementing, or enforcing the policy under analysis. Policy cannot move forward without those who initiate it through social processes or those who take on the various tasks of "making policy stick." Any analysis of policy must at least consider, for example, who the movers of a particular policy are, what their aims, motives, and/or incentives are, and what next steps toward policy initiation are both necessary and feasible. At the same time, policy analysis must include a study of the necessary next steps for installation, modification, implementation, or enforcement if the process aspects are to be adequately considered. At this point in the discussion, the emphasis is upon the reality of an action system being in place—as an essential milestone—and not so much on the interactive aspects of action. More will be said about the interest group aspects later.

The presence of an action system—an identifiable set of actors committed to taking action for the sake of promoting (or even impeding) a particular policy—is a necessary milestone in social action and, therefore, a necessary element in the process aspects of our policy analysis. A careful analysis of the action system's legitimacy, authority, leadership capacities, membership and their individual and collective status, and the overall strategies that they employ are all important dimensions of the size and shape of the action system. A consideration of these aspects of process in policy analysis helps to recognize the policy system's capacity and ability to do such things as convert issues to public concerns, bring about agenda setting in the organization or community, or determine the parameters within which the policy will take shape. In essence, this aspect of policy process analysis is the assessment of the power of the action system, a measurement of the ability of a given set of actors to effect the probable outcomes of future events in relation to the policy under analysis.

Action system

As noted above, the action system was comprised of five individuals and their associated agencies, each of which had a right to take action. After only three meetings, the goals and objectives enumerated above were more formally developed. An early strategy centered around serving primarily the indigent population of the neighborhood and the concept that the fundamental activity would only be case conferencing. The

TEAM agreed to hold to the notion that, if the agencies experienced some success in adhering to the multiagency case conferencing strategy, other agencies would come around—when and if such success became evident.

Key participants. Another milestone in the play of policy and, therefore, in the analysis of policy process, is the recruitment and participation of certain key actors in the policy system. That is, for purposes of analysis, it is not only important to identify whether or not an action system exists but to identify the participants in that action system—who they are and who or what they represent. The whole is greater than the sum of its individual parts. Hence, the action system is more than the accumulation of individual actors. Nevertheless, a determination of the nature of individual actors is essential in an effective analysis.

A definition of the membership of the policy action system would include officials with designated authority, influential media, people with technical expertise, and those who are in touch and have influence with decision makers. Designated authorities means those who hold elected or appointed offices, those named in agreements or contracts, and those who informally emerge as "the leadership." "The media" may mean those who usually come to mind—radio, television, or newspapers; however, media may also mean those who "spread the word" in various ways (e.g., through newsletters or information offices) or simply influential individuals who move about freely in the neighborhood or the office, for example, and become important channels of communication. Clearly then, influential policy actors need not always mean those holding official positions: furthermore, individuals may be influential channels by virtue of their own attributes or because of the group that they represent. Influence makers may be individuals, such as key staff, knowledgeable authorities or organizations, prestigious think tanks or research groups, or reference groups of various types. What is clear is that the presence and force of key actors not only play a part in the political processes of policy but also constitute vital milestones in the policy process.

Key participants

A key participant in the project was the TEAM chairperson, who was known to the professional community but who, as a graduate student from another county, was not seen as motivated as others might have been to serve agency or personal self-interest. The agencies involved were also key in that each had had extended experience with the client population on a daily basis, and their accumulated knowledge of client needs had credibility. The original TEAM of five had a mixture of professional and "paraprofessionals," which demonstrated to members who later joined the TEAM that professional status did not create barriers that would interfere with the team approach to case coordination. The Police Department did not have any experienced human service personnel on staff, though it had recently embarked on a neighborhood foot-patrol strategy and officers were receiving more human relations and community resource training. On the one hand, the hospital and the community mental health staff were experienced social workers, while the Transitions Detox Center (except for visiting volunteer physicians) was primarily staffed by trained volunteers. The Salvation Army mission, a multipurpose agency comprised of a range of professional and volunteer staff, served as the model for staff interaction and also contributed a meeting room for the regularly scheduled TEAM meetings.

In summary, these five agencies represented a range of professional and disciplinary orientations. As line staff from each of the agencies became more involved in TEAM interaction, an atmosphere of professional parity developed. That interaction then served as a model and linkage to their counterparts in other agencies in the ongoing TEAM program.

Interest Group Relationships

A number of factors give shape to the analysis of interest group politics in policy process. Some have to do with the sheer power or influence (i.e., the exercise of power) of particular groups; others involve the salience (attraction or valence) of particular policy-related issues for particular groups; and some involve specific intergroup activities that occur in the context of interest group interrelationships.

Power and influence. It is absolutely essential to estimate the power (i.e., the ability to control the outcomes of others' behavior) and the influence (i.e., the actual exercise of that power) of the various interest groups that are party to a policy under analysis. A precise measurement, of course, is not likely. Thus, the estimate would probably be based upon historical evidence of the actual exercise of influence behavior in the past or on speculation about what particular groups might do under hypothetical circumstances. Kenneth Gergen (1968) speaks to this matter somewhat when he discusses the concept of "personal efficacy." Efficacy might be thought of as not only the individual's but the group's capacity or ability to produce desired effects as well as its actual history or experience in doing so. Some obvious considerations here are: (1) speculation as to the likelihood of a particular group supporting or rejecting a proposed policy and (2) an estimate of whether any particular group is needed to assist in the enforcement or maintenance of a policy position. At this point, we come to an analysis of the *vested interests* various groups already possess, risk losing, or have the potential to obtain via an existing or proposed policy position.

Power and influence

As noted in the discussion regarding legitimacy, each member of the action system had authority to take action. Given the range of professional and disciplinary orientations represented in the original and, therefore, the expanded TEAM, that influence enabled newcomer individuals and agencies to identify with existing TEAM members. Perhaps one of the greatest sources of influence was the actual success of more efficient service attributed to case conferencing.

Aside from the collective goals of the agencies there were additional individual or organizational vested interests at work.

Some agencies, for example, were more interested in participating in the interagency communication network for other purposes or in maintaining an "in-the-know" posture. Another large agency actually aimed at testing the political waters regarding a single track or entry to a county-wide service system. (That fact, at one point, was a serious threat to the continued existence of the TEAM experiment.) Yet another agency used the TEAM project as an entree into a new program that it was preparing for introduction into the Middleside neighborhood. As in all coalition-type efforts, it is important for the process analyst to recognize that, in coalitions, each discrete organization has the right to maintain its own goals; coalitions are maintained when organizations can pursue common interests that derive from the goals that each organization rightfully reserves for itself.

Salience of the issue(s). Identification of the power and influence of group participants leads us to some estimate of the salience of particular issues for particular groups. The "salience" of an issue might be thought of as the extent to which any particular issue generates action because of its special meaning or value to the actor. Gergen (1968) speaks of "issue salience" in relation to individual actors in policy processes; here we are speaking to salience giving rise to group action. While individual policy initiatives are not to be ignored (indeed, they were mentioned in the previous section of this chapter), it is group action that greases the skids of *social* welfare policy action. Consequently, an estimation of the salience of the proposed or existing policy for all groups in the policy system is an essential element for effective policy analysis. In the best of all worlds, these estimates would each have sound empirical bases; that is, each would be based upon "hard" data gathered under established rules of procedure and evidence. In policy analysis, such empirical data may not be readily available. Nevertheless, one should strive for such data or, at the very least, have a conscious tally of those data that are based only on conjecture.

Salience of the issues(s)

The central issues facing the agencies were needy clients without services in the Middleside neighborhood and tremendous duplication of efforts in other areas. These salient issues were translated in practical terms into both expected client outcomes and expected outcomes for each agency. Some client-specific outcomes were: **(1)** interagency case conferencing for a coordinated treatment plan; **(2)** a broadened range of service alternatives and resources for each client; **(3)** involvement of professional services from many disciplines; **(4)** an integrated community response to client needs; **(5)** greater specificity regarding primary case management responsibility; and **(6)** a more appropriate matching of client need to agency service. Some agency-specific outcomes were: **(1)** integrated community approaches to dealing with service gaps; **(2)** coordinated agency responses to system manipulators; **(3)** strengthened interagency relationships; **(4)** clarification of agency roles in the human service matrix; **(5)** improved ability to provide clients with the least restrictive alternative; and **(6)** pooling of resources in extremely problematic client situations.

Intergroup activities. Power, influence, and issue salience might be thought of as the static aspects of interest group phenomena. However, the very construct of the interest group suggests social action, or to be more exact, social interaction. And, of course, the literature of political science is full of concepts and their illustrations of the interactive aspects of political processes.

Intergroup activities

Given the nature of the policy developed here, essentially three types of intergroup interactions emerged: (1) coming together

for the regularly scheduled case conferences convened by the
TEAM chairperson; (2) actual case activity by line staff; and
(3) informal interaction among and between agency administrators who shared the experiences of their respective staffs'
interaction with other agencies as a result of the TEAM project.

Unilateral transfers versus bilateral exchanges. Our focus here is
upon the political aspects of social welfare policy processes. Social
welfare activities tend to be unclear regarding the domain of policy
substance or the prerogatives of policy actors. This lack of clarity is
exemplified by the contrasting views of Kenneth Boulding (1967)
and Robert Pruger (1973). For Boulding, social policy involves
unilateral transfers of various commodities, whether money or services, as opposed to exchange transactions. That is, the donor is viewed
as giving up something and the receiver as obtaining something. No
exchange is presumed—just a transfer—and the commodity is said
to move only in one direction. In contrast, Pruger sees social policy
as involving *bilateral exchanges* between donors and receivers in which
a transaction involves commodities (tangible or intangible), and movement in both directions between provider and receiver. This is best
illustrated by the aphorism "There is no such thing as a free lunch."
The most debased and humiliated recipient gives up something—
dignity or freedom of choice—in exchange for assistance.

Given that what constitutes right and proper prerogatives in social
welfare policy is so universally contested, it is no small wonder that
few rules exist to serve as guides in the analysis of interest group
activities.

Unilateral transfers versus bilateral exchanges

Clearly, the agencies with the greatest incentives to actually
engage in coordination of efforts were those that engaged in

---

bilateral exchanges, while the agencies who came along in order to stay "in the know" or work on their own agendas were more likely recipients of unilateral transfers of information or intelligence. From another perspective, the underserved client population was more likely to benefit from the bilateral exchange, while those residents of the neighborhood who were intense recipients of neighborhood services were more likely to give something up as a result of the TEAM project.

Bargaining and negotiating. Bargaining and negotiating are especially characteristic of social welfare policy processes, since social welfare resources are generally obtained through debate because they are scarce or limited or needed by a variety of competing interests. This is not to say that other, more common activities are not also present in social welfare policy processes, such as initiating tradeoffs, seriality, or "satisficing" (see Lindblom, 1968). Given the constant contentiousness of social welfare policy it is particularly important to the policy analysis to assess bargaining and negotiating (and what occurs during these activities).

Bargaining may be thought of as the means by which agreements are reached between two or more parties in which the interest of each is pursued. Therefore, in policy analysis one should study the commitments made in the agreements themselves as they might enhance or hinder the policy objectives. Negotiating may be seen as a special kind of means by which bargains are obtained, and is generally characterized by particular social rules or norms. Indeed, in collective bargaining between management and labor, such negotiating is even regulated by laws. Consequently, it is valuable in the policy analysis to note what kinds of agreements (bargains) were made by various interest groups and in what way (i.e., form of negotiation) bargaining occurred.

Bargaining and negotiating

Agreements by agencies in individual case situations came about totally through a bargaining and negotiating process. The context in which bargaining and negotiating occurred not only included what agency preferences might have been but how each agency's responsibilities were perceived by their colleagues in the TEAM meetings. For example, greater specificity in designated responsibility for case management of clients on aftercare from the state hospital came about when the state hospital liaison became regularly involved, along with the staff of The Bridge and staff from the work activity training center. Agreements were negotiated in process; the absence of such agreements had heretofore been a major weakness in the service system.

Coalition building. Another special activity, related to both negotiating and bargaining, is coalition building. Coalitions are commonly found in social welfare policy processes, given the competition for scarce resources and the need for cooperation in the interest of client service. Coalitions may be thought of as temporary agreements or arrangements made by interest groups in which limited goals of each group are served while, at the same time, no group's autonomy is surrendered. For purposes of policy analysis, it is helpful to determine the particular goals selected to bind the coalition(s) together; or to observe which goals are *not* binding. It is also important to determine who the coalition's spokespersons are and to identify the policy principles articulated by those spokespersons or by the literature the coalition generates.

Coalition building

The entire TEAM project may be called a formal coalition building effort, arising out of the initiative of five agencies and resulting in an informal coalition of twenty-one such agencies.

Contracting. Finally, contracting is a special form of policy activity that has great potential for policy analysis. This includes the processes employed and the forms obtained in such contracting. Contracting may be thought of as a formal agreement upon terms. These terms, such as the resources to be employed, the conditions under which policies will be pursued, and the outcomes to be expected guide interactions between two parties. Indeed, contracts themselves may be seen as master statements or a collection of principles, each suggesting many policies which invite analysis. Given the increased reliance upon contracting in recent years, both with the specific introduction of purchase-of-service contracting supported by Title XX of the Social Security Act and the general inclination to formalize economic relationships, analysis of contract elements and contracting are grist for the mill. Some likely provisions are the usual "boilerplate" policy principles, such as the formal standing of past practices, the nature of master-slave relationships between parties to the agreement, rights and responsibilities regarding access to and provision of data and auditing, expectations regarding the form and frequency of reporting, and prerogatives regarding the movement or reallocation of funds within a budget. Other elements might relate to expectations regarding notice of termination of the contract, matching requirements for funding, limitations on subcontracting, output and outcome expectations, and rates of reimbursement.

An important point here for the analyst is that contracts themselves give explicit suggestions — by the very provisions existent within them — regarding what some of the appropriate criteria for analysis might be. Other criteria for analysis might be suggested by what provisions are *not* in the contract. Furthermore, it should be especially noted that a formal contract need not be written or in place for the analyst to use contract principles or features for the policy process analysis, since the fundamental questions to be asked have to do with what group interests are or were being served by existing principles and how those principles or provisions were arrived at.

Contracting

While this particular case illustration does not provide evidence of formal contracting taking place, there were extensive examples of interagency contracting occurring through the development of case plans in TEAM meetings. In fact, to some extent an "anticontracting" approach was ostensibly taken in the sense that "recommendations for action" were developed as opposed to specific treatment plans. To be sure, client goals were established and the participating member agencies became committed to assigning staff resources to particular client situations, and agreements to pursue particular progress goals were made. In this way, accountability to one another was established at the client or case level while specific contracting was particularly avoided.

Process Resources

The achievement of social goals requires resources. Analysis of the social welfare policy process is no different in that regard. Analysis itself requires resources. An important point for the analyst to recognize, however, is that "resources" constitute a rather broad area. In fact, many of the elements that we have already discussed might fall under the rubric of "resources." Surely, the efficacy, power, or influence of individuals or groups might be considered in any analysis of resources; so too with the ability to bargain or negotiate, or with the legitimacy of statutory law and appellate decisions. Here, however, we will include the somewhat more tangible, perhaps even quantifiable, aspects of resources for movement of the policy process, which, in turn, provide the makings for policy analysis.

People power. In assessing resources, one should identify the people necessary to the job of bringing the policy to fruition. The analyst must ask how much effort was expended and by whom, which gives some evidence of the salience of the policy for particular groups and the relative value of the principles articulated in the particular policy at issue.

People power

The process appears to have been adequately staffed in that each of the participating agencies assigned staff liaisons to the TEAM project. The initiating group was comprised of middle management staff of the core group of five agencies. Another key people resource was the person assigned to serve as chairperson of the TEAM. No voluntary group effort can succeed without at least some amount of staffing effort at group maintenance. However, given the project's commitment *not* to develop yet another layer of bureaucracy and another service, the formal logistical support of that effort was minimal in terms of ongoing staffing of the TEAM itself.

Technology. A corollary to the question of people power is that of technology, the existing skills and/or talents used in the policy process. That is to say that people's skills are considered technology, as well as mechanical or electronic technology available to the policy actors for the attainment of policy goals. Some examples of the latter are computerization of data or computer facilities, office space, and communication facilities. Communication facilities is a special case since policy principles are of no value unless they are communicated. Furthermore, an analysis of communications capacities suggests who the gatekeepers and filterers of communications are in the policy system (e.g., intergroup liaisons, spokespersons, press officers, or even messengers). Also, an analysis of communications technology leads the analyst to look for particular avenues or organs for communicating policy principles, such as newsletters, flyers, or even electronic bulletin boards as illustrations of formal channels, or informal networks of people of like interests who come together, and the ability to move the word quickly throughout a neighborhood.

Technology

Since so many different agencies were involved, this project and policy process benefited from the range of disciplinary and professional services available in the community. Given the multiproblem nature of the clientele served, a variety of staff were necessarily involved in the TEAM case coordination efforts. Staff orientation ranged from volunteers from some agencies with minimal amounts of training (e.g., the Christian Service volunteers from a neighborhood church) to highly trained staff from one of the mental health outpatient clinics. Thus, a range of problem-solving technology was brought to bear.

Finances. Access to or the use of money in its various forms is an obvious criterion for analysis of the play of policy processes. A clear illustration would be the presence of actual cash contributions to campaigns or drives. Yet another would be the ability to hire people to staff a campaign for a preferred policy outcome. There are, of course, other factors pertinent to financial resources in policy processes, such as the availability and/or use of office space or access to locations for public meetings. Another is the ability to have funds available to conduct mailings or other advertising efforts.

Finances

This policy required minimal amounts of out-of-pocket expenditures. The Salvation Army was reimbursed by the United Way for expenses incidental to making the facility available for TEAM meetings. There were some expenses for mailings and phone calls. The cost to each agency of having staff available to meet in TEAM conferencing was, of course, extensive. That staff time was lost to what otherwise would have been direct client contact. However, the benefit/cost relationship between achieving case coordination as opposed to the prior situation, though not computed, appeared to be worth the TEAM effort. Evidence of this conclusion is found in the growth of the TEAM project from five to twenty-one agencies over the nineteen-month project period.

Time. Our final criterion for resource analysis is the availability and/or use of time in the play of policy processes. Time might be seen as an asset or a liability. When adequate amounts of time are available to develop and conduct effective campaigns for system-wide support, time is an asset. When insufficient amounts of time are available, time is a liability. One can also observe how or the extent to which significant policy actors utilize time in achieving policy goals, such as being patient, playing brinksmanship politics, issuing ultimatums on short notice, or building timetables for time-consuming participatory processes.

Time

As just noted the time allocated to interagency meetings is time lost to what otherwise might have been direct service. Another time factor is the possibility of lost opportunities because staff efforts went into this project as opposed to alternative efforts. Since it is impossible to determine what opportunities were or were not foregone by each of the twenty-one agencies, this time factor cannot be obtained. Time is a necessary resource, and in this instance, one that appears to have been available, given the apparent success in drawing agencies into the process.

Congruence with Desired Values

In this section, we will apply the outline for analyzing value elements in policy analysis to our Interagency Service Coordination TEAM case illustration. This allows us to apply the Values outline to a process illustration.

1. Generic Values

a. Identity

This policy process should contribute greatly to client self-image because each citizen of the Middleside neighborhood, client or nonclient, could assume that the community as a whole was interested in the neighborhood. Residents of the neighborhood could rightfully conclude that they were being recognized as citizens who, as members of the community, were entitled to services and that the service system was taking steps to appropriately deliver those services.

b. Self-determination

Each resident of the neighborhood would, like any resident of the city, have the opportunity to receive or refuse services. Clients who were subjects of case conferencing by the TEAM gave express permission to have their situations discussed in the TEAM conferences via the legal and ethical requirement that a written and signed release of information and a statement of informed consent be obtained for each client conferenced. This requirement was automatic for some agencies and not done at all in other agencies. Consequently, development of this procedure was a major task for the policy process. One element possibly lacking in the attempt at client self-determination—at least in the collective sense—was the absence of any clients or client group in the TEAM policy process itself.

That is, client representatives were not utilized in the initiation or planning of the case coordination approach. The policy analyst would need to determine whether that client participation would have been helpful or appropriate in this policy situation.

c. Confidentiality

Confidentiality was a difficult principle in this policy process, given the extensive number and variety of service providers involved. In a formal sense, it would appear that the policy achieves confidentiality, though this is very difficult to conclusively determine in this instance. The policy analyst should use the process analysis to develop techniques whereby confidentiality could be better assured. Some possibilities are making the issue of confidentiality a topic at TEAM conferences, formalization of staff in-service training in the topical area, or further/more extensive procedures for written client permissions.

d. Individualization

A central objective in the policy observed in this process is, in fact, individualization. The policy process is aimed at developing plans and services that are unique to the needs of each client.

e. Nonjudgmental Attitude

There is a suggestion of a judgmental attitude when some clients are viewed as "manipulating" the service system; that is, when clients engage in behaviors that maximize the availability of services for themselves, they are sometimes labeled as manipulative. Such labeling may be judgmental on the part of service providers since the "manipulative" behaviors may, in fact, be indicative of resourceful clients who are able to access what is rightfully theirs in the community. One can not deny that some citizens consume inordinate amounts of community resources, inappropriately or otherwise. However, the issue of judgmental attitudes implicit in "ganging up" on some clients should at least be considered on a case-by-case basis.

2. Frameworks as the Source of Values

In this section, we will look at the implications of the theoretical approach to the problem.

In the Community Case Coordination Team, the apparent theory behind the policy process is that efficiency and effectiveness can be obtained by coordinating case planning and case management services to an indigent population in a particular neighborhood. That is, the principle driving the process appears to be one of efficiency or, perhaps, effectiveness. The analyst should be mindful of the fact that the policy does not foster strategies of *integration* of services, or the development of a *comprehensive* service for Middleside neighborhood residents; these would be entirely different strategies. The strategy employed in the TEAM process is one of bringing about coordination of efforts without building a new program or service or without altering the way in which any agency serves the neighborhood (other than participation in TEAM conferences). The presumption is that participation in TEAM conferences will bring about case coordination; the evidence appears to support the efficacy of this presumption.

3. Values in Human System Approaches

This section will review the possible values underlying human systems approaches which might be inferred in the policy process.

a. Indeterminateness

The TEAM policy process shows evidence of indeterminateness—that the end states of social processes are determined during the life of events. This is apparent in the open-ended approach of the five-member initiating system who opted for a strategy of using a pilot demonstration to bring along an undetermined group of agencies for subsequent participation. In other words, while there were some preferences as to which agencies and even which particular staff might have participated, the membership of the experiment was subsequently open. Furthermore, the resultant reports to the home agency administrative supervisors of each TEAM member were not established at the front end but, rather, were left to be subsequently determined during the life of the TEAM project.

b. Multifinality

The principle of multifinality—that similar original states could properly result in varied subsequent conditions—is evident in the approach that the TEAM took to case planning. The TEAM concentrated on developing interagency treatment "recommendations" and not hard and fast treatment plans. As the reader will note from our earlier discussion, the notion of formal case-plan contracting was avoided. Thus, the agencies involved were free to develop plans in process while, at the same time, their commitments to one another were honored to the extent felt reasonable. This approach provided an informal accountability system.

c. Nonsummativity

The principle of the whole being more than the sum of its parts is evident, to some extent, in the very notion of case conferencing. Recognition of the need for a holistic view of a person is illustrated by the acknowledgment that no single agency can adequately serve the needs of an individual. Case planning and case management is not simply a collection of individual services but an approach to client problem solving that must be coordinated if one is to provide a holistic perspective for the client.

d. Morphogenesis

The principle of morphogenesis—that human systems can change their forms and structure in process—is demonstrated in the TEAM policy process. No single agency altered its mission, goals, or fundamental procedures during or as a result of the effort. However, the nature and process of interagency interaction was fundamentally altered around activities relating to serving Middleside neighborhood residents.

e. Stochastic Processes

We stated earlier that policy provides for a stochastic process—gives order and predictability to a system. The development of the TEAM approach in this policy process gave order and predictability in a number of ways. The first is that agencies came to know, more and more, what to expect as a result of engaging in interagency cooperative case planning and case management. The second is that the client group could more readily see that agencies would be working together to provide them services. Curiously enough, the inclusion of additional agencies makes the service situation itself more—not less—predictable since the client and the participating agencies can begin to develop reasonable expectations of what services ought to be provided.

4. Discriminatory Factors

The TEAM policy process has particular implications for those who are poor and socioeconomically disenfranchised in many communities. Many clients are transient and indigent, living in high-density neighborhoods where little outreach has been pursued by a majority of local agencies. To some extent, agencies extended their efforts into the Middleside neighborhood due to their vested interest (minimizing duplication of efforts); on the other side, eliminating gaps in services was also a motivating force.

The neighborhood also has a disproportionate number of black residents, relative to the number of black citizens in the rest of the Valley Falls area. Factors of social class and race, then, appear to relate to this policy process in the sense that the poor and disenfranchised were apparent beneficiaries of the TEAM's coordinating efforts.

Summary

This has been an analysis of a policy process in which a Community Case Coordination Team in the Middleside neighborhood was developed—initially as a pilot experiment—to bring about coordinated case planning and case management for an indigent and highly transient client population. Essential milestones of the establishment of the initiating set and development of a broadly based legitimated charter were achieved, as well as demonstration of the adequacy of the pilot effort. The vested interests of individual agency participants were honored and participating organizations were not required to alter agency services or expected to commit unusual amounts of new resources to the TEAM efforts as a condition of participation. The appointment of a chairperson permitted minimal staff resources to sustain group leadership. Analysis of value elements leads the analyst to the conclusion that the generic values of social work and appropriate values of human systems were evident, although the maintenance of confidentiality was specifically identified as being at risk.

Summary

In this chapter we have reviewed some elements for policy analysis that help to explain the process aspects of social welfare policy. We addressed elements of process that should be reviewed as the milestones of process, the interest group features for analysis, and the resources to be considered in policy processes for analysis. Application of the elements has been illustrated throughout by reference to a case example involving the development of an interagency coordination team.

The case illustration in this chapter also served to review the value elements for policy analysis and provided an opportunity to also apply our Values outline to a policy process illustration.

We will now apply these processes to two case illustrations (i.e., Cases 7 and 8), using our outline "Process Elements for Analyzing Small-Scale Policy," which follows.

Remember that the essential activities in analysis are:

1. Identifying the policy problem and/or the policy goal
2. Identifying milestones in policy processes
3. Identifying interest group relations
4. Identifying process resources
5. Assessing congruence with desired values

Process Elements for Analyzing Small-Scale Policy (An Outline)

1. *The Policy and the Problem.* A clear and concise statement delineating the policy sought or the problem of concern.

2. *Milestones in Policy Processes.* A focus on the major developmental tasks undertaken or to be undertaken in the policy process.

- a. Charter and legitimacy
    - (1) Original agreement or template
    - (2) Right to take action
    - (3) Levels of legitimacy—legislative, judicial, and administrative
    - (4) Source and nature of charter and legitimacy
- b. Action system
- c. Key participants
    - (1) Recruitment and participation
    - (2) Who participates and who is represented

3. *Interest Group Relationships.* A focus on the particular groups whose interests are affected by the policy, the activities undertaken, and the interaction that occurs relevant to the policy.

- a. Power and influence
    - (1) Efficacy
    - (2) Vested interests
- b. Salience of the issue(s)
- c. Intergroup activities
    - (1) Unilateral transfers vs. bilateral exchanges
    - (2) Bargaining and negotiating

(3) Coalition building

(4) Contracting

4. *Process Resources.* A focus on the resources that are needed and/or observable in the policy process.

a. People power

b. Technology

c. Finances

d. Time

5. *Congruence with Desired Values.* See Value Elements for Analyzing Small-Scale Policy (An Outline)

Note: Recommendations, where appropriate, could be included at this point.

Case Illustrations

Case 7: Policy Process and Uniform Fee Determination

Case 7 provides an illustration of a process involving two interrelated issues. The first is the development of the Cascade County Community Mental Health Board's system-wide "Policy and Procedures for a Uniform Method of Determining Ability to Pay." This is a uniform fee determination policy and fee schedule for all local agencies operating as contractual services under the county's community mental health program. The second issue embedded in the policy program is a system-wide push for the generation of revenues. This is an effort to support continuation of services in a period of significant funding cutbacks by means of increasing program support through the billing of clients and/or their insurance carriers.

Cascade County, a county of approximately one-half million inhabitants in a standard metropolitan statistical area in a north central state, operates its county community mental health program by contracting out all direct services to various private and public agencies in the county. Board administration, planning and evaluation, and recipients' rights activities are all conducted out of the county board's offices; all direct services are operated by twenty-five other agencies through purchase-of-service contracting with the Cascade County Community Mental Health Board.

1. The Policy and the Problem

The central problems here appear to be the absence of a policy and procedures or clear guidelines for the installation of a uniform fee policy, in addition to an increasing need to develop new sources of revenue for program funding. Chapter seven of the State Mental Health Code, Act 129, provides that the State Department of Mental Health or its designees (i.e., the county community mental health boards) have the authority to establish fee schedules and bill recipients for services. The "Standards for Community Mental Health Services" subsequently published by the State Department of Mental Health provides that each county board has the responsibility for developing and implementing clearly defined mechanisms for the collection of fees from clients and third parties ("Standards," p. 29).

Approximately five years ago, the Cascade County Mental Health Board Chairperson appointed a fee policy task force comprised of the board chair, the board's executive director, directors of three agencies contracting with the Board to provide mental health services, and representatives of two noncontracting agencies in the community. This group formulated a two-page philosophy and fee policy, and a fee schedule. The policy espoused the principle that those utilizing services be asked to pay for them, that the actual cost of services should be disclosed to consumers, and that no one be denied services based on inability to pay. There was little comment on the proposed policy during its sixty-day public review but, after its implementation, widespread concern was expressed about the effect of the policy on the poor, the difficulty in assessing fees for nontraditional services (e.g., case management and respite care), and the correlation of the policy and guidelines with Blue Cross/Blue Shield procedures. The lack of specific guidelines and procedures for policy implementation, as well as the proposed fee schedule (viewed as excessively high by many agency directors) led at the time to the policy largely being ignored by contract agencies. A few agencies adopted and followed the policy; others maintained policies and fee schedules of their own; and others did not charge fees. Thus, the first attempt at establishment of a system-wide fee policy and schedule was not successful.

Budgetary constraints due to increasing program demands, the general instability of the state's economy, and State Department of Mental Health cuts in matching funds to Cascade County Community Mental Health led to a reawakened interest in fees as a source of revenue in the past year. Another key factor was the recent application by the state for federal reimbursement for certain mental health services under Medicaid (Title XIX), which would require uniform billing policies and procedures to be operational throughout the system. During this period, a reimbursement officer was hired by the board and given the responsibility by the executive director for developing a new fee schedule as well as policies and procedures for its implementation. In cooperation with the financial officer of the Board, research was undertaken rather hastily with an ad hoc task force comprised of administrative staff and clinicians from a number of contract agencies regarding the possible clinical impact of fee assessment and equitable models for collection of fees. With the initial activity of the reimbursement officer and the financial officer, upper and middle management of the Mental Health Board generated a fee policy, specific procedures for implementation, provisions for waiver, and a sliding fee schedule based on ability to pay. The earlier, two-page policy and fee schedule was replaced by a forty-three page document consisting of policy, procedures, and examples of recommended forms.

After the review period the new policy was accepted by contract agencies with little comment and apparent resignation and was quickly approved by the board. Some minor resistance was voiced, with contractees reminded that such a requirement had been allowed years previously by the Mental Health Code, mandated by the State Mental Health Department, and was already embedded in the current purchase-of-service contracts, though it had neither been implemented in principle nor monitored.

2. Milestones in Policy Processes

This section will review the key events evident in the policy process.

a. Charter and legitimacy

In both attempts at initiation and implementation of the uniform fee policy, there was a solid base of legitimacy in the actions taken. In the first attempt, by virtue of the legitimate authority vested in the role of chairperson, the board chair established a task force; in the second attempt, the Board's Executive Director initiated action in the appointment of administrative officers and another task force. Each action was formally legitimated by the appropriate charter associated with community mental health, the State Mental Health Code, Act 129. The standards that arose out of that Act even required uniform policy and procedures to be established, though processes for those actions were not prescribed. Consequently, legitimacy may be found in both legislative and administrative authority.

b. Action system

In each instance the action system was comprised of a delimited set of individuals, though the nature of each group differed. The first attempt at organizing the action system tended to be somewhat more open and collaborative in that the board chair appointed board administrative staff, directors of some contract agencies, and even included agency directors from the community who were not purchase-of-service contractees with the Community Mental Health Board. The second attempt was more of a closed system approach, with board staff developing the policy and a detailed set of procedures. However, in each instance there was opportunity for review and comment when the proposed policy was published, and final, formal approval at a regularly scheduled board meeting was required. In both events, the entire mental health system was presumably involved (or had the opportunity to be involved at some level), though the action system was much more limited in numbers and representation in the second attempt.

c. Key participants

The common policy development practice of publicizing an administrative policy for public review and comment during a specified period of time is frequently used by governmental agencies. In theory, this provides equal opportunity for public participation. In practice, it means solicitation of participation with little active recruitment and suggests little attention is given to assuring any particular representation or mixture of participants in the process. Furthermore, response or reaction to the input provided is not always guaranteed. In these two situations, however, the leverage exercised by certain actors is much more significant. In the first attempt, the key actors are identified leaders among their various constituencies. Unfortunately, their contribution was a vague and general policy. In the second attempt, the key actors are staff members whose leverage is technical information (it does not derive from elected or appointed legislative authority); however, their contribution is clear, detailed, and specific. Our analysis reveals that not only the actors, but the types of contribution they made (indicative of their roles and positions in the system), were key ingredients in the development of the policy.

3. Interest Group Relationships

This section of our analysis will focus on the particular groups whose interests are affected by the policy and the relevant intergroup actions.

a. Power and influence

Clearly the efficacy and legitimacy of the power of the board's officers and staff are rooted in the requirements of the State Mental Health Code, the standards for review, and the requirements to be met for Title XIX. The ability to exert influence beyond and outside of these areas is unquestionably connected to the board's funding role. While many of the local contractees exert some leverage through their ability to generate seed monies for local matching funds, the Community Mental Health Board is the conduit to state mental health matching funds and is the local mental health authority under the code. Each element has, in general, a vested interest in having that conduit function well; each has a stake in maximizing funding opportunities. Consequently, we see in the second (and successful) attempt at developing policy and procedures an apparent "resignation," evidence of both contract agencies' ambivalence and realism.

b. Salience of the issue

Uniform procedures establishing community-wide equity for the recipients of services, as well as the maintenance of adequate funding levels, are each issues salient to the entire community mental health system. In general, the absence of equity and a reduction in funding levels would affect all contract agencies equally. Consequently, while any one agency might not be enchanted with particular provisions, there is little argument about the necessity of the policy or its procedures.

c. Intergroup activities

In this particular policy, we find relatively little evidence of intergroup interaction. The first attempt tended to incorporate a democratic representation model, but there was little response during the period of public review and comment, and implementation was uneven and not at all uniform. In the second attempt at development and implementation, the strategy of using internal board staff precluded much intergroup activity. This is an interesting phenomenon, considering the salience of the issue. One possible explanation might be that while service agencies generally find it distasteful to install fee policies that will place more burdens on their clientele, there is actually widespread recognition of the real necessity to do so.

(1) Unilateral transfers vs. bilateral exchanges

At the agency-to-agency interaction level, the absence of apparent conflict is explained by the fact that the mutual interests of the board and contractees are, in fact, served. The board achieves its legislated and administratively-directed mandates for a uniform fee policy and procedures while contractee interests in financial support are maintained.

At the client-to-agency level, however, the unilateral nature of the exchange is enlarged. That is, the client group will now shoulder an increased share of cost. The recipients of service will be asked to bear an increased burden of the incidence of cost — at least those who have the ability to pay. Those who do not have the ability to pay will also feel the burden, as will be discussed later.

There is a mixture of incentives for agencies to participate cooperatively. For example, large agencies, or those that have automatic billing procedures in place, will likely benefit most from increased revenues, which could result in continued growth and independence. On the other hand, smaller agencies, especially those serving largely indigent clients and those with innovative, difficult-to-bill services, have to invest additional resources with little hope of recovering even their billing costs. In some agencies, this could result in lack of development, further financial strains, and inability to compete with larger agencies.

(2) Bargaining and negotiating

There is little in evidence here of bargaining or negotiating. However, some attempt was made to study issues, such as the clinical impact of a fee schedule; this is the point at which any negotiating might have taken place. In no event did contract agencies find themselves in a bargaining position.

(3) Coalition building

Given the general passivity of contractees in both attempts at fee setting, there is little evidence of a coalition process. However, given that coalitions exist when the goals of individual parties are served by cooperative efforts, the tacit approval of the second attempt, whether out of resignation or agreement, does give evidence of some consensus.

(4) Contracting
The whole process evolves around a network of services that exists by virtue of the ability of individual agencies to establish purchase-of-service contracts with a planning and funding source. (Of course, the contractual goals of each party must mesh in these instances.) The contractual goals of the Community Mental Health Board include development of alternative methods of generating revenue, compliance with the State Mental Health Code and the standards and perhaps, even movement towards the decrease in the county's dependence on state funding. In this particular instance, an additional goal might be to compensate for the lack of structure and guidelines in the former policy by providing elaborate detail and forms in the second attempt. The contractual goals of the individual contract agencies would include the maintenance of productive relationships with their funding source, advocacy for client rights, and preservation of the integrity of the agency's services. Both parties (i.e., the board and the contractee) have an interest in providing services to those most in need in an equitable, efficient, and effective manner.

4. Process Resources
This section will focus on the resources needed or observable in the policy process.

a. People power
Our analysis suggests that neither approach was lacking in necessary people power. The first and more democratic approach included a range of participants. The second and more technical approach included the persons necessary to develop an adequate policy. The success of the second approach derived mainly from the ability to develop and promulgate a detailed and technically sound set of policies and procedures that would give explicit direction to the contracting agencies.

b. Technology

As noted, the board apparently had the technical capacity to produce the policy, procedures, and guidelines in a way that was functional with respect to achieving the policy goals. This technical capacity is evidenced by the lack of negative criticism or rejection of what was produced and the fact that (for reasons noted above), there was "resignation." One could also infer that a technical rather than a more democratic approach was indicated in this instance. The latter is evidenced by the need to comply or conform with the state's application for a Medicaid certificate for Medicaid funding of selected services. A technical approach to policy and procedures would more likely result in conformity with state and federal regulations, though there is nothing to preclude that a more participatory process would be less effective.

c. Finances

Except for the cost of the actors' participation in each attempt, no out-of-pocket costs were incurred in the process of developing the uniform fees policy. The whole policy and the process surrounding it, of course, have financial implications for the board and the mental health system.

d. Time

Time was used differently in each instance. The first attempt, being more participatory in nature, used time to develop involvement and investment on the part of the ad hoc task force. The time investment during the period of public review and comment brought little return in terms of input. However, such time is not wasted since it allows input by those who wish to offer it and serves, if nothing else, as a vehicle to inform the constituency. (Thus, time as a resource, also has educational value.) The second attempt used time to develop detail and specificity.

Congruence with Desired Values

In this section, we will review the process from the perspective of our "Value Elements for Analyzing Small-Scale Policy, An Outline."

1. Generic Values

First, we will focus on the core values that might be considered or reflected in the policy process.

a. Identity

Maintaining the identity of the contract agency as an integral team member of the mental health system was enhanced more in the first approach to the policy process. The argument could also be made that the first approach promoted a greater sense of ownership and greater acceptance. The second approach, whether viewed as expedient or as a strategy to co-opt input, gives much less recognition to the role of the contractee. It could be said, however, that the role and identity of the contractee agencies are respected in each approach by the provision of the review and comment period.

b. Self-determination

Clients of mental health services in the community will have more restricted access to mental health services in the sense that there will be even more eligibility rules with which to conform. Presumably, no persons would be taxed beyond their ability to pay, but the current latitude in deciding to use mental health services will likely be curtailed.

From the agency perspective, this is a "take-it-or-leave-it" situation since the agencies are compelled to comply. The policy is not only promulgated from the top down but is a precondition of existence in the absence of alternative funding sources. Since agencies have virtually no choice in the policy decision, their self-determination is severely limited.

c. Confidentiality

Recipients of mental health services will, as a result of the policy, have to disclose more information regarding their personal finances. This will put more information into the system, thereby creating a need for additional safeguards to assure protection of confidentiality. In terms of the *process* of the policy's development, however, there do not appear to be any implications for maintaining client-system confidentiality. The policy process itself neither risks nor enhances the principle of confidentiality.

On the other hand, agencies will now be forced to develop and disclose more internal information (such as cost per units of services), in order to establish appropriate fees. Thus, the confidentiality of an agency's organizational information is at greater risk. The Mental Health Board's procedures for contract monitoring will have to ensure confidentiality for the agencies pertaining to organizational secrets.

d. Individualization

There appears to be no threat to the ability to deal with any client as a unique person with self-worth, either as a result of the policy or the process occurring in the policy's development. This would also appear to be true in regard to the contracting agencies.

e. Nonjudgmental attitude

A nonjudgmental attitude in the administration of the policy is assured, provided that the guidelines for the policy (e.g., guidelines specifying excluded income or allowable expenses) do not reflect arbitrary or capricious judgments on what clientele do with their own resources. The policy process itself did not appear to reflect any judgmental attitude on the part of the policy developers, though the procedure requiring validation of income seems to imply a lack of trust in the individual's ability to be truthful. While this procedure is practical, it runs counter to professional values; the policy objective could perhaps be achieved as well by the client's affirmation by affidavit.

2. Frameworks as the Source of Values

This section will focus on the particular values that might be implicit or are reflected in the theoretical explanations of the problem or the process.

One mental set implied in the policy is the work ethic—that those who receive benefits should properly pay for them. The establishment of a fee schedule is consistent with this attitude. The assumption that individuals utilizing services should pay for them, even though they have already helped fund them through tax dollars, is consistent with the Protestant work ethic prevalent in the community. Another view is more pragmatic—that service systems must maximize use of any and all sources of revenue, and the recipients of services merely constitute one of many such sources.

The theories implied in the process itself are fairly evident. One explanation is that participatory approaches to policy development are likely to be well received and implemented without resentment. A second is that complex and detailed policies requiring both technical skill and cooperative processes require more time to process. As noted above, the second approach appeared to be more successful, not because of its strategic superiority but because of the realities forced upon the system by reductions in the funding base.

3. Values in Human System Approaches

This section will focus on the particular values underlying human systems approaches to the process.

a. Indeterminateness

This policy would seem to fly in the face of the values associated with indeterminateness—that the end products of social processes are determined in process. In the second attempt at policy development, the policies, procedures, and guidelines were more or less handed down; there was little process. Furthermore, from the perspective of the client system, the specificity of the policy and its associated trappings leave little room for an indeterminate perspective. The opportunity for public review and comment and the formal establishment of the policy at an open and formal public meeting would introduce some element of indeterminateness. However, the nature of specific fee schedules and forms would preclude much opportunity for a participatory policy-making process.

b. Multifinality

The principle that a variety of end states can arise out of similar beginnings is somewhat honored in a uniform fee schedule since different family or client circumstances can, or should, be considered and allowed in the implementation of the policy. Thinking in terms of the policy development process itself, however, little space was provided for conceptualizing a variety of alternative outcomes. (Fee schedules become fixed, though their application throughout a system might differ.) Consequently, little evidence is found in the substance or process in policy development of anything other than a rather deterministic view of the uniform fee decision.

c. Nonsummativity

The principle of nonsummativity — that the whole is greater than the sum of its parts — is demonstrated by the fact of a *uniform* policy being established. Acknowledging the need for uniformity in a fee policy gives recognition to the fact that the implications of such a policy are system wide. Any departure from uniformity and consistency in the policy or procedures from contractee to contractee would be injurious to the entire community mental health system. This was evident in the absence of the policy to begin with, and in the first ineffective attempt to create it.

d. Morphogenesis

The ability of the community mental health system to alter its structures or processes is demonstrated in at least two ways. Perhaps because of the sequential/incremental nature of fundamental policy change, the system has evolved historically from one of total commitment to a policy of no fees for services, to a policy (albeit not largely implemented but at least sporadically embraced by some agencies), to a uniform, system-wide policy with attendant procedures and guidelines. This led to a fundamental restructuring in the funding base of the system as a whole and for most of the individual agencies.

In a second illustration relating to alterations in system processes, we observe the movement away from policy development by traditional consensual and representative processes to a more technical, unilateral process. This is a fundamental departure from the system's usual way of approaching policy and program development. The resiliency of the system is evident in at least these two illustrations.

e. Stochastic processes

The ability of the policy to order the subsequent sequencing of events or to increase the probability of future events is found in the uniform fee determination policy. At one level, the policy, with its detailed procedures, guidelines, and even newly developed forms, tremendously increases the predictive power to make things happen — to increase the probabilities of conformance in uniform fee determination. At another level, the process itself has likely strengthened the position of the Community Mental Health Board in relation to the agencies it funds. The agencies' growing compliance, and the board's clear statement of its authority, will likely impact the manner in which future contract negotiations occur, the environment in which further policy statements are issued, and the always tenuous line between the agencies' self-determination and the goals of the funding source.

On the other hand, the long-run probabilistic events may differ largely from the scenario above. The board has consistently called upon contract agencies to collaborate with each other and work cooperatively to plan and implement services. That encouragement has largely taken hold as a result of the board's power as a funding source. Now, however, if the contract agencies become increasingly more independent as a result of increases in client- and third-party fee payments, there will be a lessening of dependency on the board and perhaps less of a tendency for collaborative efforts. As the board's leverage rests less on its funding potential, it may need to establish alternative leverage based on its expertise in such areas as planning, programming or evaluation.

4. Discriminatory Factors

This section will consider implications of the content or process for issues of sexual identity and preference, ethnic and racial identity, age, and economic status.

The fee policy could result in a significant decrease in utilization of mental health services by the poor. The elderly, many of whom rely on fixed incomes and live on the margin of or in poverty, often hesitate to use mental health services, fearing social stigma. They are also often reluctant to reveal personal financial information to strangers, let alone provide verification that they are telling the truth about income. Similarly, the poor, many of whom also have strong reservations about utilizing mental health services, will be reluctant regarding the verification requirement. Of the agencies serving the poor in Cascade County, many are small; For these agencies the cost of initiating the complex billing procedures would be a financial hardship offering little opportunity for cost recovery. Thus, we could reasonably predict cutbacks in such agencies, which would result in decreased services to the poor.

The situation described above may explain the high level of resistance by these agencies during the policy development process. The policy may ultimately result in a decrease in services to the poor and the elderly and could eventuate in the merger or termination of some smaller agencies.

The policy could work its toll on female clientele of the mental health system inasmuch as women are overrepresented as clients in the system in comparison to their numbers in the county. Given the fact that being black or a single head of household, for example, geometrically increases one's chances of being poor if one is a woman, the policy could take a hard toll on female clients.

Summary

This case illustration has reviewed the development of a uniform fee determination policy by a county community mental health board for an entire county mental health system and its twenty-five contractual provider agencies. By observing two attempts at developing the policy, each with a different strategy, we have obtained additional insights.

Case 8: Policy Process and the Downtown Mall

This case illustration extends the discussion of content analysis begun on this policy topic in Case 3 and the values analysis provided in Case 6. Case 8 applies the outline, "Process Elements for Analyzing Small-Scale Policy."

1. The Policy and the Problem
The reader may recall that this situation involves a community concern over the use of the Downtown Mall by various groups in the community. There is particular concern about the relationships between the "mall people" (i.e., residents of a correctional half-way house, youths, developmentally disabled citizens working at a sheltered workshop in the area, some senior citizens, and some persons on aftercare from the state hospital), merchants, and other visitors to the mall. City Commissioner Frances LaRose proposed a policy, as follows:

> It is the policy of the City of Rapid River that all citizens of the community shall have equal access to all public facilities associated with the Downtown Mall; that the civil rights of no citizen of the community will be violated by any policy or procedure related to any activity of any public or private group while associated with the Downtown Mall; and that all ordinances of the city and laws of the State and Federal governments shall be observed insofar as those ordinances and laws pertain to conduct of citizens on the mall.

Our analyses in Case 3 and Case 6 offered the possibility of a complementary policy that would provide social service supports to some of the "mall people" and a public education program for others associated with the mall. The goal of each approach is to create an environment in which everyone in the community finds the Downtown Mall an attractive and satisfying place while, at the same time, the rights of all citizens are honored, the responsibilities of all are properly carried out, and the opportunities for community pride and development are maximized.

The mall, a combination of pedestrian walkways on a closed thoroughfare and arcades housing shops and meeting places, was constructed with both public and private funds. Some city agencies and businesses guard their investments jealously. Some see the mall people as a threat to the ongoing viability of the mall; others view them positively, seeing the creation of a mall environment that is functional for all elements of the city as a challenge. Our present analytic task is to gain understanding about the process aspects of policy development in this situation.

2. Milestones in Policy Processes
This section will review key events evident in the policy process.

a. Charter and legitimacy
The key concepts providing impetus to policy action here are entitlement to free access, protection of property rights, maintenance of the public good, equal opportunity for participation, and provision of adequate supports to all elements in the system. The latter are all potential elements in the charter—the valued ends that motivate policy action. While competing priorities surround these valued ends at any one point in the life of the policy process, they will have to be pursued in an integrated fashion if the policy process is to succeed.

Each of these conceptual goals has its own source of legitimacy. The regulatory and enforcement approach of Commissioner LaRose's proposal is based on the right and responsibility of city government to take legislative and administrative action. The service approach is legitimated by mandates for service agencies—particularly state and local public agencies—to provide more than custodial care for its clientele. In fact, these agencies are mandated to provide services as the least restrictive alternative to institutional care.

The City Commission has the unquestionable right to take the action implied by Commissioner LaRose's proposal and, while some citizens may not approve of the particular strategy, commission prerogatives in this proposal are not at issue. The service agencies may have to educate funding sources and/or various publics regarding the propriety as well as the responsibility to undertake the services strategy; nevertheless, the agencies possess the necessary legitimacy, if not the actual support, to take action.

b. Action system

The group initiating change in the policy system is comprised of an active member of the Downtown Merchants Association, Commissioner LaRose, and a staff member of the Human Relations Office of the city administration. There have been some encouraging preliminary discussions with the chief of police, the director of the Community Mental Health Board, and the president of the Rapid River Adult Foster Care Home Owners Association. But the impetus for action has come primarily from the original three: one merchant, the city staff member, and Commissioner LaRose have clearly been the generating force for policy change.

c. Key participants

The regulatory and enforcement strategy required by Commissioner LaRose's proposal requires the broader participation and cooperation of many key elements, such as the police and court agencies, as well as the entire downtown business community. Key decision makers and proximate policymakers in all of these areas must be involved to arrive at a workable policy.

The service and enforcement strategy requires participation of correctional, mental health, public welfare, school, transportation, and housing agency officials. The participation of local officials in these areas would be appropriate, at least in the early stages. Due to the authority structure in funding and program approvals, state-level officials may also have to be brought in at a later time.

The key participants mentioned thus far will need to play either technical roles such as developing plans and procedures or interactive roles such as bringing various essential elements together. At least two other significant elements are present in this policy process — the various media in the community and the Community Welfare Planning Council, a companion agency of the United Fund. Each of these elements will play system spanning or integrative roles. The Community Welfare Planning Council has the opportunity to bring together numerous key decision makers from a variety of organizations and associations in the community, many of whom are intricately involved in decisions regarding the design and finance of public and private health and human service programs. The integrative function of the media will not only be crucial in helping the public to understand the problem but also in determining the approaches to resolution that the public will support.

3. Interest Group Relations
This section will focus on particular groups whose interests are affected by the policy and consider relevant group interaction.

a. Power and influence
In a legal sense, the City Commission unquestionably has the power to control the outcomes of citizens' behavior with respect to establishing viable ordinances. However, the influence of the commission — the actual exercising of that power — depends upon the commission's ability to be an *effective* leader. Within its legal boundaries, the commission controls the policies and procedures of the Public Safety Department, the Human Resources Office, the Transportation Department, and all affairs pertaining to use of the public portions of the mall.

The issue of power — the ability to control the behavior of others — held by the merchants rests more on the personal efficacy of certain individuals, which is based upon local history that includes many issues other than the mall and the many inter-dependencies found among and within the business community. The leadership that the business community brings to bear on problem resolution will probably emphasize a combination of future commercial development, recognition of the needs of all citizens, and prudence in financial investment.

The power of the health and human services elements of the community is extensive in terms of *their* ability to control the outcome for the mall people. This power relates directly to the condition of the mall people in that agency policy, proce-dures, and resources intimately affect the nature and quality of services provided. However, the service agencies' ability to exer-cise that power (their influence) is greatly controlled by many other elements in the community. Some merchants, city offi-cials, the Community Welfare Planning Council, and the media *all* have many opportunities to exercise control over the commu-nity's agenda and the level of funding for virtually all social services programs.

b. Salience of the issue

Perhaps the most important dynamic in this policy problem is the salience of the issue. The "problem" of the Downtown Mall has high valence, i.e., value and investment, to a whole range of elements in the community. Whether one is a responsible pub-lic official, an entrepreneur, a service agency staff member, one of the individuals under scrutiny, or merely a citizen observer, the "Downtown Mall problem" is important. The issue cuts across geography, ideology, income, and time. This level and quality of issue salience suggests that *something* will certainly happen in the way of policy change. The investment is too great for too many people for policy action not to occur.

c. Intergroup activities

The broad salience and potentially integrative nature of this particular issue suggest that extensive intergroup relationships are necessary. Issues of public access, successful commerce, the special needs of particular population groups, community aesthetics, and pride are all intertwined, as are the groups that represent those interests and/or responsibilities. To date no ongoing task force or coalition exists to deal with these problems. The city manager's office, the Community Welfare Planning Council, or even one of the special interest agencies could assume leadership in bringing these elements together. However, no institutional arrangements are in place in the community to bring these various elements and interests together on a regular basis: their interaction is likely to be dictated by ad hoc strategies for solving particular problems.

Our analysis will now consider some particular aspects of intergroup interaction.

1. Unilateral transfers versus bilateral exchanges. Were only one of the policy approaches (i.e., regulation and enforcement or supportive services) to be taken, the reward of opportunity and burden of sacrifice would be unilateral. If only the regulatory and enforcement approach were taken, there would be a bilateral or multidirectional "giving up" of many existing ways of dealing with the problem. For example, a specific "mall person" whose behavior violated the rights of others would be forced (more directly) to give up such behavior. However, this would not solve the problem of the dissatisfaction that some people feel about other, legal behavior on the mall. If only the supportive service strategy was taken, the burden would rest only on the mall people to either change their behavior or cease to frequent the mall.

The tandem policy approach suggests a bilateral (more democratic) sharing of responsibility for change. All elements— the city, merchants, and the mall people—would have to participate in various ways to resolve the problem. The rest of the public, hopefully all participant-observers, would also have to make certain adjustments.

There are incentives for each of these elements to make the necessary adjustments. A refusal to participate and make such changes could signal the ascendancy of any one group and impede the community goal of providing an environment that is attractive and satisfying to all elements concerned.

2. *Bargaining and negotiating.* The main vehicles for policy change will be extensive negotiating among all elements. Particular issues for negotiations would involve the City Commission, city manager, and the Department of Public Safety addressing the clarity of the policy and the adequacy of resources to be provided for its regulation and enforcement. Given the probable changes in working conditions for the police force, some collective bargaining efforts may be necessary to alter some of the terms in existing agreements. Commitments would have to be made by and with individual business people and the Downtown Merchants Association on the negotiating strategies to be employed. Turf issues are also likely to arise: negotiation about service domains and obligations would be necessary for the health and human services agencies.

3. *Coalition building.* The nature of the problem, given its diverse auspices, authority, investment, and incentives unquestionably speaks to the necessity of formal coalition building. However, it will be extremely important to recognize that each party in a coalition has a right to expect that individual and/or group interests will be respected and not surrendered to the goals of the coalition. Thus, group self-interests will be recognized, but all in the context of achieving the community goal.

4. *Contracting.* Inasmuch as some of the local funding agencies (e.g., mental health) provide services by contracting with existing community agencies, it would be necessary to contract for certain services identified in the policy process, e.g., behavioral management training and transportation skills training. Furthermore, many local agencies' contracts with state agencies would need to be renegotiated or approved spending plans would have to be modified. Such contractual changes may require new funding and in others an authorization to transfer resources from one program line to another.

Another contracting issue could arise in that one agency or a coalition of agencies may have to assume contractual responsibility to oversee and/or coordinate future plans and policy. The probable parties to such a contract are unclear at this time.

4. Process Resources

This section will focus on the resources needed or observable in the policy process.

a. People power

The salience of the issue for the community has generated a range of interest in seeking a solution. The self- or group-interests of the range of elements in the community has meant and will assure active participation in problem resolution. Efforts of key partisans will not be lacking!

b. Technology

The regulatory aspects of Commissioner LaRose's policy approach will require new efforts in monitoring to assure citizens' rights, which may entail developing a monitoring and compliance mechanism of some sort and putting reporting procedures in place. The enforcement aspects of monitoring will undoubtedly require the addition of more uniformed foot and car patrols in the Downtown Mall area.

The supportive services strategy will require staff experienced in behavior training, operation of either daytime activity programs or day treatment services, developing and packaging public education programs in the human service area, and operating a crisis counseling service that would be immediately available for trouble situations. These are some of the activities that will demand new programs and staff with additional skills, plus the requirements of space, virtually all of which will need to be in the downtown area.

c. Finances

Regulatory and enforcement costs could come from community block grants, while other costs could be borne by shifting some city staff from other programs. Such shifting would affect staffing at the city manager's office, the city Department of Transportation, and the Department of Public Safety.

Costs for supportive services could come in part from the city's general revenue sharing funds. Funding from the correctional services area and the mental health system would likely entail a transfer of state hospital funds budgeted for local programs. This would be possible by reducing the local share of the charge back to the county inasmuch as the support programs would presumably allow for reduced institutional costs, thereby channeling some funds for community programming. That is, the county's net cost for care would be lessened, since the county would be paying for community care rather than institutional care. Some financial support would be available in the form of reduced rental costs for locating services in the downtown area since some vacated facilities adjacent to the mall would be available at very reasonable rates.

The opportunity costs of doing nothing would be considerable to all elements. Some would argue that the avoidance of regulation and enforcement could mean the loss of the central commercial district, and that the absence of supportive services will surely mean higher institutional care costs for some mall people who are otherwise maintained in the community.

d. Time

Time is a valuable commodity in this problem resolution since much will have to occur by way of citizen participation and in program planning. The costs of time in public review and debate will be an invaluable investment in terms of ultimate support. Interagency cooperation and planning will require considerable time but will have long-range effects in bringing agencies together to serve the community in this problem area, an area heretofore neglected. Moreover, successful service efforts over time could create a ripple effect that would expand community support for health and human services in general.

---

5. Congruence with Desired Values
Refer to Case 6 for a review of the policy and the problem in the context of value elements.

Summary
This case illustration has reviewed the process elements of policy development regarding the distribution of rights and privileges involving the city's Downtown Mall. A two-pronged approach to the problem, regulation and enforcement of citizen behavior, along with providing supportive services to the mall people, has emerged. The content and value elements of this issue were reviewed in cases 3 and 6, respectively.

7

Essentials in Presentation of Policy Analysis

In chapters 4 through 6, we focused entirely on the elements of policy *analysis*. Our sole concern has been what goes into the analysis of content, process, or the values implicit or explicit in social welfare policy. A range of elements have been identified for the analyst's consideration, first an analysis of the substantive content of actual or proposed policy content, then a review of the essential value issues to be considered in social welfare policy, and finally an analysis of the processes that occur in the development of policy. Thereafter, a number of detailed illustrations were provided. The reader has no doubt found that our analyses in each of these three areas have been detailed and lengthy. However, we cannot apologize (one cannot ignore the complexities of the real world). Our message now is to note that if we are to communicate our analyses to others, we must include issues of form and style in our presentation of these analyses.

Our presumption here is that we analyze policy in order to inform, teach, influence, and perhaps even persuade. Indeed, as Paolo Freire (1972) has noted, all education is a political act, and policy analysis is certainly aimed at educating others. We are not so naive as to suggest that policy analysts are value-free technicians able and desirous of cranking out enlightenment. As professionals policy analysts not only engage in these activities for personal edification or professional development but as a service to others, whether a client group, an agency director or supervisor, a policymaking board, a county commissioner, city council members, or a state legislator. However, the analysis of social welfare policy is but one part of the task of professional social welfare policy analysis; the other part is the task of effective communication of policy analyses to those we serve. Policy analysis is merely an academic exercise if we are not able to effectively communicate the analysis to people who need to be informed, persuaded, or educated.

In citing a study conducted by the University of North Carolina Department of City and Regional Planning, Ziter noted that policy practitioners coming from all levels of government felt inadequate in the communication and process skills that their work required of them (Ziter, 1983). Yet, in Ziter's own study with public welfare officials in Utah, and with the North Carolina sample, policy analysts reported spending from eighteen to twenty-five percent of their time providing written and oral presentations to professionals and approximately one-third of their time providing written and oral presentations to laypersons (Ziter, 1983, p. 47). In a study of oral, public presentational skills of social workers in the state of Michigan, Flynn and Jaksa (1983) found that both managers/administrators and direct service practitioners felt that they lacked necessary skills in presentation of policy material and were highly motivated to develop these skills through in-service training or staff development. Presentational skills, then, are very much complementary to the exercise of policy analysis skills.

Much of this presentational activity takes place in political arenas. As Mahaffey (1972) points out, certain barriers exist for social workers, for example, in working in these environments. Some of these barriers are limited knowledge of governmental structure and process, a disdain or aversion to "politics," lack of patience with procedures, and an inability to empathize with the many viewpoints presented by decision makers. Yet the proper form and style of policy presentations are very much interrelated with these environmental realities.

In this chapter, we will focus on three particular types of presentations of policy analyses: (1) the organization of written legislative analysis, (2) the presentation of oral testimony, and (3) the development of position statements. These three forms of presentation are most commonly used as the vehicles by which policy analyses are communicated in the social welfare context.

Legislative Analysis

For our purposes here we refer to legislative analysis as the analysis of policy or policy proposals that are made or under consideration by those who make policy decisions in a legislative arena. The most obvious environment for such presentations is state senates or houses of representatives. We are often called upon to make policy analyses available to state senators or representatives, or to their representatives—who might be conducting studies or investigations. However, these same analyses might also go to state administrative agencies that are in the process of becoming knowledgeable about the issues encompassed by our analyses.

Furthermore, legislative analysis is not restricted to the arena of state legislatures. Legislation and legislative analysis occurs in city councils, county commissions, and the board rooms of various voluntary and private organizations, such as the United Way and community councils. These are precisely the types of small-scale, local-level arenas in which policy analysts are called upon to communicate their products. When any of these groups are in the process of decision making, legislation in its own particular context is being developed and policy analysis is one of the essential techniques for helping those decision makers who are involved in developing such legislation.

Giving Testimony

Human services professionals are sometimes called upon to provide their analyses during formal studies or investigations.* On these occasions, the analyst (or some person representing the organization associated with the analysis) is usually called upon to make an oral presentation. These presentations of policy analysis make demands upon the style and form of communication. (These demands will be discussed in Chapter 9.) Testimony can be provided in a range of environments such as: a city council's hearings on allocations for general revenue sharing or block grant funding for human services; a community mental health board's ad hoc task force; or a state commission. These are only a few examples.

---

*Our treatment of the topic of giving testimony here does not include testimony in an administrative hearing or a court of law. These situations are of a different type and purpose; they are primarily to decide issues at law by employing rules of evidence in making decisions concerning fact. Our treatment here refers solely to testimony in *legislative contexts*.

Position Statements

Position statements are another way of communicating policy analyses. They may be directed at legislative sessions or during the conduct of hearings. Position statements may also be issued to the general public or to news media. They may take the form of lengthy and detailed position papers, brief press releases, letters to the editor of newspapers, or they may be presented to specific individuals. A position statement is more likely than legislative analysis or testimony to have the intention of influencing by both informing and taking a stance on a particular issue. Position statements present certain considerations in addition to those presented by legislative analysis and the giving of testimony. These matters will also be considered in Chapter 10.

Organizational and Interorganizational Analyses

The reader is reminded that the outlines for content, values, and process (see chapters 4, 5, and 6) may also serve as models for style and content for presentational purposes. However, we must add the caveat that these outlines are too detailed and, most of all, jargon bound for special purpose use, such as providing analyses to state representatives or city council members, giving testimony to a county budget and finance committee, or issuing a position paper for an action group. The outlines, while practical for internal use as models for presentation, are primarily intended as guides for surveying the essential elements of content, process, and values. The reader is reminded that, when policy analysis is conducted at the service or request of another, the analysis must be "packaged" in a way that effectively communicates what has to be said; otherwise, the analytic effort has value only to the analyst and not to those who will depend on it for taking action.

Policy analyses conducted for one's supervisor, agency executive, board of directors, or interagency action group are preferably presented with the detail and in the form of the outlines of analysis in Cases 1 through 8. That level of detail may be appropriate when it is "kept in the family," so to speak. In these instances, much depends on the time available, conventions or expectations in a particular agency for conveying information, the amount of detail expected, and so forth. What we wish to focus on in this and in subsequent chapters are those situations that require special style and form in the vehicle conveying the analysis.

Essential Characteristics of Policy Presentations

Social welfare policy analyses must be knowledgeable, thorough, and technically sound. However, it would be erroneous to assume that each analysis possessing these characteristics will automatically be positively received. The approach used to convey an analysis, in order to be effective, must first and foremost have credibility if it is to have the desired impact upon its target. Credible analyses can be characterized as those which are perceived by the receiver to include a sufficient number of the essential elements relevant to the issue(s), are comprehensive and inclusive of the appropriate variables and information and yet, are provided in a form and style that are comfortable and usable. Before providing direction on the form and style of legislative analysis, testimony, and position papers, this chapter will explore some of the features of form and style that are generic to all three types of policy presentation instruments.

The Form of Policy Presentations
There are a number of possible formats for policy presentations. For example, legislative analysis and position papers differ in shape and/or structure. However, some issues of form should be addressed in the development of *all* policy presentations. These issues are: (1) identification and sponsorship of the analysis, (2) simplicity and clarity of the policy statement, (3) the presentation's basis in sufficient historical or contemporary background; (4) balanced argument; (5) projections of impact; and (6) to some extent size or length of the policy document or oral presentation.

Identification and sponsorship. The presentation should first offer a clear statement identifying the author(s) of the analysis and the agency, organization, or group sponsoring it. The identification of the analyst could include job title (and mailing address if giving a presentation to a public body at a public hearing) but should not include details such as other titles, and should be devoid of credentialism. Often opportunities arise to offer other information on one's preparation or credentials relevant to the issue at hand and credentialism is not the proper or effective way to establish credibility. On the other hand, credibility is in part established by being clear about the organizational base from which the analysis emanates. Here it is important to identify your unit, office, agency, or group so that the target of the presentation has the proper context for your analysis.

The policy statement. The next item of form to consider is that there be a clear statement "up front," in brief but adequate terms, of the proposed policy or the remedial action being proposed. Generally speaking, a policy analysis is aimed at an individual or a group of decision makers who are considering or are about to take some action. That action may even be to maintain the current status or form of an existing policy. Nevertheless, the reader or listener should be clear in his or her mind at the outset, regarding what the policy under analysis is about and, particularly, what action is proposed or favored. In fact, as a matter of form and strategy, it is well for the analyst to consider physically placing the policy statement and/or proposed action in the very beginning and again at the end of the presentation. Placement at the beginning is not only a practical aid to those asked to consider the analysis, it is also an aid in establishing the analyst's credibility since the reader or listener is clearly informed of what the analyst is proposing. Additional placement at the end of the presentation provides another way of summarizing the issues, the analysis, and the proposed action.

Recognition of background issues. Very few issues in the area of policy analysis stand alone and are not in some way interdependent with previous or contemporary issues in the system. The policy presentation should, again as briefly as possible, give some recognition to those issues when they are relevant. This recognition communicates a number of things to the target of the presentation: first, that the analysis is based upon a knowledgeable and informed understanding of the issue(s) surrounding the policy under consideration; second, that the analyst has the interest of the target in mind by providing orientation or education about related matters or is at least reminding the target of the relevant issues involved; and third, that the analyst is attempting to be helpful in establishing his or her credibility by providing concrete evidence that he or she takes the interest of the target listener or reader at heart, and is not simply pursuing some unknown self-interest.

Balanced argument. In some instances the analyst is not expected to take a position or to offer recommendations, but in others the opposite is true. It is, of course, extremely important for the analyst to be clear about this expectation—to be clear about the charge or the assignment, and the position or role in which he or she has been placed. Put simply, the analyst should be clear about his or her own rights and responsibilities, depending on the authority and assumptions under which the analysis is being provided.

It is generally worthwhile to know what the issues are in a balanced argument and whether those "opposites" are actually articulated in the presentation. At the very least, by "doing one's homework," the analyst is more knowledgeable, better prepared to answer follow-up questions, and again, gains credibility for being knowledgeable and honest. At the other end of the continuum, when the presentation of analysis is not aimed at urging social action or at persuasion, the analyst should present arguments for, as well as against, the relative merits of the choices or courses of action under consideration. After all, policy analysis has as its purpose the enlightenment of people in the process of problem solving. While it is true in argumentation and debate—and in political struggle—that it is incumbent upon the proponent of an idea or action to offer the "warrant" or convincing claim or proof, honesty and adequacy of information are still key in presentation of policy analyses. Clearly if one is taking a position, there is no expectation that that individual will provide convincing arguments for "the other side." However, when taking a position is not the function of the analysis, a balanced presentation is essential.

Projections of impact. Assuming that most decision makers are honest people trying to meet their responsibilities and do their job, the analyst plays a key supportive role. The decision makers should be well advised about the impact of a particular choice or course of action, and the policy analyst should be helpful in "speculating out loud," so to speak, about the potential effects of the decision. It is also important to consider the possible unintended as well as intended effects of the decision. This does at least two things for the target of the presentation. It helps to put the decision back into perspective. People do not make choices just for the sake of making decisions; rather, choices are made because people want some outcome to occur. By providing statements of impact the analyst helps to focus on the fundamental purpose of the decision and the accompanying analysis. A second function of identifying impact is that it is consistent with the complementary functions of the decision maker and the analyst. The decision maker needs information to make the best decision possible in all good faith; the analyst is there to provide that information. By shedding light on both intended and unintended possible consequences of the policy action, the interests of both parties (decision maker and analyst) are served.

Size or length. It is very difficult to give any rules of thumb regarding size or length except to say that the presentation should be as short as is reasonably possible but yet include all necessary information. Generally more space and time are available for the more lengthy and detailed analytic presentations provided for internal use. Prior experiences about what the agency, the staff, or the group usually needs helps us to determine what is appropriate. Furthermore, when something is developed internally, it can always be reduced in time or size with early feedback.

Complex detail cannot be irresponsibly reduced to meaningless minima. Yet, the analyst must acknowledge the reality that he or she may have little time on the stage when the actors are busy people, perhaps themselves playing many roles. When the analyst has been invited to provide an analysis, and if there are not a number of competing issues or interests involved, it may be reasonable to "think big" to some extent and not be parsimonious. In such instances the analyst plays more the role of a consultant. However, in many policy analysis situations, there is limited time and space and the policy analyst is in competition with others for those resources. Consequently, we might think in general terms of legislative analyses being approximately two single-spaced or four double-spaced typewritten pages. Testimony, which should be available in both oral and written forms, should be no longer than five minutes. (If those receiving testimony or conducting the hearing desire more time, especially for their own questions and interchange, it is their prerogative.) The oral and written presentations should contain the same information. Position papers probably vary the most in length. When directed at the media, they should be no longer than one and one-half pages. If a position paper relates to a very technical matter and is being presented to a study commission or committee, the paper can and should be much longer than the other types of presentation.

The Style of Policy Presentations

Other considerations in presentation of policy analyses are equally important; they cannot be classified as matters of form, layout, or particular categories of content. These considerations might be called the *logical necessities* of policy analysis, and they should be reflected in policy presentations. Patti and Dear (1975) refer to the necessity of being timely, balanced, responsive to the request, and focused on relevant alternatives. We will focus here on the requirements of objectivity, languaging, targeting, inclusiveness of key variables, consistency with relevant values and goals, and appropriateness to the policy under study.

Objectivity. A policy analysis, professionally provided, should aim at being objective and factual. This is not to say that a policy presentation, where appropriate, cannot make recommendations and take positions. However, even when positions are taken, the analysis and its manner of communication should be as objective as possible and based upon best estimates of what is factual. This means that the analysis and its presentation must be descriptive and analytical and that "feeling" arguments (e.g., "I feel" or "we feel") are neither appropriate nor helpful in achieving the desired ends. We do not mean that values do not enter into analysis. Indeed, we have stressed that point in earlier chapters. Mahaffey (1972), in speaking of lobbying, makes the point well in noting that values and philosophy can only be maintained by social action that proceeds with clearly defined objectives by carefully relating means to ends. This suggests that valued ends are pursued in a context of norms requiring objectivity and specificity.

Languaging. The policy analyst has a difficult task, since the subjects of analysis are often complex problems involving very technical issues. However, to the degree possible, the analytic presentation should employ words that the average individual would understand. With the omnipresence of the photocopier and visual media, and now the advent of computer transfer of text files, the audience for one's analytic presentation grows and becomes indeterminable. While the target or primary audience must be kept in mind, it is often impossible to know by whom or how an analysis will be used at some point in the future. Furthermore, explanations contained in the analysis should, as much as possible, be complete, simple, and fully understandable.

Targeting. As was just noted, the policy analyst must always have the particular target of the analytic presentation in mind. This factor is primarily emphasized by Dear and Patti (1981) and Kleinkauf (1981). This could mean determining what particular issues might be relevant or what perspectives might be important to the person or group commissioning or receiving the legislative analysis, testimony, or position paper. Recognition of these factors is important in the key words, idioms, special symbols, or images that are used in the presentation. Policy analyses are not only undertaken for resolution of a problem; they are also undertaken for people. The people who are targeted for analyses must be kept in mind when deciding how to communicate the analysis.

Smith (1979) has stressed the importance of knowing, for example, a legislator's role conception (or orientation) as a key variable in the decision process. For instance, Smith notes that a legislator's self-concept may be that of facilitator, neutral person in an issue, or resister of change. From another perspective, the decision maker may be more program- than policy-oriented. Knowledge of these role conceptions is very helpful in developing and presenting the analysis.

Inclusiveness of key variables. The previous chapters—devoted to content, process and values—had as their purpose the task of being reasonably inclusive of the variables generally thought to be relevant to all social welfare policy analyses. It is the analyst's responsibility to determine which of these elements are essential and to show the target of the presentation that the relevant elements or variables have been adequately considered. At a minimum this would include consideration of who the proposal or policy is designed for, what the existing level of need is, the level or scope of the remedy recommended, its cost, delivery mechanisms, resource requirements, and method of administration. Two other special considerations are often overlooked, the first of which is offering suggestions, or at least giving recognition to what possible measures might be established a priori to assure the decision maker that the accountability needs can be honored. Making suggestions also gives the analyst an opportunity to be creative and offer evaluation approaches that could be considered humane, appropriate, or consistent with the values of the profession. The second special consideration is that changes in policy often create a ripple effect regarding need for subsequent administrative rules or guidelines for programs or people ultimately pursuing the policy goal. Consequently, the style of policy analysis presentations should make visible, to the extent possible, the implications of a policy decision in terms of future needs for change.

Consistency with values and goals. We have already said a good deal about values in policy analysis. What we want to emphasize here is that the presentation of policy analyses should be made in ways that are consistent with dominant social and professional values. When the policy choices are in conflict with those values, the policy analyst has an obligation to make such realities known to the target of the presentation. In the same vein, the analysis should help the analyst and the target see the extent to which the proposed policy or option might actually be in concert with the original goals set forth by the overriding policy or the program currently in existence. First and foremost the policy choice must relate to and not be in conflict with the basic needs of individuals or groups.

Appropriateness. Lastly, we will consider the category of appropriateness since certain matters must be attended to in presenting an analysis that speak to the question of good common sense. Here, for example, the analyst should remember that the analysis and its presentation must reflect the fact that social problems that are rooted in multiple causes cannot generally be remediated by one simple approach. Or, complex problems cannot be solved by simple solutions reflected in naive policy. Another consideration is that massive needs usually require massive amounts of resources. Yet another consideration is that the policy solution proposed or selected must be internally consistent with companion policies related to the same problem. Given the truism that all things in real life are interrelated, no policy stands totally alone.

Summary

This chapter has drawn attention to the fact that analyses are not only conducted about problems or choices but are also conducted for people. Furthermore, issues involved in the communication of analyses must be addressed to maximize the effectiveness of the analysis. This chapter has set forth a number of essential elements in presentation of policy analyses, particularly those matters related to questions of form and style. Those elements are summarized in the general outline, "Form and Style in Policy Presentations," which follows. Subsequent chapters will include more specific guides to providing legislative analyses, giving testimony, and presenting position papers.

Form and Style in Policy Presentations (An Outline)

1. *The form of policy presentations*

a. Identification and sponsorship
b. The policy statement
c. Recognition of background issues
d. Balanced argument
e. Projections of impact
   (1) Intended
   (2) Possible unintended
f. Size and length

2. *The style of policy presentations*

a. Objectivity
b. Languaging

c. Targeting
d. Inclusiveness of key variables
   (1) For whom the policy proposal is designed
   (2) Existing level of need
   (3) Level or scope of remedy
   (4) Cost
   (5) Delivery mechanisms
   (6) Resource requirements
   (7) Method of administration
   (8) Evaluation
   (9) Need for consequent rules or guidelines
e. Consistency with values and goals
f. Appropriateness

8

Legislative Analysis

This chapter will deal with the task of developing legislative analyses—those policy documents aimed at informing and/or influencing those involved in the decision-making process in legislative arenas. We particularly want to remind the reader that these decision processes occur at the local level; thus, by "legislative analysis" we are not only referring here to analyses of propositions being considered by state and federal legislatures. In the practice of social welfare policy at the local or small-scale level, there are a number of situations in which policy practitioners require written presentational skills that can effectively convey policy analyses. Some of these possibilities were mentioned briefly in chapter 7. For example, a member of an interagency coalition may be asked by the United Way board of directors to develop an analysis of a proposed new policy for governing United Way membership requirements. A social action group may need to develop a formal written analysis for presentation to a county board of commissioners considering a policy decision to reorganize the county's human services system. A staff member of a city human relations department may be called upon to present an analysis of a proposed city ordinance regarding the use of a particular block grant program or the limitations to be placed upon a tax abatement policy. A neighborhood organization may wish to present its analysis of a proposed zoning ordinance to a planning commission. These are but a few examples wherein human service professionals have an opportunity to become a part of the legislative process through the preparation, development, and presentation of legislative analyses.

Legislative Processes

Our purpose here is to provide practical aids in the development and presentation of legislative analyses, not knowledge or skill regarding participation in legislative processes. However, it is important to recognize the fact that effective legislative analysis does not occur in a vacuum. It happens in the context of local customs and rules about how legislative proposals are introduced; how they are formally (and informally) considered and/or adopted, how lobbying occurs, and so forth. Legislative analysis is not a static technical skill and event; it is a dynamic and processual phenomenon. Legislative analysis also takes place in the context of lobbying—knowing how a proposition becomes official policy or a bill becomes law. Other related concerns might involve knowing how to tap into a decision-making network, knowing how to draw upon informational resources, and being able to determine the proper timing for intervening into the process with one's analysis. While these concerns are themselves topics of a whole range of literature, it would be well to consider a few of them in the special context of legislative analysis.

Lobbying

Lobbying is that set of events that surround the bringing of organized information and influence to bear upon the decisions suggested by a legislative proposal. As mentioned earlier, there are a number and variety of factors involved in effective lobbying. However, in relation to legislative analysis, we must stress that there is homework to be done by the policy analyst which is really a part of the development of legislative analyses (see Dear and Patti, 1981). The analyst should try to determine when and why the proposal was introduced, by whom, and for what reasons. Formal drafts of the proposal must be obtained. Thus, one must do a considerable amount of work prior to developing the analysis.

A very important step is to determine, perhaps through a committee aide, legislative assistant, the city or county manager's office, or the agency's public communications officer, the sequencing or timing of a number of key events. For example, the analyst needs to know the routines used by a decision-making group vis à vis the sequencing of important events, such as whether, when, and how the matter is first considered by a particular committee, subcommittee, or administrative office. Being knowledgeable about these events/factors not only provides early opportunity to gather information but also helps the analyst to begin building his or her own timetable for when the analysis must be completed and may also offer some suggestion regarding the content as well as style and form likely to be most effective. Having attended to these details, the policy analyst might be able to clarify any questions about committee procedures and timetables and, consequently, be in a better position to determine the best time(s) to introduce the legislative analysis.

We have provided a general characterization of the need to tune into the process of lobbying. The key concept here is that each legislative process has its own peculiarities, and legislative analysis demands learning what they are; legislative analysis is thus one part of the lobbying process.

Use of Informational Resources

A good analyst recognizes personal and organizational limitations and routinely develops and uses regular sources of information. A good habit to develop is to routinely contact the proposers of a policy or piece of legislation (e.g., legislative aides or administrative assistants, council members, directors, etc.), not only to solicit their opinions but to ask for references regarding their sources of information. When governmental policy is being proposed, the administrative branch is also likely to be preparing analyses. It is helpful at such times to identify, for example, the person or office within the State Department of Health, or the city's planning department, or the public liaison officer who serves as a contact person, in the absence of or in addition to using one's own organization's internal resources. Then, of course, there are the usual library and computerized resource systems. Newsletters of associations or various interest groups are excellent resources in helping the analyst determine the positions held by competing interests surrounding a policy decision.

A Habit of Doing One's Homework

There are volumes and courses of study surrounding the whole area of legislative and other political policy processes. Our task here is not to summarize them. Rather, it is to develop helpful outlines for analysis—at this point legislative analysis in particular. The key point is that the associated activities such as lobbying and resource utilization are not one-time events. Effective, thorough, and credible legislative analysis are a reflection upon the individual's or group's sensitivity to the processual aspects of the policy effort. The analysis is also a reflection upon those who routinely, as a matter of course, make it their business to become familiar with these processes and resources so that their analyses have a "goodness of fit" with the milieu. When the proposed legislation, ordinance, or policy appears to be outside of the analyst's realm, he or she is well advised to bring in those who understand or are sensitive to key issues, procedures, or symbols in that particular policy environment. Put simply, get someone to help with the homework.

A General Outline for Legislative Analysis

As with all presentations of policy analysis, the legislative analysis document must address the standard set of who, what, when, where and why questions—sometimes called the "five 'W's." Then, too, the analyst should at least consider the whole range of elements suggested in previous chapters using the content, process and values guides. However, for the analysis to be reasonably considered by busy people who are likely to have a number of analyses to review, it must be *packaged* in a way that meets the mutual needs of both the provider and the reader of the analysis—the analyst (or the group that the analyst represents) and the decision maker. To be reasonably well received, the analysis cannot be a simplistic summary of complex events; neither can it be a voluminous dissertation. It must reflect work that has thoroughly considered a wide range of issues in sufficient depth; yet, the legislative analysis must also be compact and to the point.

The standards described above may seem impossible to achieve. Nevertheless, the outline on the following pages attempts to be as thorough as the analyst ideally should be. This outline has been applied by many students and the author, over time and in its many forms, to a variety of legislative policy situations. There are other forms to be used, especially if one is completing a policy analysis as a staff member of an administrative agency of government. However, we should first look at a more generalizeable format for legislative analysis. After that, a case illustration will be provided.

Statement of the Policy Proposition(s)/Provision(s)

As with all other types of analyses, the legislative analysis should begin with a clear, uncluttered, and brief statement of the law, rule, policy, proposition, or guideline that is being proposed. What is being proposed or is under consideration should be uncomplicated and clear to all who read the analysis. It should be stated in only one or two sentences and should be as free as possible from jargon or without reference to concepts that would be unknown to the reader, particularly to those readers who are decision makers—but also the general public.

The Proposer(s)

The person(s) or group(s) sponsoring the policy proposal should be identified, particularly in terms of their formal positional titles and/or organizational affiliations.

Authority or Legitimacy

The analysis should identify, early on, the statute, ordinance, board directive, licensing requirement, or other source of authority or legitimacy for the existing and proposed action that has a bearing upon the action to be taken. Identifying the source of authority will suggest the opportunities and/or constraints for action that might exist and help the decision makers to more readily determine their prerogatives and range of latitude.

General Concepts

This is the main body of the analysis. This portion should clarify and enumerate the concepts that particularly relate to this particular proposal. This is where the analyst can summarize the shape and nature of the problem that exists or characterize the proposal offered as a remedy. This section should make clear why this particular approach is proposed and how the methods or means proposed are presumed to be particularly suitable to the matter under study. This is also the point at which factual data can be brought in, along with an explicit discussion of the value considerations. Some possibilities for discussion are the way the problem is stated, to the implications of the means to be employed if approval or passage is obtained, and/or to the departure from or congruence with prior conceptualizations of the problem or ways of dealing with the issue.

The analyst should take care to bring out the background factual data while giving focus to the central issues. Specifics concerning implications for financing for the target, client or service systems, and the possible arguments for or against the proposal, should come later and separately in the analysis.

Intended and Possible Unintended Effects

Next, the analysis should speak fairly and objectively to the intended and possible unintended effects of the proposal upon the target, client and service systems, indicating the potential impact upon each. It should also shed light on the potential ripple effect upon existing administrative rules, guidelines, companion policies, or other requirements or programs associated with the proposal.

Fiscal Implications

Assuming that human cost issues have been addressed, fiscal implications should then be considered. The analysis should not only shed light upon the revenue and expenditure aspects of the proposal, but also upon the fiscal implications of *not* taking action (i.e., the opportunity costs).

Advantages and Disadvantages

This section should list, in very concise fashion, the arguments both for and against the proposal, unless the analyst is trying to persuade the readers or listeners to adopt a recommended course of action. In that case, the burden of raising counterarguments rests with the proposal's critics. The analyst should also identify which groups and organizations, if any, have taken positions for or against the proposal or any of its provisions. Preparation and presentation of this material is helpful for the analyst in development of the background information and serves as a practical support service to the decision maker as well.

Recommendations

Depending upon the charge and task given to the policy analyst, this section should be the only point at which the analysis purposely takes a position. If the analysis is developed at the request of an executive director or a board of directors, the recommendations may suggest what the agency should do, and why. On the other hand, if the analysis is being prepared for a county commissioner or state representative, the recommendations may speak less directly to organizational interest and more to a range of interests. The important point here is that the analyst may be expected to take a position, and have every right to make recommendations, but these recommendations must be identifiably separate from the rest of the analysis.

Author's Identity

The final statement should identify the author of the analysis, not only to provide a signatory but also to offer a convenient way of announcing to the reader who might be contacted for further information. Cosignatories may be required in some administrative agencies; this matter will be addressed when we consider analyses provided by administrative agencies of government.

Our outline, then, would be as follows:

A General Outline for Legislative Analysis

1. Statement of the Proposition(s)/Provision(s)
2. The Proposer(s)
3. Authority or Legitimacy
4. General Concepts
5. Intended and Possible Unintended Effects
6. Fiscal Implications
7. Advantages and Disadvantages
8. Recommendations
9. Author's Identity

We will apply "A General Outline for Legislative Analysis" to the illustrations in Cases 9 and 10. Case 9 deals with a uniform fee schedule proposed by a community mental health board and is analyzed from the perspective of a contract agency offering field-based services to elderly citizens. Case 10 deals with analysis of a piece of state legislation, written from the perspective of a local substance abuse services agency, involving the decision of whether to make application as a local screening program.

Before beginning, however, we will discuss one other legislative analysis situation with its own set of distinguishing characteristics. This is the situation wherein the policy analyst, a staff member of an administrative agency of government, is asked to provide an analysis of a piece of proposed legislation. Often, when a piece of legislation is proposed by a legislator (e.g., a state senator or representative, city commissioner or council member, or county official), a civil servant employee is called upon to provide an analysis of the policy proposal. This situation differs from the others in that the administrative agency (e.g., the State Department of Public Health, the City Planning Department, or the County Human Services Department) is also a part of government. That agency may currently administer some aspect of the program to which the legislative proposal is addressed and/or may have some responsibilities in the future regarding that proposal.

In some instances, this situation may bring a set of factors into play that are somewhat different than those discussed at the beginning of this chapter. The legislative analysis will become a public document and may be taken by some as being the department's (i.e., the administrative agency's) position on the policy proposal. A question may arise about the agency's role or position in the policy proposal, i.e., whether the agency sponsored, supports, or opposes the bill. (Also, an analysis should give some estimate of the general effect of the proposal upon the responsibilities already assigned to the administrative agency.) The analysis may, on the one hand, be developed solely for top-level agency management or, on the other hand, may serve as an informational piece for all agency staff members, other agencies, and/or the general public. Consequently, while the analysis may be developed by the policy analyst, the document itself may be signed or countersigned by a designated responsible agency official. The actual analyst may or may not be identified as an additional source of information. Those elements discussed earlier in regard to other legislative analyses would also be considered in such an analysis as well as the following questions:

1. What is the bill number or title of this proposal and who is the sponsor?
2. What existing legislation, rules, or policies are directly related to this bill/proposal?
3. Was the bill/proposal introduced at the agency's/department's request?
4. For whom is the bill/proposal designed and what is their need?
5. What is the intent of this bill/proposal and what are some possible unintended effects?
6. What are the potential programatic and fiscal implications of this bill/proposal?

7. What are the values implications?
8. What are the arguments for and against (or advantages and disadvantages) of this bill/proposal?
9. What is recommended as the agency's position?
10. Who is the author?
11. Who is the agency's responsible person?

With these questions in mind, the following checklist should be of value in providing an analysis of proposed legislation written from the perspective of a governmental administrative agency. This checklist will be applied in Case 11.

A Checklist for Legislative Analysis by Governmental Administrative Agencies

1. Bill number and sponsor
2. Related legislation and/or rules
3. Agency's role in the request
4. Target of bill and level of need
5. Intent of the bill
6. Potential programatic and fiscal implications
7. Values implications
8. Arguments for and against the bill
9. Agency's position
10. Author/signatory
11. Responsible person

Case Illustrations

Case 9: Legislative Analysis—Uniform Fee Schedule

The following case application will demonstrate the fact that legislative analysis at the local, small-scale level need not be restricted to policy developed by a state or federal legislature. We will use our illustration from Case 7 on uniform fee determination as the example.

The reader might recall that, in the Case 7 situation, the Cascade County Community Mental Health Board had established a system-wide policy for all contracting agencies, entitled "Policy and Procedures for a Uniform Method of Determining Ability to Pay." In this illustration of a legislative analysis we will take the perspective of Seniors, Inc., one of the twenty-five local agencies contracting with the Mental Health Board. Seniors, Inc. provides services in the mental health system's outpatient services category, which in this situation consists of a variety of field-based mental health services to citizens fifty-five years of age or older. Among these services are case and program consultation, educational services, counseling and psychotherapy, case management, volunteer services, and information and referral services. You are one of the program managers of the agency and have been assigned the task of providing an analysis of the Community Mental Health Board's proposed policy, which has been circulated among contract agencies for a sixty-day review and comment period.

1. Statement of the Proposition

The Community Mental Health Board has proposed a policy stating that those receiving services from the mental health system shall be assessed a fee to contribute to the cost of services provided. A sliding scale based on ability to pay is proposed, and a procedure for fee waiver is established so that individuals not able to pay will not be refused service. The recipient of service is required to present verification of income and, if full or partial fee waiver is requested beyond that provided by the sliding scale, the individual is to present verification of hardship. Refusal to do so will result in the recipient being billed for the full amount of services. Individuals having insurance carriers that provide reimbursement for mental health services are required to sign a standard assignment of benefits/release of information form or incur the cost of services themselves. Proposed procedures outline methods for implementing the policy, the process wherein exceptions may be made, and a description of the fee waiver process.

2. The Proposer

Impetus for the policy has come from the Cascade County Community Mental Health Board which, in turn, has been required by the State Department of Mental Health to take policy action in this area.

3. Authority or Legitimacy

The authority for such an action is clearly provided in Chapter Seven of Act 129, the State Mental Health Code, which provides that the department (or its designees) have the authority to establish fee schedules and bill recipients for services. Furthermore, the "Standards for Community Mental Health Services" provide that each county board has the responsibility for developing and implementing clearly defined mechanisms for the collection of fees from clients and third parties ("Standards," p. 27). While the proposed policy is within the state department's and Cascade board's authority, there is some question about whether Section 4 of the "Standards" contains certain constraints. Provisions allowing the use of fee collection agencies to secure payment on delinquent accounts may, in fact, be a violation of Section 4 of the "Standards," which protects clients from disclosure of their identity as service recipients to any organization or individual without their written permission. This limitation on agency authority needs further clarification.

While the proposed action is within the legal prerogative of the local board, this policy and set of procedures is a radical departure from the historical posture of community mental health regarding client fees. The relatively unilateral nature of the policy, while within the authority of the Cascade board, is also a radical departure from normally accepted community practice in Cascade County.

4. General Concepts

This policy is directed at two separate but associated issues related to the community's mental health system. The first is the Cascade Board's desire to develop uniformity in fee-setting and billing and collection procedures within the service system. The second has to do with generating new sources of revenue in order to maintain the level of client services in the face of reductions in available state dollars. The emphasis is on placing more responsibility for payment upon the recipient and/or third parties (including Title XIX) and more responsibility for implementation upon the contract agencies. Presumably, the policy is also aimed at achieving equity among the recipients of services in the state and the county.

The sliding scale approach is presumably aimed at pegging fees to the individual's ability to pay and is also based upon the assumption that such an approach will not be a deterrent to a person seeking or receiving services. The policy's procedures concerning verification are also presumptive of the fact that individuals cannot be counted upon to provide accurate financial information short of proof through such means, for example, as providing an affidavit attesting to the accuracy of information provided.

5. Intended and Possible Unintended Effects

The intended effects of the proposed policy would appear to be fundamentally fiscal in nature—to expand the financial resource base of community programs. While some professional literature suggests that therapeutic and/or motivational value may be attached to fee-charging, this does not appear to be an intended effect here.

However, the policy could result in a significant decrease in utilization of mental health services by various target populations. The elderly are often hesitant to utilize mental health services, fearing social stigma; many rely on a fixed income; others are reluctant to reveal personal financial information to strangers. Additionally, many minority clients and those of lower socioeconomic groups already have reservations about the mental health services' responsiveness to their needs and would be even less likely to seek services. Thus, this policy initiative could further deter many individuals from utilizing programs that are available.

The proposed policy could also deter development of innovative mental health programming. Workers in field-based settings such as nursing homes, apartments, and residential facilities would have to engage clients in fee determination discussions in an atmosphere where such conversations would be neither comfortable nor appropriate, and in many cases could be detrimental to the development of a therapeutic relationship. An alternative might be for clients to travel to an office setting (thereby defeating the purpose and style of field-based approaches), or perhaps initiation of such approaches as telephone/mail contacts. The latter would also probably discourage service utilization, would not increase revenues, and the staff time required would still need to be funded.

The policy appears to be conceptually based upon the image of practices traditionally found in outpatient clinics and hospital settings. In services fundamental to Seniors, Inc., such as case management and consultation, the client is sometimes the family, sometimes an organization, or even the mental health system. The goals and services are not easily cost billable to the client or a third party. An unintended effect may be a move backwards into traditional approaches to providing clinical services to individuals.

6. Fiscal Implications

Assuming the maintenance of the same level of case activity, the policy would generate new revenue or at least replace revenues lost through reductions in state funding. Sources of such revenue would be individuals and third party payees. Funding generated would differ from agency to agency, depending upon variations in cost per unit of service, the economic level of the clientele, and the uniformity of criteria actually applied in assessing full and partial fee waivers.

All contract agencies would incur billing costs and increased reporting costs. Those agencies without such procedures in

place would incur substantial front-end costs, generally ranging from $7,000 to $12,000 annually.

7. Advantages and Disadvantages

Possible advantages of the proposed policy would include
increased funding for mental health services and greater
independence for Cascade County contract agencies. Also,
those who utilize service would more routinely pay for at least
a portion of the cost directly, an approach which may be more
attractive to the taxpayer. Lastly, the policy would assure uniform procedures, thereby increasing the likelihood of systematically obtaining certification for Medicaid billing.

Disadvantages would include the startup costs for the contract agencies, both financial and with respect to staff morale,
each of which could result in a deterioration in the quality of
services offered. There may be reduction in service utilization
by some high-risk or high-need groups, e.g., the elderly, the
poor, and minorities. Some innovative field-based programming
may be discouraged due to the difficulty of implementing the
policy in nontraditional settings. Finally, this radical departure
from encouraging individual program development and
management by community agencies may fundamentally alter
the service system's manner of cooperation in program planning and provision.

8. Recommendations

The following recommendations might be considered by
Seniors, Inc.:

a. That the Cascade County Community Mental Health Board
   be encouraged to delay implementation of the policy until
   more detailed information is available on the assessment
   of possible outcomes for all agency clientele.
b. That analysis continue in special areas of consideration, especially service utilization by the elderly, the poor and minority
   citizens; also, the financial cost of implementation should
   be further assessed in light of the current budgetary strains

already felt due to reduced allocations in each of the agencies.

c. That the County Board obtain an attorney general's opinion on recipients' rights issues concerning confidentiality and the use of fee collection agencies.

d. That a task force be convened, comprised of contract agency personnel, Cascade Board staff, and other appropriate community groups to: **(1)** consider and examine other sources of revenues, and **(2)** review other means of adapting current and proposed fee policy procedures.

(Signed)

Position or Title

Date

Case 10: Legislative Analysis — Screening Application

The application of the legislative analysis outline in Case 9 illustrated a policy that was developed and proposed by a local funding agency and analyzed from the perspective of a contract agency. In Case 10 we will look at another situation often requiring legislative analysis, i.e., when an agency needs information on the content of a piece of legislation prior to making a decision or taking a position.

In Case 10, Crisis Services, Inc., an agency that provides alcohol and drug abuse rehabilitation services in downtown Arapahoe City, is exploring the possibility of becoming a designated screening agency for the State Department of Substance Abuse Services. Before making application to the state, the executive director of Crisis Services, Inc. has asked for an analysis of the legislation and appropriate recommendations.

1. Statement of the Provisions

Public Act 410 (P.A. 410), particularly Section 222(8), provides that, before imposing sentence upon an individual for particular violations, the court shall order screening and assessment by a person or agency designated by the State Department of Substance Abuse Services to determine whether the individual is likely to benefit from rehabilitative services, including alcohol or drug education, and alcohol or drug treatment programs. The court may order the individual to participate in and successfully complete one or more appropriate rehabilitative programs and require that the person pay for the costs of the screening, assessment and rehabilitative services.

2. Proposer(s)

This law, introduced in the last session of the state senate as Senate Bill 803 by Senator Ralph Kline (D., Crystal City), was part of a "package" of three bills supported by the State Department of Substance Abuse Services aimed at stiffening the penalties for drunk driving in the state. The primary organization supporting the legislation, in addition to the State Department, was People Against Drunk Driving (PADD), a national organization with local chapters in the state.

3. Authority or Legitimacy

This program is authorized by state law, particularly P. A. 410, Section 222(8). Should Crisis Services, Inc. become a designated screening agency, authority would derive from P. A. 410 and the administrative rules developed under that act and administered by the State Department of Substance Abuse Services.

4. General Concepts

P.A. 410 requires, after someone has been convicted on either a charge of Operating Under the Influence of Liquor (OUIL) or Operating While Intoxicated (OWI) that, prior to sentenc-ing, the court shall order that individual "to undergo screen-ing and assessment by a person or agency designated by the Department of Substance Abuse Services" to determine whether he/she might benefit from an alcohol or drug treat-ment and/or rehabilitation program. If the screening and assessment agency determines in the affirmative, then the court may order, as a part of the sentence, that such person suc-cessfully complete one or more such programs.

The basic purpose of the "package" of three drunk driving laws enacted during that period was to attempt to decrease the high number of deaths and injuries on state streets and highways caused by drunk driving. The basic assumption under-lying P.A. 410 is that stiffer punishment of drunk drivers is not enough; they also need treatment and/or rehabilitation so that they will no longer be a public menace when they are driving.

5. Intended and Possible Unintended Effects
a. On targets (persons convicted of drunk driving)

Persons convicted of drunk driving who may not other-wise be willing to get treatment or rehabilitation will now be required in many cases to seek such services. P. A. 410 pro-vides a very strong incentive for such persons. The law will hopefully result in a decrease in the number of deaths and in-juries and in an increase in the number of persons treated or rehabilitated. Private medical and automobile insurance car-riers will need to determine whether they will cover the costs of court-ordered assessment, treatment, and/or rehabilitation, which could result in higher premiums. The courts, particu-larly probation departments, will need to work more closely with substance abuse treatment centers (such as Crisis Serv-ices, Inc.), which, in turn, should bring about increases in staff workloads.

If a person has neither sufficient funds to pay the costs of screening, treatment, or rehabilitation nor a third party to pay such costs, this legislation could impose a very real hardship—particularly on low income groups. It could result in refusals of or negative attitudes toward services.

b. On intended service systems

P. A. 410 will likely increase the number of clients who come for services to agencies prepared to deal with these problems. Given the current economic situation, P. A. 410 may counter the effects of reduced state funding cutbacks by helping such agencies survive current funding difficulties. On the other hand, the legislation could cause even more financial difficulties for these agencies since some may be confronted with clients who refuse services or clients who are unable or unwilling to pay for services already received. Furthermore, whether or not they are able or willing to pay, clients coerced into obtaining services are not likely to cooperate fully in the service process.

6. Fiscal Implications

If the Detoxification Unit of Crisis Services, Inc. were to become qualified by the Department of Substance Abuse Services as a screening agency, a staff person who meets the state's qualifications for screening agents would have to spend time with persons referred from the courts. Therefore, we will need to determine: **(1)** how many OUIL/OWI (i.e., "drunk drivers") would be referred to the agency for screening and assessment each month; **(2)** whether the county court would be willing to collect the screening fees from the offender and then reimburse the agency; and **(3)** what the standard fee for screening and assessment would be. Current estimates obtained in discussions with state agency personnel suggest an average of fourteen cases per month for this agency, that the billing process may be negotiable, and that the fees have yet to be established.

Since these costs must ultimately be paid by the offender, the financial burden on those who do not have adequate insurance coverage, especially the poor, will be substantial. Unless the courts are willing to underwrite the costs in those instances, it will be difficult for substance abuse agencies to admit such persons into their programs and survive financially.

7. Advantages and Disadvantages

There are some merits in making application to become a screening agency under P. A. 410. Although becoming a screening agency may not be cost-beneficial per se (given the potential difficulty in collecting screening fees), the agency might receive clients for the Detoxification Unit and the Turnaround Program who might not otherwise come to these programs. Also, from a public relations standpoint, it would be useful to become a screening agency, if for no other reason than to develop a closer working relationship with the courts. Finally, it would be consonant with the goals of the agency to become an active part of a statewide effort to reduce deaths and injuries caused by drunk driving.

There are also sound arguments against making such application. First, it probably would not be cost-beneficial — at least at the outset — until some of the aforementioned problems are resolved. A major portion of at least one staff person and perhaps a number of staff persons' time would be required at the outset and screening fees would probably not cover these costs. Second, the agency could find itself receiving an increase in the amount of "difficult" or unwilling clients due to the coercive aspect of the legislation.

8. Recommendations

The agency would do well to continue negotiations with the local court, since the latitude for working within the provisions of state law seems to reside at the local level. This particularly pertains to the considerations mentioned earlier regarding the expected rate of referrals/intake, the court's willingness to collect fees, and the actual fee schedule related to our agency's cost per unit of service. Keeping in mind our agency's mission, and the potential effects on community relations, the agency should continue to explore the matter.

(Signed)

Title or Position

Date

Case 11: Legislative Analysis—Rule Impact Statement

In Case 11, the state legislature is considering a bill aimed at improving the economic climate affecting opportunities for the development of small businesses. The bill is in the House Commerce Committee and, while it may seemingly be unrelated to social services affairs, it could unquestionably affect two existing statutes involving the licensing and regulation of out-of-home care facilities for children and vulnerable adults. As a staff member in the State Office of Regulatory Services, you have been asked to prepare a legislative analysis of the bill for review and possible approval by the director of the office and the director of the State Department of Social Services. We will use "A Checklist for Legislative Analysis by Governmental Administrative Agencies" in this analysis.

Date

1. Bill Number and Sponsor
House Bill 6077 is sponsored by Representative King et al. and, at this writing, is being considered by the House Commerce Committee.

2. Related Legislation and/or Rules

The proposed legislation would amend P. A. 508, the State Administrative Procedures Act, by altering the procedures under which administrative rules are developed and promulgated by the state's administrative agencies as those rules pertain to small businesses. The proposed legislation would also result in alterations in P. A. 118, The Child Care Facilities and Programs Act and P.A. 222, The Adult Foster Care Facilities Act. Consequently, the rules for Operation of Child Day Care Centers, Children's Foster Care, and Child Care Institutions would also be affected.

3. Department's Role in the Request

The bill was not introduced at the department's request.

4. Target of Bill and Level of Need

This bill has been designed for owners of small businesses in the state. It includes small businesses operated as for-profit child care facilities and is designed to benefit the small, independent entrepreneur by reducing regulatory requirements on business operations.

5. Intent of the Bill

This legislation would require administrative agencies to prepare a "small business economic impact statement" when proposing new rules. The purpose of such statement would be to assess the cost impact of proposed rules on small businesses. The legislation also encourages administrative agencies to reduce unnecessary costs to small businesses by such actions as reducing compliance requirements and exempting these businesses from the proposed rule where appropriate. An example might be exemption of a child day-care center from minimum parking space requirements.

There is no evidence that the intent of the bill is to include such business activities as the provision of out-of-home care. However, "small business," as defined by House Bill 6077, would include virtually all of the child day care, child residential care, and adult residential care facilities currently licensed by this department.

6. Potential Programatic and Fiscal Implications

a. This bill would affect all licensees providing day care or residential care for children, and for adults in residential or long-term care. In this state, those licensees serve more than 150,000 children in day care homes and child care centers, over 5,000 children in residential child caring institutions, over 300,000 children in summer camps, over 20,000 adults in residential care facilities and 35,000 adults in long-term care facilities.

b. The bill could reduce the level of protection to the vulnerable citizens served by these licensees if the definition of "small business" in H. B. 6077 is not altered.

c. This bill would affect the State Departments of Public Health and Mental Health with respect to their regulatory responsibilities and in terms of the citizen populations for which they provide programs.

d. The bill would not result in any savings to the department. Considerable staff resources would be required to research the economic impact of proposed rules on the providers of residential or day care, long-term care, and medical services. Substantially lengthened rules would probably be required in many situations, resulting in considerable cost to state government. Consequently, this legislation would require additional staff.

7. Values Implications

To some extent, this bill is an expression of free enterprise and the maximization of opportunity for the small business entrepreneur. It also represents a creative attempt to generate business activity in the state and, therefore, to increase state revenues, and is an expression of current political attitudes toward government regulation. However, unless the bill is altered to specifically exclude providers of out-of-home care from the definition of "small business," the bill is not consistent with the mission and goals of the department, i.e., providing protection for vulnerable citizens.

8. Arguments For and Against the Bill

Given the present climate of economic activity in the state, a boost to the business community would be very welcome at this time. It would also necessitate looking at existing administrative rules and, perhaps, require a reassessment of the need for some of these rules. On the other hand, lacking a redefinition of "small business" to exclude providers of out-of-home care, the bill is unacceptable to the department in its present form, because it interferes with the protection of children and vulnerable adults in out-of-home care situations.

9. Department's Position

The Department supports the proposed legislation, with amendments, for the following reasons:

The bill clearly intends to reduce the regulatory burden faced by small businesses. In the present climate of economic uncertainty and hardship, this may be an important goal. While the department does not oppose such an intent, it cannot support this bill as it presently stands because of the adverse effect it would have on the vulnerable citizens served by the licensees and the services provided by various private and public agencies.

This proposed legislation is not designed with health or human services issues in mind. It is not appropriate to subsume the provision of out-of-home care under the definition of "small business" as provided in the proposed legislation. It is believed that, over a period of time, the health, safety, and welfare of hundreds of thousands of vulnerable children and adults receiving care from some of these facilities would be jeopardized as a result of this legislation.

The Department recommends that H. B. 6077 be amended, specifically by addition of the following language in Section B (2): "excluding those persons or businesses that provide day care and residential care for children and adults, as provided for in P.A.118 and P.A.222"

Director
Office of Regulatory Services

Director
State Department of Social Services

Prepared by:

(Signed)
Title or Position
Date

9

Giving Testimony

While chapter 8 dealt with the development and organization of written legislative analyses as a technical support function, chapter 9 will deal with oral presentations of policy analyses. Generally speaking, the policy analyst could present the analysis of social welfare policy in oral fashion in such forums as a speech to a community group or professional association or a radio interview. Public communications involve special considerations and the policy analyst would do well to prepare for the unique requirements of each. However, these matters are properly the topic of another time and space; each, in itself demands specific public communications skills. For our purposes, we will focus on the giving of testimony as a means of communicating policy analyses.

Some essentials of presentation were considered in chapter 7, particularly those matters having to do with form and style. However, the political contexts of oral presentations via testimony in a policymaking environment demand special consideration.

Types of Testimony Situations

Giving testimony occurs in three basic situations, i.e., judicial, administrative, and legislative. The first refers to testimony in a court of law and may generally be thought of as oral presentations having to do with the search for and affirmation of facts; consequently, giving testimony in the judicial situation is not generally a policy analysis function. Though there may be times when an expert witness is asked to give opinions on policy-related matters, oral presentation of policy analysis is not the main function of testimony in judicial situations.

Legislative testimony is most likely to occur during the development of proposed legislation, ordinances, and municipal policies and is what most of us commonly think of as "giving oral testimony." When the policy practitioner gives testimony it is also likely to occur in administrative situations. It may occur in quasi-legal situations such as the conduct of fair hearings, appeals from administrative action, and development of administrative rules. The first is similar to the search for facts in judicial hearings and is not the focus of this chapter; the third, e.g., hearings on proposed administrative rules or the presentation of policy positions on budget matters, are both situations wherein the policy practitioner may be called upon to give testimony. The latter are situations in which the policy analyst is called upon to orally present the analysis of social welfare policy.

While the outlines provided in preceding chapters may serve the analyst well in preparing for oral testimony, the actual oral presentation will likely be relatively brief and short. Considerations of time and length are extremely important and even limiting. Nevertheless, the need to communicate the basics of who, what, when, where and why is no less important or compelling.

Basic Essentials of Giving Testimony

Beyond the basic "Five 'W's," Wilcox (1973) has noted the special characteristics of most technical oral presentations. For the policy analyst, this means being aware that the analysis is likely to be directed at a narrow, special audience, such as a committee or staff group, but not ignoring the presence of unintended audiences. Since testimony-giving is often time-limited, there are very real constraints on what should be included or emphasized. Also, testimony is likely to demand instant understanding, unlike a written report that can be reread or discussed. Consequently, special attention must be given to the use of the voice, the use of language, and the use of transitions and imagery.

A most important distinguishing characteristic of testimony is that its intent is apt to be persuasion rather than communication of facts. This is not to say that a values orientation and/or social change are not inherent in other forms of policy analysis. However, persuasion is generally both the explicit and implicit purpose in legislative and administrative testimony. This is perhaps why Haskitt gives particular attention to the need for credibility in giving testimony.

According to Haskitt, the provider of oral presentations must obtain a high rating in three essential credibility areas: competence, trust, and enthusiasm. Since testimony-giving is listener-centered, the analyst must help the listener to accept not only the content of the analysis but the personality and/or technique of the person providing it (Haskitt, 1973). Consequently, the presentation of policy analyses in these situations makes special demands of form and style as well as substance. In speaking of the presentation of testimony at budgetary hearings, Wildavsky emphasizes its unique interactive nature and even speaks of the analyst's wisdom in role playing or rehearsing the hearing and the testimony in advance (Wildavsky, 1964).

Rules of Thumb for Testimony (A Checklist)

Given these overall considerations, the following rules of thumb are offered as a checklist in developing or preparing testimony that involves policy analysis. The policy analyst, in offering testimony, should:

1. Recognize the importance of protocol for some people and in some situations. It is generally best to assume that protocol is important for everyone until or unless the analyst learns otherwise. This means maintaining a demeanor which, without being officious, stiff, or arrogant, conveys firmness and confidence.
2. Not be dogmatic. There will probably be value dilemmas or ethical choices to be made in a particular position.
3. Visualize dealing with both a listener (through judicious use of words, symbols, images, and phrases introducing new concepts) and a reader (by using explanatory headings, obvious outlines and/or numbered or labeled items).
4. Remember that, in real life, only small gains are possible or probable. Many competing interests shape a compromise, and no analyst is likely to be magically persuasive.
5. Be aware that he or she may have to return to deal with the same set of actors about the same or other issues.

6. Be critical of ideas or concepts but not of people and rarely of organizations. The key here is to know how to disagree without being disagreeable as a person or as a group. This means, among other things, not using ad hominem arguments, avoiding the use of straw man approaches, and not resorting to the "imperial we." At the same time, be firm and clear about one's own position.

7. Educate those receiving the testimony about the essential front-end assumptions of his or her position and provide the necessary basic information without talking down to people or being pedantic.

8. Be truthful, and avoid expressing personal opinions.

9. Speak slowly, audibly and distinctly, avoiding jargon, sarcasm, and gratuitous humor.

10. Do preparatory homework by learning about the positions of those who will hear the testimony, having a working knowledge of both the central and peripheral issues involved, and, *especially,* being technically prepared in the subject area.

11. Be specific regarding concerns and the proposed remedy.

12. Anticipate the probable criticisms.

13. Be prepared to share written copies of the testimony with hearing committee members and the media.

14. Follow up the testimony with a note or message of some kind to the hearing officers, expressing appreciation and, once again, briefly reiterating the position.

While this checklist is by no means inclusive of all that might be considered, it can serve as a basic inventory of considerations, as well as a tickler for other matters for the analyst to consider when providing testimony. Regardless of the particular list of dos or don'ts that might be used, the important point is that a variety of interactive considerations, in addition to the substantive content and process elements, are brought to bear in the testimony environment.

Organization of the Testimony

The next consideration is the organization of the analysis. The least ambitious approach could include a statement of the identity of the person or group offering the testimony, a brief position statement, and a summary of background information, followed by an explicit statement of recommendations for action. The testimony should be preceded and followed by an expression of appreciation for the opportunity to be heard and an offer of help by the person providing the testimony.

A more elaborate, though not complex, format has been suggested by George Sharwell in which a brief introduction is followed by a body of testimony comprised of three main parts. The first is a statement of the most important point, including the rationale for the position taken and mention of the flaws in opposing arguments. The second is mention of the least important point, along with its rationale and the flaws in opposing arguments. The third part is the second most important point, along with its rationale and the flaws in opposing arguments. The testimony ends with a brief closing statement. The two strategies, which are not mutually exclusive, aim at "winning" on the merits of one's own argument, or by default in showing that the opposing views are not (as) credible (Sharwell, 1982). It should be noted, however, that Sharwell's outline was recommended particularly for legislative testimony presentations to a state legislature.

Given that our interest here is in the more general question of giving oral testimony in a variety of situations, we do not recommend a particular format. However, for "all seasons" purposes, the following checklist might be considered adequate for structuring the giving of most testimony, keeping in mind that the analyst might make appropriate adjustments as indicated by the particular circumstances.

A Checklist for Legislative or Administrative Presentations of Testimony

1. Identification of the person or group offering the testimony
2. Statement of appreciation to the hearing committee
3. Brief statement of position
4. Summary of issues, including lack of merit in alternatives
5. Statement of recommendations for action or preferred position
6. Offer of future assistance by the person or group

Case Illustration

Case 12 provides a simple and uncluttered sample statement of testimony given by Mrs. Alice Willer, president of L. R. Vincent Homes for Children, Inc., concerning a state house bill regulating the practice of surrogate parenthood. The testimony is being given before a hearing held by the house judiciary committee.

Case 12: Giving Testimony— Surrogate Parenting (Con)

Testimony by

Mrs. Alice Willer, President
L. R. Vincent Homes For Children, Inc.

before

The House Judiciary Committee
State House of Representatives

on

H. B. 5293 – The Surrogate Parenthood Bill
(Date of Presentation)

Mr. Chairman, and members of the Committee, I am Mrs. Alice Willer, President of L. R. Vincent Homes for Children, Inc. The L. R. Vincent Homes is a nonprofit service offering substitute care for children, organized by a statewide federation of local agencies, each of which is guided by a citizens' board of directors. We thank you for giving us this opportunity to present our views on House Bill 5293.

The member agencies of L. R. Vincent Homes across the state strongly oppose in principle the practice of surrogate parenthood and strongly oppose the Surrogate Parenthood Bill.

H. B. 5293 is not in the best interests of the child since:

1. only the wants of the childless couple are considered,
2. the physical, emotional, social, and legal protection needed by the child is denied,
3. the likelihood of subsequent legal entanglement for the child is created, and
4. the status of the child is relegated to that of a commodity.

H. B. 5293 is also not in the best interests of the other parties involved since:

1. all parties are vulnerable to subsequent unpredictable legal actions,
2. the natural emotional attachment of the mother to the new-born infant is denied,
3. a dual class system for adoption will be created due to the economic realities involved, and
4. the identity of each of the parties is not adequately protected.

L. R. Vincent Homes for Children, whose mission is to provide protection and appropriate care for the unprotected child, and whose concerns also extend to the safeguarding of human welfare in general, cannot support H. B. 5293 as an amendment to the continuance of the present adoption code. We urge your complete rejection of this bill.

Thank you, again, for your time and consideration. May we also extend our offer to assist you in any way in your study of this matter. We have provided the Clerk of this Committee with copies of our statement, attached to which is the name, address and telephone number of our Executive Director and myself, should you wish to contact us further.

10

Position Statements

Position statements are yet another way of communicating policy analyses. Whereas testimony is offered orally, position statements are offered in writing. Furthermore, position statements, as the name implies, are unequivocally a manifestation of a person's, group's, or organization's stand on a particular issue. While a legislative analysis or testimony may provide a clear position on an issue, the analyst need not take a position in either instance, since both may be for the purpose of providing technical education. In the case of position statements, however, the express purpose is persuading or taking a stand.

The term "position statement" is used here to mean policy analyses that are committed to writing and aimed at persuading decision makers to choose a specific course of action. Therefore, we include what are generally referred to as position papers — which may be relatively brief statements or lengthy documents. Also included are news releases, which can also serve as notices of testimony having been given or a position statement having been released. (On the other hand, a press release may stand alone as an announcement of a newsworthy event.) Another example of a position statement might be a letter, such as a letter to a decision-making group or to the editor of a newspaper. Each of these instruments serves as a unique vehicle for presenting the analysis of social welfare policy.

As with the more detailed or inclusive applications of the content or process outlines (see chapters 4 and 5), or with the development of legislative analyses or testimony, position statements must also be concerned with credibility, accuracy, and knowledgeability, and must pay attention to matters of style and form. Again, the context of the situation will determine some unique aspects of style and form. The position statement, however, allows the furthest deviation of all presentation forms from the expectation of a balanced argument or position. This is not to say that the position statement can ignore facts, realities, or the use of common logic; it does mean that a position statement, identified as such and not introduced deviously, is expected to take sides on an issue. Consequently, the person or group offering the analysis needs to determine whether or not they have the right or authority to take the position and whether the desired (social action) outcome will be positively served. Given the legitimacy for taking action via a position statement, the analyst must be cognizant of the fact that analysis then moves to purposive change in a way that is more goal-directed, assertive, and unilateral than other forms of policy analysis. This is important to remember since, once the analyst chooses to attach more value to a particular position and use the analysis and the associated technical information and process skills to achieve the desired end, the risk of the analysis losing credibility becomes greater. It is easy to become righteous or sanctimonious when one has studied a matter thoroughly and a position has been carefully thought through. If the analyst is mindful of this risk, the opportunity for effective use of the analysis is enhanced.

Discourse Management

Steiner (1977) has suggested that policy development is given direction by what he calls the process of "discourse management." Discourse management is said to be comprised of three elements: (1) descriptive premises, (2) value premises, and (3) prescriptive conclusions. Discourse management is the process in the development of social policy wherein the descriptive and value premises of analysis are integrated with prescriptive conclusions. Descriptive premises are the statements that the analyst derives from observation, study, and classification of what is analyzed. One might say descriptive premises are the conclusions reached from observing empirical phenomena as a result of one's policy analysis. Value premises, on the other hand, are statements which communicate the preferences of the person making the observations. For Steiner, prescriptive conclusions (i.e., statements of what ought to be done or what course of action should be taken) should be derived from careful development of descriptive and value premises. Overemphasis or exclusion of any of these elements of discourse management impedes policy development (Steiner,

1977). A position statement properly developed and presented is not only a vehicle available to the analyst but, given adequate and balanced attention to the elements of discourse management, it can be an effective tool for social action and change. An effective policy analyst will be clear in identifying and separating the descriptive premises from the value premises and will base the conclusions chosen upon a logical connection between the three elements of discourse management. The presentation of position statements forces the analyst to clearly articulate the premises and desired conclusions and fosters responsible dialogue. This is not to deny the other power and influence aspects of social policy processes; it merely gives focus to the value of these technical and processual aspects of policy, and position statements have a particular function in this regard.

Types of Position Statements

Tropman and Alvarez (1977) identify at least four different types of written instruments used in social welfare policy related work. The first two deal with relatively specific and known audiences: correspondence, such as letters, agreements, memos; and program records, such as minutes, logs and reports. The last two tend to have less clear targets or audiences. These are publicity documents, such as flyers, brochures, or newsletters; and substantive documents, such as position papers or study reports. Each of these types and examples has some relationship to the presentation of policy analyses. For our purposes here, the applications with particular implications for the communication and presentation of analyses are position papers, press releases, and letters.

Standards and Pitfalls in Form and Style

Before proceeding, we will consider expectations and dangers inherent in written position statements that go beyond the essentials considered in earlier chapters. Some of these relate to all three approaches; some are unique to the particular type of presentation. Bromage (1973) makes the point that some issues in written communication may be either pitfalls or effective tactics, depending upon their conscious use. These tactics evolve around the use of:

1. *Abstract words.* These require the reader (or listener) to visualize the concept and supply the specifics. They may be effective in some circumstances or leave too much to the reader, depending upon the issues, the nature of the reader, and other factors.

2. *Passive voice.* This could separate the identity of the person taking the position from the issues involved in the position; it could also make the statement less personal, which may or may not be desirable depending upon the particular circumstance. The general rule is that position statements are written in the third person.

3. *Bland language or cliches.* These tactics may also depersonalize or, in the case of cliches, help the reader see what he/she expects or hopes to see; they may also make the position taken or its associated arguments appear sterile or trite.

4. *Jargon.* It is not a good idea to unnecessarily use jargon. However, jargon sometimes makes the simple seem complex or vice versa. Jargon may help move the process to a desirable outcome from a political perspective but it does not enlighten the general audience.

5. *Weasel words.* Words that qualify or hedge tend to deal less with facts and more with opinions and judgments. As a general rule, it is better to state what is considered fact — as fact — and be clear about one's values and valued positions.

6. *Silence.* Silence is sometimes used as a means of purposely communicating one's position — by ignoring an alternative or another point of view, for example. However, silence is risky when it is interpreted as unfamiliarity with the issues involved.

In summary, these tactics can be used to obscure or to effectively manage the nature and/or flow of communication. Bromage makes the point that, if the tactics of obfuscation are used for political purposes, the real overall strategy is gamesmanship (Bromage, 1973). In policy analysis, one seldom has the right to make a personal decision about political strategies in using position statements. Decisions about gamesmanship strategies are policy decisions themselves and are to be made by the group or person having the authority to make them, i.e., the group using the analysis for its purposes. While the policy analyst may be an integral part of strategic action planning, the analysis itself is the property of the decision-making group, and its manner of communication is the prerogative of that group.

Once again, virtually all authoritative literature in this area stresses the importance of including the "Five Ws": who, what, when, where, and why. This is especially true in press releases since the media often cut the release from the bottom up. Therefore, it is essential that the "Five 'W's" be minimally but adequately covered in a first paragraph if the essentials of a particular position are to be told.

In all instances it is extremely important to proofread one's work and check for accuracy of facts, spelling, titles, and the like. Sometimes professionals can destroy their credibility by sloppiness in this area, regardless of the technical soundness of the position statement provided.

Position Papers

Position papers are position statements that generally provide detail and specificity arising out of an analysis and are aimed at both enlightening and/or educating as well as influencing. The position paper tends to be a declaration of a policy stance and may include resolutions or formal recommendations for action, or may serve purposes such as being a boilerplate preamble to a charter, a contract, or a formal agreement between organizations. Position papers tend to be issued by associations or organizations, and seldom by individuals. Consequently, the policy analyst's major role in position papers is to assure the group or organization that the statement is correct and suitable in style and form. Sometimes a position paper serves as an aid to developing group positions and group processes since its development helps a group or organization to sharpen its own understanding of goals or purposes. Position papers demand specificity and, in turn, rely upon the organization's own clarity regarding its preferences and priorities. This serves both internal and external functions for the organization since internal elements become better informed about policy positions and priorities as a result of the position paper development, and external elements become educated about the stance of the organization.

The following checklist is suggested for position papers. It should be noted that either these or other headings should be used for the actual paper so that the reader is provided with a visual aid, giving direction to what the writers of the position paper wish to stress.

A Checklist for Position Papers

1. Identification of the sponsor of the position paper
2. Brief summary statement of the position taken
3. Indication of when the position is taken or the circumstances under which the position applies
4. Indication of where the problem occurs and the circumstances under which the remedy offered by the position is likely to be helpful
5. Statement of rationale for the position taken
6. Identification of person or organization for further contact

News Releases

A news release is an instrument aimed at encouraging and helping the media to utilize the position statement and reaching a mass audience. While a news release may include a large portion of what actually constitutes a position paper, it can achieve useful goals by merely calling attention to the essentials of a position. Or the news release may only call attention to the fact that an event has occurred in which a position was taken or announced by the group presenting its policy analysis.

A news release is one of the technical tools of professional communicators and the policy analyst seriously interested in communicating policy analyses through this medium would do well to consult the professional communications literature, particularly as it relates to public relations. However, there are some essentials that can be considered here in the context of presenting policy analyses.

An excellent publication on relationships with media is available from the Office of Human Development Services of the U.S. Department of Health and Human Services entitled, *It's Time to Tell: A Media Handbook for Human Services Personnel* (USDHHS, 1981). This publication is aimed at a number of public relations tasks that go beyond the presentation of policy analyses. It includes many helpful hints about the use of news releases. The following discussion is taken largely from this pamphlet as well as from various experiences in developing news releases.

To be received positively by the media and the audience, a good news release must not be a disguised advertisement for a position but a report of an actual event. The lead paragraph must contain the essentials of the "Five 'W's" since the media, given their time or space constraints, often do their cutting from the bottom up. If the basics are at least minimally stated in the first sentence or paragraph, the essentials of the position will be communicated. Subsequent information might be labeled with a heading such as "Additional Facts" or "Supporting Statements" and may or may not be used in the story actually printed or presented on the air. Nevertheless, by including such material, the analysis is not lost and the media source may use some of the additional material, either then or at a later time, particularly when issue resolution is prolonged or the policy issue has a long life.

While the basic essentials of style and form also apply to news releases, there are some special considerations here. The release must be headed by a dateline and a byline, thereby indicating when, where, and by whom the release is provided. Names, addresses, and phone numbers should be included in case the media seek clarification. The double-spaced document should use an inverted pyramid format. Standard white 8½ by 11 inch paper should be used, with pages numbered (e.g., Page 2 of 2, etc.), and the word "more" at the bottom of a page when more follows. The end of the release should have the single word "end," or the symbols "###" or "-30-" at the conclusion. Abbreviations are not generally used.

As long as the "Five Ws" are the lead sentence or paragraph, it is not necessary to use a particular outline for a news release. The outline for legislative analyses or position papers might be used for the remainder of the release.

Letters

Letters tend to be directed at an individual or narrow audience. They range from conveying a position to an agency or government official or to the editor of a local newspaper. The broader the readership, the less technical the analysis should be. Aside from the general conventions of sound writing and exposition, there are some special considerations in letters conveying policy analyses.

Since policy analyses conveyed by letter are often directed to persons holding office or in administrative positions, it is important to properly address the person to whom it is written. Failure to do so may unintentionally communicate naivete, sloppiness, or lack of sophistication — each of which could inadvertently sabotage the analyst or the group sponsoring the analysis. The communication should be timely; it should be conveyed well enough in advance of the decision point so that the decision maker can benefit from the input and not be embarrassed by learning of your position too late in the decision process. As with other positions, the letter should be clear and specific as to preference or objections and, above all, what you are requesting the addressee to do. Obviously, the same clear and cogent rationale provided in other analyses should be included.

Letters to editors or public officials sometimes have a tendency to berate the office-holder and occasionally are couched in threatening language, implying removal of future support. Such approaches are generally counterproductive and, while it may have some place in the politics of policy processes, they have nothing to do with providing sound policy analyses. Furthermore, it is probably arrogant (and for most of us, naive) to allege or pretend to wield vast amounts of political influence.

The following case examples will provide an illustration of a position paper, two different news releases, and a letter.

Case Illustrations

Case 13: Position Paper — Surrogate Parenting (Pro)

In Case 12, we provided an illustration of testimony-giving, using Mrs. Alice Willer's testimony opposing House Bill 5293 regulating the practice of surrogate parenthood. Her organization, the L. R. Vincent Homes for Children, Inc., was opposed in principle to the practice of surrogate parenthood and strongly opposed the bill. In Case 13 we will use that topic as a vehicle for illustrating a position statement, this time providing a statement in support of the principle of surrogate parenting and H. B. 5293. The bill, as before, is being considered by the House Judiciary Committee. A statewide action group, the State Alliance for the Prevention for Genetically Transmittable Diseases, has issued a position paper, as follows.

Surrogate Parenting

A Position Statement by the State Alliance for the Prevention of Genetically Transmittable Diseases

We, the members of the State Alliance for the Prevention of Genetically Transmitted Diseases, declare our support for the legalization and regulation of surrogate parenting in the state.

Central Position

The Alliance is concerned with protecting the rights and interests of those individuals who seek surrogate parenting as an alternative and for those children who are born out of surrogate parenting agreements.

Opportunity

We urge the state legislature to provide for an open forum of public debate on this issue and to adopt legislation which adequately addresses the concerns and issues involved in surrogate parenting. We believe that the widest possible dialogue on the issue could take place if the House Judiciary Committee would hold hearings on H. B. 5293 at various locations throughout the state.

Affected Group

There are many people in our state who, because of a number of health reasons, are unable to conceive healthy children of their own or for whom adoption is not a viable option. Some children are currently victims of questionable surrogate parenting practices and the state should meet its obligation in extending protection to such children.

Rationale

The State Alliance for the Prevention of Genetically Transmittable Diseases recognizes that surrogate parenting is a highly complex, legal, moral, and socio-psychological issue. It is compounded by the fact that there is no current legislation or legal precedent to regulate this uncharted area. We strongly urge the state legislature to enact legislation on surrogate parenting which will establish provisions for the following concerns:

1. To establish the parental rights and responsibilities of a natural father and his spouse for a child conceived through the artificial insemination of a surrogate, i.e., to ensure the assumption of responsibility regardless of the child's psychological or physical condition;
2. To establish the legal status of a child conceived through the artificial insemination of a surrogate, i.e., to ensure that the child will be considered the legitimate child of the natural father and his spouse;
3. To provide for the termination of parental rights of a surrogate, i.e., to ensure that the surrogate shall sign a consent agreement to terminate her parental rights and responsibilities upon the birth of the child;
4. To prohibit any person from engaging in certain unethical conduct, such as arranging a surrogate birth for unreasonable economic gain;
5. To require that certain documents be filed with the state registrar for the purpose of allowing the child access to hereditary information on the surrogate mother, and for making available the identity of the surrogate mother in the event of her consent, such as providing that each surrogate birth acknowl-

edgment, consent, revocation, or contract shall be notarized and filed with the state registrar;

6. to provide for mental screening of the parties involved, i.e., the surrogate mother, the spouse of the surrogate mother, and the adopting parents.

Conclusion

The State Alliance for the Prevention of Genetically Transmittable Diseases is fully aware of the argument against surrogate parenting, namely, that surrogate parenting is a potential "pandora's box" of problems and conflicts. Nevertheless, we strongly feel that this should be no reason to prohibit surrogate parenting as an alternative for those couples who are either unable to give birth to a child or do not wish to transmit particular diseases to their offspring. Simply because an issue presents problems is no reason to avoid addressing it altogether. Such logic is totally inappropriate and inadequate. We submit that, in fact, many of the existing precedents and much extant legislation on custody in the areas of foster care and adoption provide guidelines and examples, from which appropriate legislation can be drafted to regulate surrogate parenting. As foster care and adoption were new frontiers years ago, so today is the life-giving alternative of surrogate parenting. We urge the state legislature to support and adopt these measures.

Date:

For further information, contact:
    Margaret Michelle, M.D., Chair
    State Alliance for the Prevention
        of Genetically Transmittable Diseases
1001 Main Street
This City, This State
(717) 347-8899

Case 14: News Release — Surrogate Parenting (Pro)

We will now use the position paper developed by the State Alliance for the Prevention of Genetically Transmittable Diseases as an illustration of a news release for Case 14. The reader will note that although Case 14 covers the basic "Five Ws" requirement, the two instruments differ greatly in size and detail.

For Immediate Release

Date:

From: The State Alliance for the Prevention of Genetically Transmittable Diseases, Margaret Michelle, M. D., Chair, 1001 Main Street, This City, This State, (717) 347-8899.

    The State Alliance for the Prevention of Genetically Transmittable Diseases will be presenting a position paper in favor of legalization and regulation of surrogate parenthood to the State House Judiciary Committee on Tuesday, March 10, 1984, at 3:00 p.m. at the State Capitol Building, Room 204, Capitol City, This State. The Alliance is "concerned about protecting the rights and interests of those individuals who seek surrogate parenting as an alternative and for those children who are born out of surrogate parenting agreements," said Peter Dale, Alliance spokesperson. The meeting is open to the public and all interested persons are urged to attend or contact the Alliance Chairperson, Dr. Margaret Michelle at (717) 347-8899.

###

The news release in Case 14 is an example of a policy analysis presentation aimed at giving notice of an event that was meant to inform and persuade or to urge others to action. In other situations a policy analysis may have been completed and a news release might serve as an opportunity for more generalized public relations.

Case 15: News Release—Agency Energy Audits

Case 15 is an analysis of energy conservation concerns regarding local United Way agencies. In this situation, the vehicle of a news release provides an opportunity of informing the community that the United Way and its member agencies are acting responsibly through efficient and effective use of voluntary contributions. The United Way has studied the recent decision by the State Public Utilities Commission mandating the state's utility companies to provide energy audits to homeowners. The United Way has conducted a review of energy consumption and costs among member agencies and is urging the State Public Utilities Commission to include human services organizations in that mandate. This case illustration also makes the point that news releases need not restrict themselves to proposed policy changes under consideration by legislative bodies but are also appropriate in instances involving both public relations and the influence process in making administrative agency policy.

For Immediate Release

Date:

From: The Cummings County United Way, Harold Kelly, President, 129 South West Street, This City, This State, (233) 764-6666.

The United Way of Cummings County hopes to enlist the aid of the State Public Utilities Commission in urging the commission to require that utility companies in the state provide energy audits to human services organizations, effective January 1 of next year. The commission recently mandated that utility companies provide these audits to homeowners.

In issuing the statement this morning at the City Center, Madelyn Brown, Executive Director of the United Way, noted that the United Way and its affiliate agencies have contacted and exhausted all potential sources offering energy assistance to human services agencies. The organization found that there are no available sources, although schools, hospitals, local governments, and public care buildings are eligible for energy assistance grants under Title II of the National Energy Conservation Policy Act.

In the past year in Cummings County, energy costs consumed one-third of United Way's total allocation to its affiliate agencies. Continued rises in the costs of energy will increasingly divert funds from services to maintenance. United Way is, therefore, requesting that the State Public Utilities Commission's mandate of energy audits for households be extended to human services organizations. This effort is one of many steps being taken by the United Way to aid human services agencies during the energy crisis.

-end-

Case 16: Letter — Agency Energy Audits

We will now use the content of the news release on the energy audit, which indicated the United Way's intent to enlist the aid of the State

Public Utilities Commission, to communicate by letter to State Representative Bridget Green. While the letter in Case 16 is provided primarily to illustrate the form and content of letters conveying a position, the reader should note the courtesy and good politics involved in formally informing a state legislator from the area about the group's activity.

Date

The Honorable Bridget Green
State Representative, Third District
State House of Representatives
City, State   ZIP

Dear Representative Green,

We are pleased to inform you that the Board of Directors of Cummings County United Way has urged the State Public Utilities Commission to require that utility companies in the state provide energy audits to human services organizations, effective January 1 of next year. Our recent press release is enclosed. We have requested that the audits currently mandated for homeowners be extended to human services organizations. In our judgment, this step is necessary because all potential sources of help offering energy assistance to human services agencies have been exhausted. Energy assistance grants under Title II of the National Energy Conservation Policy Act available to schools, hospitals, local governments and public care buildings are not available to the United Way and its affiliate agencies.

As you are perhaps aware, energy costs have consumed one-third of United Way's total allocation to its affiliate agencies. Continued increases in energy costs will increasingly divert funds from services to maintenance. This is one of many steps being taken by the United Way to aid human services agencies during the energy crisis. We would hope that you could be of assistance in urging the commission to take this action.

Once again, we would like to take this opportunity to thank you for the interest that you have continually shown in the work of the United Way and in the programs of many of our affiliate agencies. Should you have any questions or concerns regarding this or any other matter, please do not hesitate to call me (office—388-2864; home—385-9223) or our Executive Director, Ms. Madelyn Brown.

Sincerely,

Harold Kelley, President

Note: The letter should be on letterhead stationery that displays the agency name, address, and phone number.

11

Utilities and Imperatives

Policy is often made by those who seize opportunity. Better policy is made by those who seize opportunity and are adequately informed. If the policy practitioner is to be adequately prepared for the occasion, then policy analysis must become a way of life. Sound policy analysis is not just an occasional academic exercise or a hobby for curious people. Policy analysis is a continuous process that must become, at least in some form, part of the routine of the social practitioner. While the level of analysis may range from only a glimpse at the source of a policy's legitimacy to the detail of alternative policy choices, policy analysis must become part of our practice routines. Policy drives what we do in meeting social agency responsibilities. This is as true for the direct service practitioner as it is for the planner or the administrator; only the level of focus differs.

The Task of Policy Analysis

The task of the policy practitioner is to be informed and to help others to be informed—clients, colleagues, other decision makers, the general public, or whomever. Through adequate policy analysis we become better advocates for client groups; we provide valuable information for program planning; we guide the development of positions for social action; and we become active participants in organizational maintenance or change.

The policy practitioner can participate in and influence the shaping of social welfare policy, but he or she must be an active participant in the process to do so. The making of policy at the local or small-scale level is highly idiosyncratic and demands the participation of those who are in a position to know or uncover the details. This is a major part of providing social services, whether efforts are instigated by a formal assignment or charge for analysis, or moved by meeting the professional obligation of being "in the know."

The Ethical Imperative

We have been speaking thus far in pragmatic terms about the need to know and the utility of analysis. The purpose of policy analysis goes beyond functional utility, however. For example, the Code of Ethics of the National Association of Social Workers (1979) provides a clear mandate for the social worker to develop professional competence: "The social worker should accept responsibility or employment only on the basis of existing competence or the intention to acquire the necessary competence." At first glance, the direct service worker, planner, community organizer, or administrator may assume that competence refers only to the acquisition of technical knowledge and skill directly related to method of practice. While this is where the emphasis for professional development should be placed, social welfare policy provides the legitimacy, the limits, or the opportunities for the application of that practice knowledge and skill. Policy analysis, at least at some level of detail, must become a part of that practice competence if practitioners are to meet ethical obligations for sound professional practice.

Levy (1976) has said:

> The social worker should know what he is capable of and what he is not capable of and accordingly make the appropriate choice or provision — withdrawal, referral, counsel, guidance, consultation, and so forth — in the best interests of clients and anybody else toward whom he has attributable responsibility. (1976, p. 119)

It might be added that the practitioner must not only make the appropriate choice but also the appropriate adjustments, and policy analysis is one of the tools available in making these practice decisions. Furthermore, the ethical responsibility is there to take such action. As noted above, the Code of Ethics mandates the acceptance of professional responsibility to engage in practice that is either based upon existing competence or the intention to acquire such competence. Inasmuch as policy embodies the principles upon which such practice is made possible, then policy analysis must become a regular and important aspect of the practitioner's intervention decisions.

What Next?

The first action step for professional development is to make policy analysis part of the practitioner's conscious routine. This means that policy analysis must become a regular part of case assessment and planning, needs assessment, organizational analysis and development, social action, or whatever the problem system/task environment. Since most social workers meet their professional responsibilities at the local and/or small-scale levels, the second step will require that they familiarize themselves with their environments in new ways, since they are not used to seeing their worlds from a policy perspective. This suggests the necessity of a number of "trial runs," so to speak. The third step is to acquire skill through experience and dialogue with others over policy analysis products at the small-scale level. If this experience and dialogue is to take place, each practitioner must take initiative.

The Need for Staff Development

Few supports are available for the acquisition of policy analysis skills at the present time, particularly with respect to small-scale policy analysis. This book is one attempt to confront this problem. Also, while small-scale policy analysis has become the responsibility of many working in human services, the subject is not likely to be found in their job descriptions and is generally not part of staff development or in-service training programs. It is as if the tasks of policy analysis have just "crept in." Yet policy analysis is an integral part of development and survival in local-level human services and most of us play a part in such analyses whether we know it or not.

To make policy analysis a part of the professional practitioner's routine, we need to make its actuality more visible. Why? Because this would legitimize related efforts in the area of staff development. If staff are actually engaged in policy analysis activities, and accountable for those tasks, and if agency development and survival are dependent on the adequacy of those analyses, then we should move to effective staff development efforts in that area. We could start with those policy activities already engaged in by local social and human service practitioners. Some of these activities are cited by Ziter and the North Carolina study (Ziter, 1983) or in the study by Flynn and Jaksa (1983). These or other policy activities could be the focus of efforts for staff development or training. If social policy analysis at the local level is to be advanced, the activities engaged in by practitioners need to be codified so that systematic development of the practitioners' skills can be obtained.

A Common Language for Policy Analysis

Another area for further exploration and development is the expansion of the range of practice literature. While writing this book, we were surprised to find that a substantial body of literature concerning small-scale policy analysis was not immediately available. After all, social work as a discipline has its roots in social policy as well as direct services, yet social policy practice appears to be the least well developed. On the other hand, some human service fields (public administration, for example) are long on policy but short on direct services practice. What we appear to need is some sort of process whereby there is interdisciplinary, or at least multidisciplinary, interaction that might speed up the process of synergistic creation. Perhaps we could benefit from a synthesis arising out of an interdisciplinary dialectic or, better yet, a morphogenesis of human services policy practice arising out of a common language. Kenneth Boulding (1968) has argued that general systems theory offers an opportunity for an interdisciplinary language; perhaps the construction of commonly understood outlines for analysis, founded upon general systems principles, can provide a vehicle for this interchange and this morphogenesis.

The Relationship of Computer and Information Technology

Another possibility for development might be found in computer and information technology. There is, fortuitously, much in the way of available technology that might assist us in these tasks. The tremendous amount of data already collected (though perhaps not coded as we might like or as accessible as might be desired), means that a wealth of information is already at our disposal. There are mounds of data residing in many management information systems that are relevant to our interests. Then, too, in determining our own models or outlines, we will better know a priori what data to collect and what form to put it in.

We need to explore more of what computer technology offers by way of policy analysis. We are starting to see more use of computer simulation in social welfare (see, for example, Luse, 1980; 1982). This writer has been able to apply the general experimental simulation model of EXPERSIM, created by CONDUIT, to four social welfare policy process simulations for instructional purposes (Flynn, in press). As these and other models are developed, they can be applied to analysis in agency practice. Simulations do not provide answers to policy questions, of course, but they do help us to specify variables, shape questions, and reduce fuzzy thinking. Computerized simulations and gaming are valuable heuristic devices to help clarify what the analysis is really about.

A related area offering some promise are computerized decision support systems (e.g., Boyd et al, 1981; Jaffe, 1979) in which algorithms are developed, based on what has been learned in the field. These systems store experiential data and allow the computation of probabilistic outcomes from a related group of variables. While these systems have related primarily to direct service practice, such as making judgments about adoptive placements and providing in-home relief services, their applicability to policy analysis is rather obvious. Such systems require the specification of the variables assumed to be relevant, and necessitate the collection of a data base comprised of historical events. The modeling comes in making repeated heuristic investigations, an approach that is highly compatible with policy analysis. A possible corollary of this approach is that it would move us to exploit more of what the quantitative models can offer to small-scale policy analysis.

Summary

In this book, we have reviewed models of content, process, and values that have been applied to large-scale policy systems and identified what may be considered essential elements of outlines for analysis. We constructed three outlines for small-scale analysis for application to substantive areas, and we offered a number of case examples as illustrations. The case illustrations ranged from issues immediately related to direct practice for the individual practitioner to organizational and interorganizational policy matters. We also considered particular issues of form and style in specific situations in which policy analyses are presented externally, or "outside of the agency," including the development and application of checklists for legislative analysis, giving testimony in legislative settings, and developing position statements such as position papers and news releases.

This chapter has reviewed the functional utility and ethical imperatives of policy analysis at the small-scale level and considered some steps that might be taken to further develop our abilities in this area. Clearly, we have a great deal of work to do but the challenge promises equally great rewards.

Appendix

A Composite Outline for Analyzing Content, Process, and Value Elements for Small-Scale Policy

A. Content Elements

1. *The Policy Problem and/or Policy Goals.* A focus on the definition or delineation of the particular problem or the specific policy that is to be analyzed. Identification should include in writing, at the outset, the source or location of the policy in terms of its base(s) of legitimacy and its location(s).

    a. The policy statement
    b. Contemporary issues
    c. Historical antecedents
    d. Targets of concern
        (1) Client and target subsystems
        (2) System maintenance, control, or change
        (3) Efficiency in coverage
    e. Explicit or implicit theories
    f. Topography of the policy system

2. *Criteria for Review or Choice.* A focus on the generic criteria to be used in the analysis, particularly with regard to the clients and targets affected by the policy.

    a. Adequacy, effectiveness, and efficiency
    b. Equity, equality, and fairness
    c. Individualism and the work ethic

    d. Impact on rights and statuses
    e. Identity and self-determination
    f. Eligibility
    g. Feedback

3. *System Functioning.* A focus on the organizational, administrative, or environmental functioning of the policy system and the interaction of components in that system.

    a. State of system boundaries
    b. Patterns of communication
    c. Tension, variety, and entropy
    d. Interface constraints
    e. Functioning of feedback devices
    f. Dynamic adaptation
    g. Authority, influence, and leadership
    h. Resistance to change

4. *Major Strategies.* A focus on two levels. First is the major strategy employed in the particular policy option(s) taken; second is the particular strategies employed in implementation of the policy itself.

    a. Overall approaches
    b. Resources allocated
    c. Types of benefits for clients and targets

5. *Feasibility.* A focus on the elements that help achieve resolution of the problem or attainment of the policy goal.

    a. Legality
        (1) Legislative
        (2) Judicial
        (3) Administrative
    b. Resource requirements and availability
    c. Power and influence
    d. Rationality
    e. Environmental impact
    f. Newly perceived self-interests

B. Process Elements

1. *The Policy and the Problem.* A clear and concise statement delineating the policy sought or the problem of concern.

2. *Milestones in Policy Processes.* A focus on the major developmental tasks undertaken or to be undertaken in the policy process.

  a. Charter and legitimacy
    (1) Original agreement or template
    (2) Right to take action
    (3) Levels of legitimacy: legislative, judicial, and administrative
    (4) Source and nature of charter and legitimacy
  b. Action system
  c. Key participants
    (1) Recruitment and participation
    (2) Who participates and who is represented

3. *Interest Group Relationships.* A focus on the particular groups whose interests are affected by the policy, the activities undertaken and the interaction which occurs relevant to the policy.

  a. Power and influence
    (1) Efficacy
    (2) Vested interests
  b. Salience of the issue(s)
  c. Intergroup activities
    (1) Unilateral transfers vs. bilateral exchanges
    (2) Bargaining and negotiating
    (3) Coalition building
    (4) Contracting

4. *Process Resources.* A focus on the resources that are needed and/or observable in the policy process.

  a. People power
  b. Technology
  c. Finances
  d. Time

C. Value Elements

1. *Generic Values.* A focus on the core values that should be considered or reflected in policy content and process.

   a. Identity
   b. Self-determination
   c. Confidentiality
   d. Individualization
   e. Nonjudgmental attitude

2. *Frameworks as the Source of Values.* A focus on the particular values that might be implicit or reflected in the theoretical explanations of the problems as defined or the strategies selected by the policy option(s).

3. *Values in Human System Approaches.* A focus on the particular values underlying human system approaches to the problem or the policy.

   a. Indeterminateness
   b. Multifinality
   c. Nonsummativity
   d. Morphogenesis
   e. Stochastic processes

4. *Discriminatory Factors.* A focus on the implications of the content and the process of policy for issues of discrimination based on gender or sexual preference, ethnicity or social class, race, economic or handicapping condition, or age.

Note: Recommendations, where appropriate, could be included at this point.

References

Anderson, Ralph E., and Irl E. Carter. *Human Behavior and the Social Environment: A Social Systems Approach.* 2d ed. Chicago: Aldine, 1974.

Beistek, Felix. *The Casework Relationship.* Chicago, Ill.: Loyola University Press, 1957.

Boulding, Kenneth E. "The Boundaries of Social Policy." *Social Work, 12* (Jan. 1967): 3-11.

Boulding, Kenneth E. "General Systems Theory—The Skeleton of Science." In Walter Buckley, *Modern Systems Research for the Behavioral Scientist.* Chicago: Aldine, 1968. Pp. 3-10.

Boyd, Lawrence, Jr.; Robert Pruger; Martin D. Chase; Marleen Clark; and Leonard Miller. "A Decision Support System to Increase Equity." *Administration in Social Work, 5*(3/4) (Fall/Winter 1981): 83-96.

Bromage, Mary C. "Gamesmanship in Written Communication." In Richard C. Huseman et al., eds., *Readings in Interpersonal and Organizational Communication.* 2d ed. Boston: Holbrook Press, 1973. Pp. 526-30.

Buckley, Walter. *Sociology and Modern Systems Theory.* Englewood Cliffs, N. J.: Prentice-Hall, 1967.

Carrier, John, and Ian Kendall. "Social Policy and Social Change—Explanation of the Development of Social Policy." *Journal of Social Policy, 23* (July 1973): 209-24.

Cates, Jerry R., and Nancy Lohman. "Education for Social Policy Analysis." *Journal of Education for Social Work, 16*(1) (Winter 1980): 5, 12.

Cloward, Richard A., and Frances F. Piven. *Regulating the Poor: The Functions of Public Welfare.* New York: Vintage Books, 1971.

Cox, Harvey. *The Secular City: Secularization and Urbanization in Theological Perspective.* Rev. ed. New York: Macmillan, 1966.

Dear, Ronald B., and Rino J. Patti. "Legislative Advocacy: Seven Effective Tactics." *Social Work, 26*(4) (July 1981): 289-96.

DiNitto, Diana M., and Thomas R. Dye. *Social Welfare: Politics and Public Policy.* Englewood Cliffs, N. J.: Prentice-Hall, 1983.

Dolgoff, Ralph, and Donald Feldstein. *Understanding Social Welfare.* New York: Harper and Row, 1980.

Dolgoff, Ralph, and Malvina Gordon. "Direct Practice and Policy Decisions." *Journal of Social Welfare,* 5 (Spring 1976):5–13.

Dye, Thomas R. *Understanding Public Policy.* 4th ed. Englewood Cliffs, N. J.: Prentice-Hall, 1981.

Easton, David. *A Systems Analysis of Political Life.* New York: Wiley, 1965.

Flynn, John P. "A Guide for Mapping and Analysis of Small-Scale Social Welfare Policy." *Administration in Social Work, 31* (Spring 1979):57–63.

Flynn, John P. "Local Participation in Planning for Comprehensive Community Mental Health Centers." *Community Mental Health Journal,* 9(1) (Feb. 1973):3–10.

Flynn, John P. "MERGE: Computer Simulation of Social Policy Process." *Computers in Human Services* (in press).

Flynn, John P., and James Jaksa. "Social Workers' Public Communication Skills: A Research Report." *Journal of Continuing Social Work Education,* 2(3) (1983):9–15.

Frederico, Ronald C. *The Social Welfare Institution: An Introduction.* 3d ed. Lexington, Mass.: D. C. Heath, 1980.

Freire, Paolo. *Pedagogy of the Oppressed.* New York: Herder and Herder, 1972.

Galper, Jeffrey H. *The Politics of Social Services.* Englewood Cliffs, N. J.: Prentice-Hall, 1975.

Gergen, Kenneth J. "Assessing the Leverage Points in the Process of Policy Formation." In Raymond Bauer and Kenneth Gergen, eds., *The Study of Policy Formation.* New York: The Free Press, 1968. Pp. 181–203.

Gil, David G. "A Systematic Approach to Social Policy Analysis." *Social Service Review,* 44(4) (Dec. 1970): 411–26.

Gil, David G. *Unravelling Social Policy.* Rev. ed. Cambridge, Mass.: Schenkman, 1976.

Gilbert, Neil, and Harry Specht. *Dimensions of Social Welfare Policy.* Englewood Cliffs, N. J.: Prentice-Hall, 1974.

Haskins, Ron. "Social Policy Analysis: A Partial Agenda." In Ron Haskins and James J. Gallagher, eds., *Models for Analysis of Social Policy: An Introduction.* Norwood, N. J.: Ablex Pub. Corp., 1981. Pp. 203–26.

Haskitt, Harold O., Jr. "When Speaking from Manuscript: *Say* It and *Mean* It." In Richard C. Huseman et al., eds., *Readings in Interpersonal and Organizational Communication.* 2d ed. Boston, Mass.: Holbrook Press, 1973. Pp. 518–25.

Heffernan, Joseph W. *Introduction to Social Welfare Policy*. Itasca, Ill.: Peacock, 1979.

Hoos, Ida R. *Systems Analysis in Public Policy: A Critique*. Berkeley, Calif.: University of California Press, 1972.

Jaffe, Eleizer D. "Computers in Child Placement Planning." *Social Work, 24*(5) (Sept. 1979): 380–85.

Kahn, Alfred J., ed. *Shaping the New Social Work*. New York: Columbia University Press, 1973.

Kahn, Alfred J. *Theory and Practice of Social Planning*. New York: Russell Sage Foundation, 1969.

Kammerman, Shiela B., and Alfred J. Kahn. *Social Services in the United States: Policies and Programs*. Philadelphia, Penn.: Temple University Press, 1976.

Keefe, Thomas. "Beyond Radicalism: An Historical-Materialist Framework for Social Policy Curriculum." *Journal of Education for Social Work, 14*(2) (Spring 1978):60–65.

Kelley, Joseph B. "Educating Social Workers for a Changing Society: Social Policy." *Journal of Education for Social Work, 11*(1) (Winter 1975):89–93.

Kleinkauf, Cecilia. "A Guide to Giving Legislative Testimony." *Social Work, 26*(4) (Jul. 1981):297–303.

Levy, Charles S. "The Ethics of Management." *Administration in Social Work, 3*(3) (Fall 1979):277–88. (a)

Levy, Charles S. *Social Work Ethics*. New York: Human Sciences Press, 1976.

Levy, Charles S. *Values and Ethics for Social Work Practice*. New York: National Association of Social Workers, 1979. (b)

Lewis, Harold. *The Intellectual Base of Social Work Practice*. New York: Haworth Press, 1982.

Lindblom, Charles E. *The Policy Making Process*. Englewood Cliffs, N. J.: Prentice-Hall, 1968.

Lindblom, Charles E. "The Science of Muddling Through." *Public Administration Review, 19* (Spring 1959):79–88.

Luse, F. Dean. *OUTPST: Education/Simulations for the Human Services*. Park Forest, Ill.: F. Dean Luse, 1982.

Luse, F. Dean. "Use of Computer Simulation in Social Welfare Management." *Administration in Social Work, 4* (3) (Fall 1980):13–22.

Lyon, Paul. "Ideology in Social Welfare Policy Instruction: An Examination of Required Readings." *Journal of Sociology and Social Welfare, 10*(3) (Sept. 1983): 376–90.

Mahaffey, Maryann. "Lobbying and Social Work." *Social Work, 17*(1) (Jan. 1972):3–11.

Mayer, Robert, and Ernest Greenwood. *The Design of Social Policy Research.* Englewood Cliffs, N. J.: Prentice-Hall, 1980.

MacRae, Duncan, Jr., and Ron Haskins. "Models for Policy Analysis." In Ron Haskins and James J. Gallagher, eds., *Models for Analysis of Social Policy: An Introduction.* Norwood, N. J.: Ablex Pub. Corp., 1981. Pp. 1–36.

McGill, Robert S., and Terry N. Clark. "Community Power and Decision Making: Recent Research and Its Policy Implications." *Social Service Review, 49*(1) (Mar. 1975):33–45.

Meenaghan, Thomas M., and Robert O. Washington. *Social Policy and Social Welfare: Structure and Applications.* New York: The Free Press, 1980.

Miller, James Grier. *Living Systems.* New York: McGraw-Hill, 1978.

Moroney, Robert M. "Policy Analysis Within a Value Theoretical Framework." In Ron Haskins and James J. Gallagher, eds., *Models for Analysis of Social Policy: An Introduction.* Norwood, N. J.: Ablex Pub. Corp., 1981. Pp. 78–102.

National Association of Social Workers. *Code of Ethics.* Silver Springs, Md.: National Association of Social Workers, 1979.

Patti, Rino, and Ronald B. Dear. "Legislative Advocacy: A Path to Social Change." *Social Work, 20*(2) (Mar. 1975):108–14.

Pincus, Allen, and Anne Minahan. *Social Work Practice: Model and Method.* Itasca, Ill.: Peacock, 1973.

Polsby, Nelson. *Community Power and Political Theory.* New Haven, Conn.: Yale University Press, 1963.

Prigmore, Charles S., and Charles R. Atherton. *Social Welfare Policy: Analysis and Formulation.* Lexington, Mass.: D. C. Heath, 1979.

Pruger, Robert. "Social Policy: Unilateral Transfer or Reciprocal Exchange." *Journal of Social Policy, 24* (Oct. 1973):289–302.

Quade, E. S. *Analysis for Public Decisions.* New York: American Elsevier, 1975.

Reamer, Frederic G. *Ethical Dilemmas in Social Service.* New York: Columbia University Press, 1982.

Reamer, Frederic G. "Ethical Dilemmas in Social Work Practice," *Social Work, 28*(1) (Jan.-Feb. 1983):31–35.

Romanyshyn, John M. *Social Welfare: Charity to Justice.* New York: Random House, 1971.

Ross, Robert, and Graham L. Staines. "The Politics of Analyzing Social Problems." *Social Problems, 20* (Summer 1972):18–40.

Sharwell, George R. "How to Testify Before a Legislative Committee." In Maryann Mahaffey and John Hankes, eds., *Practical Politics: Social Work and Political Responsibility.* Silver Springs, Md.: National Association of Social Workers, 1982. Pp. 85–98.

Smith, Virginia. "How Interest Groups Influence Legislators." *Social Work, 24*(3) (May 1979):234–39.

Sower, Christopher; John Holland; Kenneth Tiedke; and Walter Freeman. *Community Involvement: The Webs of Formal and Informal Ties that Make for Action.* Glencoe, Ill.: The Free Press, 1957.

Steiner, Joseph R. "Discourse Management: Key to Policy Development." *Journal of Sociology and Social Welfare, 4*(7) (Sept. 1977):1025–32.

Stokey, Edith, and Richard Zeckhauser. *A Primer for Policy Analysis.* New York: Norton, 1978.

Tierney, Kathleen J. "The Battered Women Movement and the Creation of the Wife Beating Problem." *Social Problems, 29*(3) (Feb. 1982):207–20.

Tripodi, Tony; Phillip Fellin; and Henry J. Meyer. *The Assessment of Social Research.* 2d ed. Itasca, Ill.: Peacock, 1983.

Tropman, John E., and Ann R. Alvarez. "Writing for Effect: Correspondence, Records and Documents." In Fred Cox et al., eds., *Tactics and Techniques of Community Practice.* Itasca, Ill.: Peacock, 1977. Pp. 377–91.

U.S. Department of Health and Human Services, Office of Human Development Services and the Office of Family Assistance. *"It's Time to Tell: A Media Handbook for Human Services Personnel.* No. 0-324-000. Washington, D. C.: U. S. Government Printing Office, 1981.

von Bertalanffy, Ludwig. *General Systems Theory.* New York: George Braziller, 1968.

Warren, Roland L. *The Community in America.* Chicago, Ill.: Rand McNally, 1963.

Warren, Roland L. *Social Change and Human Purpose: Toward Understanding and Action.* Chicago, Ill.: Rand McNally, 1977.

Warren, Roland L. "Truth, Love and Social Change." In Roland L. Warren, *Truth, Love and Social Change.* Chicago, Ill.: Rand McNally, 1972.

Whitaker, William H., and Jan Flory-Baker. "Ragtag Social Workers Take on the Good Old Boys and Elect a State Senator." In Maryann Mahaffey and John W. Hanks, eds., *Practical Politics: Social Work and Political*

Responsibility. Silver Spring, Md.: National Association of Social Workers, 1982. Pp. 161–80.

Wilcox, Roger P. "Characteristics and Organization of the Oral Technical Report." In Richard C. Huseman et al., eds., *Readings in Interpersonal and Organizational Communication*, 2d ed. Boston: Holbrook Press, 1973. Pp. 509–17.

Wildavsky, Aaron. *The Politics of the Budgetary Process.* Boston: Little Brown, 1964.

York, Reginald O. *Human Service Planning: Concepts, Tools, and Methods.* Chapel Hill: University of North Carolina Press, 1982.

Ziter, Mary Lou P. "Social Policy Practice: Tasks and Skills." *Administration in Social Work,* 7(2) (Summer 1983):37–50.

Index